The White Buddhist

Religion in North America
Catherine L. Albanese and Stephen J. Stein, editors

William L. Andrews, editor. *Sisters of the Spirit: Three Black Women's Autobiographies of the Nineteenth Century.*

Mary Farrell Bednarowski. *New Religions and the Theological Imagination in America.*

David Chidester. *Salvation and Suicide: An Interpretation of Jim Jones, the Peoples Temple, and Jonestown.*

David Chidester and Edward T. Linenthal, editors. *American Sacred Space.*

Thomas D. Hamm. *God's Government Begun: The Society for Universal Inquiry and Reform, 1842–1846.*

Thomas D. Hamm. *The Transformation of American Quakerism: Orthodox Friends, 1800–1907.*

Jean M. Humez, editor. *Mother's First-Born Daughters: Early Shaker Writings on Women and Religion.*

Carl T. Jackson. *Vedanta for the West: The Ramakrishna Movement in the United States.*

David Kuebrich. *Minor Prophecy: Walt Whitman's New American Religion.*

John D. Loftin. *Religion and Hopi Life in the Twentieth Century.*

Colleen McDannell. *The Christian Home in Victorian America, 1840–1900.*

Ronald L. Numbers and Jonathan M. Butler, editors. *The Disappointed: Millerism and Millenarianism in the Nineteenth Century.*

Richard W. Pointer. *Protestant Pluralism and the New York Experience: A Study of Eighteenth-Century Religious Diversity.*

Sally M. Promey. *Spiritual Spectacles: Vision and Image in Mid-Nineteenth-Century Shakerism.*

Russell E. Richey. *Early American Methodism.*

A. Gregory Schneider. *The Way of the Cross Leads Home: The Domestication of American Methodism.*

Richard Hughes Seager. *The World's Parliament of Religions: The East/West Encounter, Chicago, 1893.*

Ann Taves, editor. *Religion and Domestic Violence in Early New England: The Memoirs of Abigail Abbot Bailey.*

Thomas A. Tweed. *The American Encounter with Buddhism, 1844–1912: Victorian Culture and the Limits of Dissent.*

Valarie H. Ziegler. *The Advocates of Peace in Antebellum America.*

The White Buddhist

The Asian Odyssey of
Henry Steel Olcott

Stephen Prothero

Indiana University Press
Bloomington and Indianapolis

A portion of this book appeared as "Henry Steel Olcott and 'Protestant Buddhism,' " in the *Journal of the American Academy of Religion* 63.2 (Summer 1995).

Chapter 2 of this book is a revised and expanded version of my article, "From Spiritualism to Theosophy: 'Uplifting' a Democratic Tradition," *Religion and American Culture: A Journal of Interpretation* 3.2 (Summer 1993) 197–216. Copyright 1993 by The Center for the Study of Religion and American Culture. Reprinted by permission.

The paper used in this publication meets the minimum requirements of American National Standard for Information Sciences—Permanence of Paper for Printed Library Materials, ANSI Z39.48-1984.

Manufactured in the United States of America

Library of Congress Cataloging-in-Publication Data

Prothero, Stephen R.
The white Buddhist : the Asian odyssey of Henry Steel Olcott / Stephen Prothero.
p.   cm. — (Religion in North America)
Includes bibliographical references and index.
ISBN 0-253-33014-9 (alk. paper)
1. Olcott, Henry Steel, 1832–1907.   2. Buddhists—United States—Biography.   I. Title.   II. Series.
BQ976.L36P48   1996
294.3′092—dc20
[B]   95-22092

1 2 3 4 5   01 00 99 98 97 96

For My Wife, Edythe E. Nesmith

"Olcott Day in India"

Stand we awhile in silence here apart,
Heads bowed and hands in worship at our breast,
And strong within our heart
Great reverence, for here they laid to rest
Amid the bosom of the kindly flame
All of the earthly part
Of him whom Lanka oweth more than fame.

He came no alien spirit from the West
To live unloved among us, nor to wind
The net of foreign creeds
About our children's hearts, nor subtly blind
Their spirits to the shame of faithless deeds
And drunkenness in culture's clothing dressed;—

Nay as a welcome guest
He came to Lanka. With strong gentle hand
He healed the sick; yet a far greater gift
Brought, to once more uplift
Our dying nation in our listless land.

For now no longer is Lord Buddha's praise
Forgotten by our people; children sing
In glad procession down our bannered ways
And bear their offering—
Fragrance of blossom and of incense sweet—
Unto the temples of our Lord once more,
And at His blessed Feet
Their reverence and gratitude outpour.*

*This poem was written on behalf of a group of Buddhists gathered at Olcott's Memorial in Adyar, Madras, India in 1920 to celebrate the anniversary of Colonel Olcott's death. It appeared in F. G. Pearce, "Olcott Day in India," in S. W. Wijayatiklke, *Buddhist Annual of Ceylon* (Colombo: Bastian, 1920) 1.16.

Contents

Preface

A screenwriter friend informs me that there are no more than a dozen or so distinct comedies to be told. Everything else is variation on a theme. Among the most popular comedies is the "fish out of water" tale. The recipe is a rather simple one. Take a sympathetic protagonist out of his or her native habitat, plop 'em down in an unfamiliar place, and hijinks are sure to ensue.

This book is a "fish out of water" tale. It chronicles the passage of a New Yorker from America to Asia in an age in which "East" and "West" were in the process of inventing one another. The "fish" is Colonel Henry Steel Olcott (1832–1907), a nineteenth-century Renaissance man—theosophist, attorney, agricultural reformer, spiritualist, reporter, drama critic, cremationist, editor, investigator of Lincoln's assassination, and indefatigable spirit—who was the first American of European descent to formally convert to Buddhism. The "water" is nineteenth-century America, more precisely the Gilded Age culture of New York City's literary elites through which Olcott swam for roughly the first half of his life. The land onto which our fish then flops is British India and Ceylon (now Sri Lanka), where Olcott spent the last half of his life building the Theosophical Society and attempting to reform Buddhism, Hinduism, and, at times, even Zoroastrianism and Islam.

Although the narrative that follows may seem comedic at times, it has three serious purposes: first, to present a sympathetic yet scholarly interpretation of Olcott's adult life, especially his work on behalf of Buddhism and Hinduism in Asia; second, to use that life as an opportunity to interpret the broader nineteenth-century American encounter with the religions of Asia; and, third, to commend to scholars in religious studies the linguistic category of "creolization" as a useful device for analyzing situations of cultural contact and interreligious interaction.

I suppose I should admit from the start that this is a work not only of history but also of criticism. While I am sure that some wonder why I do not criticize Olcott more harshly here, I am equally certain that many of the theosophists who assisted me so graciously in researching the book will be disappointed that I have chosen to find faults in a man who spent the better part of his life pursuing the laudable aim of bringing together people of different races and religions into one "Universal Brotherhood of Humanity." Some explanation of my stance may be in order here.

Preface

This book began as a dissertation for the Committee on the Study of Religion at Harvard University but it was crafted to a great extent in the library at the Harvard Divinity School. During my time at the Divinity School, I first became intimately acquainted with the rhetoric of what I have come to call "religious liberalism." Chief among the tenets of this faith is the affirmation made famous by Mahatma Gandhi (but articulated much earlier by the theosophists, Olcott included, who influenced him) that "All Religions Are True." A first corollary of this tenet is the mandate for religious tolerance.

Although I was initially attracted to this informally established Harvard Divinity School faith, I eventually came to mistrust it. The religious liberals I met typically underscored the differences between themselves and religious conservatives. But as I got to know liberals and conservatives alike, these differences largely evaporated. I met fundamentalists and charismatics who were in many ways more open-minded than my liberal friends. And I came to see that many religious liberals were zealous missionaries in their own way, as eager to coax evangelical Protestants out of their views on the Bible and Muslim traditionalists out of their commitments to jihad as they were to convert conservatives of all stripes to their gospel of the equality of all religions. Both religious liberals and religious conservatives, I came to believe, hoped in the end to homogenize the world, to lay straight (or, at least, straighter) the multiform hills and valleys of religious belief and practice. Both, in short, fundamentally mistrusted the radical diversity of religious expression that had attracted me to the study of religion in the first place.

As a result of my experiences, I now approach religious liberalism with the same sort of "hermeneutics of suspicion" that liberals typically use when approaching religious conservatives. This book is informed, therefore, by a fundamental mistrust of schemes, however well-intentioned, that begin by judging all religious traditions to be true and end by determining that something is gained when the dizzying diversity of religious beliefs and practices is reduced, however imaginatively, to one core tradition.

Having criticized what I see as the *Zeitgeist* of the Harvard Divinity School, I would be remiss if I did not acknowledge some of the people there and at Harvard University proper who, whether they breathed deeply of that *Zeitgeist* or not, helped to bring this book into being. Professor William R. Hutchison, who exemplifies most of the virtues of religious liberalism and none of its faults, served as the director of my dissertation and has read numerous revisions of the book. Dr. Hutchison, who patiently endured my not infrequent itchings to light out for non-academic territories, has a well-deserved reputation for allowing his students the all-too-rare freedom to pursue projects that, like my own, range well beyond his chosen field of American Protestantism. To his willingness to allow me to follow my own "inner light," I am extremely grateful. I am also appreciative of the assistance I received from Dr. David D. Hall and Dr. Diana Eck, both of whom served as readers of the dissertation. Their helpful comments, along with criticisms I fielded from anthropologist Nur Yalman, Buddhologist M. David Eckel, Islamicist William A. Graham, Jr., and fellow members of Harvard Divinity School's New World Colloquium, pushed the book in fruitful directions I would not otherwise have taken it.

Although this book took shape during my years of graduate study, in many ways it was gestated during my stint at Yale College, where Richard Wightman Fox taught me that doing history consisted not of memorizing dates but of interpreting conflicts and Sydney Ahlstrom convinced me, as no one else could have, that the history of religion in America was as fascinating as it was vast. Other professors and graduate students at Yale who supported my interest and advanced my expertise in the study of religion and the field of American Studies include Wayne Meeks, Elizabeth Blackmar, Robert Westbrook, and Dana Robert.

More recent contributors to the book include a number of scholars who have applied, however modestly, Walt Whitman's justifiably famous prophetic admonition—"Unscrew the locks from the doors! / Unscrew the doors themselves from their jambs!"—to our field of American religious history by pressing beyond "mainstream" Protestantism to considerations of "nonmainstream" topics. Catherine L. Albanese, whose *America: Religions and Religion* (1981) solidified her place as the "dean" of this new school of scholars, read at least two full revisions with her keen eye for problems in theory and interpretation, and I have incorporated many of her suggestions into the book. Stephen J. Stein, who along with Albanese serves as an editor of the Religion in North America series at Indiana University Press, also gave my entire manuscript careful and provocative readings on multiple occasions. Richard Seager, my closest colleague and friend during my graduate school years, read the entire work at various points and more than anyone else helped me chart my interpretive course. Finally, Thomas Tweed and Robert Ellwood, also specialists in Asian religion in America, contributed useful comments on the book at various stages in the revising process, as did South Asian specialist Ananda Wickremeratne.

I received much-needed financial support for this project from a number of sources, including the Woodrow Wilson National Fellowship Foundation, which supported my entire graduate education with a Mellon Fellowship in the Humanities, and the Lilly Endowment, which provided dissertation-writing support. Georgia State University, my institutional home for the past few years, granted me release time as I was revising the dissertation into a book. The Frederick Sheldon Travelling Fellowship Fund and the Sinclair Kennedy Travelling Fellowship Fund provided resources for a research trip both to Great Britain, where I dug around in the British Library, the India Office Library, and the Public Records Office for material on Olcott, and to India, where I spent a number of memorable months at the Theosophical Society headquarters at Adyar, just outside Madras, reading through a vast array of materials, including Olcott's letters, diaries, and personal papers.

At Adyar I incurred debts to members of the Theosophical Society who made my research stint in India both pleasant and productive: Mrs. Radha Burnier, International President; Mrs. Norma Sastry, Accommodations Officer; Mr. Conrad Jamieson, International Secretary; Miss Carin Citroen, Assistant to the President; Mrs. Dorothy Abbenhouse, U.S. President; Miss Sharanya Mohani, Administrator of Leadbeater Chambers; and all the welcoming faces who listened to and commented on my "Olcott Day" lecture on February 2, 1989. I must especially thank Burmese-born George Sein, who provided me with an outsider's view of India, and Sunderi and Sarda, who by welcoming my wife and me into their home welcomed us both into the sacred heart of India. Among the many theosophists who assisted me with my work after I was back in the United States is John Algeo, a professor of English at the University of Georgia who is now serving as the president of the American Section of the Theosophical Society.

As I amassed library fines on three continents I also became indebted to a bevy of librarians and archivists, each of whom cheerfully dug up crumbling tomes for me on Colonel Olcott: in India, Mrs. Seetha Neelekantan, Librarian of the Adyar Library and Research Center, and Mr. Baden Offord and Sri S. S. Varma, Officers-In-Charge of the Theosophical Society Archives at Adyar; in England, employees of the Public Records Office, the British Library, and the India Office Library; and in the United States, a host of assistants at the National Archives, the National Anthropological Archives at the Smithsonian Institution, New York University, the Boston Public Library, the New York Public Library, the American Antiquarian Society, the Olcott Library and Research Center, and my "home" libraries at Harvard University, Yale University, Smith College, and Georgia State University.

I must also thank my parents, Dr. and Mrs. S. Richard Prothero, my sister, Laurie Sperry, and my brothers, Eric, Dan, and David Prothero, for making the home in which I grew up a place where learning was fun, and my wife,

Preface

Edye Nesmith, and my daughter, Molly Prothero, for making my adult home a place where research and writing are not only possible but enjoyable.

Finally, I would like to extend my gratitude to an artist who was undoubtedly my relative, a Mr. Prothero who resided at 21 Upper Bedford Place in London in 1900. In July of that year, according to Olcott's diary, the Colonel sat for Mr. Prothero for a period of nearly two weeks for a portrait in pastels. I have wondered many times what that portrait looked like, but I always imagine Mr. Prothero hoping to please Olcott with his work yet simultaneously insisting on rendering as accurate a portrayal as possible. This portrait of mine has taken considerably longer than two weeks, but I see my task as analogous to Mr. Prothero's. I have attempted to paint an accurate picture of Olcott, flaws and all, yet I have sought throughout to make my rendering something that he himself might have viewed as persuasive if not entirely flattering. As I conducted my research, I was comforted to learn that Olcott was a generous man who typically found something good to say about even his staunchest critics. I would like to think that he would have something good to say about the portrait I have painted here.

Introduction

Each year on February 17, Buddhists throughout the South Asian island of Sri Lanka light brass lamps and offer burning incense to commemorate the anniversary of the death of an American-born Buddhist hero. In Theravada temples, saffron-robed monks bow down before his photographs, and boys and girls in schoolhouses across the country offer gifts in his memory. "May the merit we have gained by these good deeds," they meditate, "pass on to Colonel Olcott, and may he gain happiness and peace."[1]

In India, Colonel Henry Steel Olcott (1832–1907) is remembered every year on February 2, the day of his birth. Early in the morning, just after the hot sun rises above the river that winds its way through the suburb of Madras where Olcott made his home, hundreds of poor Hindu children attending the schools that Olcott founded a century ago march two-by-two down crowded city streets, then past a coconut grove to the headquarters of the Theosophical Society that houses his statue. The icons of Olcott they carry are draped with garlands and the morning air they breathe is filled with hymns praising his auspicious name.

Disinterested historians describe Henry Steel Olcott as the president-founder of the Theosophical Society, one of America's first Buddhists, and an important contributor to both the Indian Renaissance in India and the Sinhalese Buddhist Revival in Ceylon (now Sri Lanka).[2] Less objective observers have allotted Olcott an even more central place in sacred history. A prime minister of Ceylon, for example, praised Olcott as "one of the heroes in the struggle for our independence and a pioneer of the present religious, national and cultural revival." And other ardent admirers have determined that Olcott was a bodhisattva, a reincarnation of the third century B.C.E. Buddhist emperor, Ashoka, and/or a reincarnation of Gautama Buddha himself.[3]

In the land of his birth, Olcott has been less graciously received. The *New York Times* denounced him during his lifetime as "an unmitigated rascal"—"a man bereft of reason" whose "insanity, though harmless, is, unfortunately, incurable."[4] The *Dictionary of American Biography*, noting that Olcott has been considered "a fool, a knave, and a seer," concludes that he was probably "a little of all three."[5]

In the face of such disparate judgments, scholars frequently step forth to proffer ostensibly objective assessments. But despite the intimation of one historian of religion that Olcott may have done more than any other American to inspire and sustain American interest in Buddhism, to say nothing of direct appeals from specialists in both Buddhist Studies and American Studies for a critical study of Olcott,[6] none has been forthcoming.[7] This lacuna would undoubtedly have pleased Olcott himself, who rebuffed the only writer who asked him to authorize a biography. "I considered such things trash," Olcott explained in a curt notation in his diary, "Ephemera!"[8]

Olcott would undoubtedly have been less than delighted with this bit of ephemera, but he might have taken some comfort in the fact that it does not amount to a full-blown biography. Olcott's childhood is largely ignored here, as is his private life and much of his theosophical work. The focus of this project is Olcott's adult life, especially his work in Asia on behalf of Buddhism and Hinduism. Thus the book represents not so much a biography as a case study in cultural and religious contact or, more specifically, an examination of the complexities and ambiguities of the nineteenth-century American encounter with Asian religious traditions.

The decision to craft this sort of book instead of one of the many others that could have been written about Olcott was motivated to some extent by the sources. Olcott's diary, now housed at the Theosophical Society headquarters in Adyar, a suburb of Madras, India, is as skimpy on private matters as it is exhaustive on public events, and it does not begin until 1878, when Olcott was already well into his forties. Many entries in the book were made, moreover, not by Olcott himself but by friends who evidently read it, so even that most private of documents was in many respects an open book. Several other factors also played a part in shaping this text. The emphasis on Olcott's Buddhist and Hindu work over his theosophy was motivated largely by the existing secondary literature, which is as skimpy on the Buddhist and Hindu side as it is weighty on matters theosophical.[9] This book seeks to address this historiographic imbalance by weighing in more heavily on Buddhist and Hindu matters and largely avoiding the various squabbles between theosophists and their detractors that have occupied both theosophical and non-theosophical historians since Olcott's time. Finally, the decision to forego an exhaustive biography was motivated by my personal interests. Olcott *is* interesting and important as a man, and certainly deserves the full biographical treatment this work does not attempt to provide. But he is most compelling, at least to this author, as an example of a culture broker existing simultaneously in two distinct worlds. Olcott has lived, in short, the challenges that now face all of us who are attempting to come to grips with the problem of religious pluralism. Far earlier than most, Olcott knew how utterly false was Rudyard Kipling's famous dictum that "East is East, and West is West, and never the twain shall meet." In many respects, he paved the way for America's collective glance eastward in the 1960s and 1970s and the New Age interest in Asian religions of today.

Olcott is an appropriate figure for a study in cultural and religious contact because of his liminal standing between "East" and "West." A descendant of the Puritans, Olcott was born to Presbyterian parents in Orange, New Jersey, in 1832. As a young man, however, he renounced Protestant Christianity. He became a spiritualist and then a theosophist before moving to India in 1879 and formally embracing Buddhism in Ceylon one year later. From his mid-life passage to Asia until his death in Madras in 1907, Olcott functioned as culture broker between Occident and Orient, facilitating the commerce of religious ideas and practices between America and Asia even as he helped to bring into the world's religious marketplace a wholly new spiritual creation.

In an age inundated with grand schemes, Olcott fashioned one of the grandest of metanarratives.[10] According to Olcott's *grand récit*, Kipling's dictum regarding the essential separateness of East and West was decidedly false; Occident and Orient were coming together in a great union that would approximate, on the one hand, the glory that was ancient India and, on the other, the grandeur of the kingdom of God to come. As a result of this marriage of the technological West and the spiritual East, a "Universal Brotherhood of Humanity" was waiting to be born.

One of the most intriguing facts of Olcott's life is that though he repudiated Protestantism as a young adult, his writings evinced until his death an obsession with a Puritan heritage that both repelled and attracted him. In an article in the *National Review*, Olcott derided his "Puritan ancestors who slashed, basted, and hanged the Indians, the witches and the Quakers for alleged compacts with the Evil One."[11] But he praised the Puritans as frequently as he damned them, citing their courage in the face of adversity and their refusal to compromise their cherished beliefs.

A few years before his exodus to Asia, Olcott repaid at least a portion of his debt to his Puritan ancestors by authoring a genealogical volume entitled *The Descendants of Thomas Olcott* (1874). He concluded the book's preface with as solemn a hymn of praise as a faithful son could offer his pious and democratic forebears. "The country cannot afford to lose the history of any one of the brave men," Olcott began, "who for conscience sake abandoned home, and all that made life sweet, for a new land where, for the privilege of worshipping God in their own way, they had to pay the price of deadly perils overcome, sufferings endured, poverty, cold, sickness and all that makes life hard and bitter." And it was Olcott's appointed task to save the "brave men" of his clan for the sake of posterity. According to Olcott, all patriotic Americans should celebrate the Puritans' passage to the New World, because it was the Puritans who paved the way for liberty on the continent. "Untitled and poor though they may have been," Olcott concluded, "they were the best of their stock and, as William Stoughton said in his election sermon of 1668: 'God sifted a whole nation that he might send choice grain into the wilderness.' "[12]

By invoking in this volume what Perry Miller has identified as the myth of the Puritan "errand into the wilderness,"[13] Olcott placed himself squarely in the midst of an expanded Puritan saga. If it had been the duty of his ancestors faithfully to follow the dictates of conscience across the perilous Atlantic, then it was his duty to set their story down. Shortly after Olcott fulfilled that obligation by publishing his genealogical volume, he decided that he too was "choice grain," and set off on an errand of his own into the Asian wilderness. Years later he stood as a Buddhist in a temple in Kyoto, Japan. While reciting in broken Pali his Buddhist vows, Olcott recalled again his Puritan blood:

> I could not help smiling to myself when thinking of the horror that would have been felt by any of my Puritan ancestors of the seventeenth century could they have looked forward to this calamitous day! I am sure that if I had been born among them at Boston or Hartford, I should have been hanged for heresy on the tallest tree.[14]

Placed side-by-side, these references to Olcott's Puritan forebears might seem to introduce a rather straightforward mainstream-to-margins story of an American Protestant turned Asian Buddhist. But this tale, though plausible, cannot be convincingly told. Despite his frequent claims to stand, like some *homme universel*, above the fray of sectarian religion and national loyalties, Olcott never shook his roots in American Protestantism. He carried with him on his passage to India and Ceylon a boatload of American and Protestant baggage, which he neither fully unpacked nor entirely discarded.

If Olcott's life cannot be pressed into the service of some "insider-to-outsider" tale of an American Protestant turned Asian Buddhist, how ought his story be told? The argument presented here is that while Olcott was clearly not a "mainstream" religious figure, his story is in no way marginal to mainline developments in American religion and culture. Olcott's adult life is best understood, in other words, not as a repudiation but as an outgrowth of nineteenth-century American Protestantism. His errand to Asia ought to be seen as an extension of both the Puritan errand to America

Introduction

and what William Hutchison has identified as the errand of nineteenth-century American Protestant missionaries to the world.[15] It thus demonstrates, however paradoxically, *both* the pluralization of American religion in the late nineteenth century *and* the simultaneous persistence in that period of Protestant influence.

To note that Olcott's adult life is the story of an American Protestant abroad is to set the stage for the drama that is to follow, but it does not quite amount to a plot. That plot will begin to unfold only as we examine a few guiding questions. What exactly was Olcott's adult faith? What were his religious behaviors? Finally, how successful was he in inculcating his beliefs and behaviors among the Asians he encountered?

Olcott himself provided a simple if ultimately unsatisfactory answer to the first question. His mature faith was, in his words, "pure, primitive Buddhism."[16] But Olcott was no simple adopter of some static Buddhism. He was, in fact, at least as much a "converter" of Buddhism as he was a "convert" to it. Banishing from his Buddhism elements of the tradition that he found offensive, Olcott had no compunctions about introducing foreign elements that he was convinced any true religion could not do without. Olcott's adult faith was, therefore, both something less and something more than the traditional Buddhism of Ceylon. Although he emphasized elements within traditional Theravada Buddhism that were to him familiar, he neglected, and in many cases rejected, elements of that tradition that appeared to him as strange. Meanwhile, he freely incorporated into his newfound faith beliefs and behaviors from his American Protestant past. Olcott stood, therefore, much closer to the American Protestant mainstream than might be suspected. His faith, I will argue, represented a creative "creolization" of American Protestant and Asian Buddhist norms and organizational forms.

Continuities between Olcott's Asian adulthood and his American Protestant youth are clear in Olcott's thought, which emphasized values, such as adaptationism, cultural immanentism, progressivism, optimism, and activism, that historians of American Protestant theology have long recognized as the salient features of the liberal Protestant mainstream.[17] The proximity of Olcott's thought to the theologies of his American Protestant contemporaries is most marked, however, in his clearly ecumenical obsession with constructing unity out of diversity and his staunch commitment to reform. Before his passage to Asia, Olcott worked to unify a nation rent in two by the Civil War. And in 1875 he and Russian-born Helena Petrovna Blavatsky established the Theosophical Society in New York City, in an attempt to unite all true spiritualists under the banner of improving spiritualism. By the time of his arrival in India in 1879, however, Olcott had effectively retooled the Theosophical Society from an American society for spiritualist reform into an international organization committed to gathering practitioners of all the world's faiths into one nonsectarian family. While in Ceylon, Olcott labored to unite monks of the island's three competing Theravada Buddhist sects into a nonpartisan "Buddhist Ecclesiastical Council" and to gather lay Buddhists of all stripes into nonsectarian "Buddhist Theosophical Societies." Later he worked to knit Mahayana and Theravada Buddhists across Asia into an "International Buddhist League" and to gather Buddhists from East and West into a "United Buddhist World." Finally and most dramatically he endeavored to gather all human beings into one great pan-religious and transnational "Universal Brotherhood of Humanity."

Despite all the ways in which his thought paralleled the theologies of his American Protestant contemporaries, Olcott's connections to his American Protestant past are most evident in his actions. Throughout his sojourn in Asia, Olcott patterned his behaviors after American and Protestant models, which he then used to legitimate those same behaviors. When Olcott organized the Theosophical Society, he did so on a federal model, after the manner of the United States of America, complete with a written constitution and himself as the organization's Lincoln-like president; when he established the *Theosophist* as the official magazine of the Theosophical Society, he did so in accordance with what he termed the "American plan" of cash payment in advance; and when he worked to popularize the "Buddhist Flag" he did so with the hope that it would serve "the same purpose [for all Buddhists] as that of the cross does for all Christians."[18]

Though Olcott viewed himself as a defender of Buddhism and Hinduism against their Christian missionary despisers, his actions mirrored those of his hated missionaries at nearly every turn. Like them, he authored and distributed catechisms, promoted the translation of scriptures into vernacular languages, established Sunday Schools and other educational institutions, founded youth organizations (e.g., Young Men's Buddhist Associations), wrote and distributed tracts and periodicals, conducted open-air revivals, and organized his converts into parish-like branches. Also like them, he tended to define particular religious traditions exclusively in light of the doctrines enunciated in their scriptures. As a result, he too despised popular rituals as utterly extraneous to true religion.

What Olcott mimicked most strongly, however, was the missionaries' activistic emphasis on social reform. Toward the end of Olcott's sojourn in Asia, the American Protestant missions theorist Robert E. Speer bragged that foreign missions had "promoted temperance, opposed the liquor and opium traffics . . . checked gambling, established higher standards of personal purity, cultivated industry and frugality, elevated woman," opposed slavery, "organized famine relief, improved husbandry and agriculture, introduced Western medicines and medical science, founded leper asylums and colonies, promoted cleanliness and sanitation, and checked war."[19] Olcott's laundry list of reforms was nearly as long. He too preached temperance, women's rights, animal rights, and peace while laboring to introduce western agricultural, medical, and technological innovations to the Orient.

Olcott's optimism and activism, his desire to construct unity out of diversity, his commitment to reform, his progressivism and cultural immanentism mark him not only as an American Protestant but as a particular sort of American Protestant. Theologically, Olcott shared more with liberals such as Horace Bushnell than with evangelicals like Charles Finney. And socially, Olcott demonstrated affinities not with working-class Protestants but with that tradition's genteel elites. The religious ethos that Olcott imported to Asia was, therefore, no generic American Protestantism. It was, on the contrary, the sort of liberal Protestantism that flourished in genteel social circles in Gilded Age America.

Both Olcott's intellectual ties to Protestant liberalism and his social connections with gentility are evident in his repeated efforts to "uplift" the masses. First in the United States and later in Asia, Olcott labored to transform the supposedly vulgar masses into respectable ladies and gentlemen of "character" and "culture" by instilling in them what Matthew Arnold referred to as "the best that has been thought and written in the world." In the United States, Olcott concentrated on "uplifting" spiritualists out of both ignorance and immorality. Later, in Asia, he focused on "uplifting" Hindus and Buddhists by liberating them from sectarianism, superstitions, and unseemly rituals. In this way, Olcott participated in what Norbert Elias has identified as "The Civilizing Process."[20]

In addition to noting that Olcott creatively combined Asian and Western, Protestant and Buddhist elements in constructing his adult faith, this study attempts to interpret exactly *how* Olcott combined these disparate traditions. And it argues that Olcott's "Protestantized" Buddhism is best understood as a "creolization" of liberal American Protestantism and traditional Theravada Buddhism. In referring to Olcott's adult faith as a "creole" faith I am borrowing an interpretive tool from the field of linguistics. To linguists, a creole language is a new linguistic creation (from the Latin *creare*, "to create" and the Portuguese *criar*, "to raise, e.g., a child") that emerges

The White Buddhist

when individuals from diverse speech communities come together, typically in colonial settings, under the hegemonic authority of a host language. In the case of Haitian creole, for example, slaves from various West African language groups met under the hegemonic authority of French-speaking colonists. What resulted from this contact situation was a simplified new creole language that creatively combined elements of both French and West African languages. One key facet of languages such as Haitian creole is their tendency not merely to combine these elements but to do so in a specific way. Typically, the lexicon or outer form of the new creole language is derived almost entirely from the host language, while the language's inner form (its grammar, syntax, morphology, etc.) emerges almost as strongly from common elements in the émigrés' substrate languages. Linguistic theory regarding creole languages thus articulates an important fact about linguistic transformation: individuals seem to be almost as insistent about clinging to inherited grammatical forms as they are comfortable with adopting new vocabularies.[21]

Seizing on the fact that other cultural forms function like languages in colonial settings, some anthropologists and cultural historians have begun to refer to the "creolization" of colonial cultures in an attempt to explicate how cultural transformations occur in conditions of cultural contact. For example, in a study of a slave community in All Saints Parish in the South Carolina low-country, anthropologist/historian Charles Joyner has discerned, in addition to linguistic creolization, an analogous creolization of crafts, foodways, housing, and work patterns. According to Joyner, these slaves creatively combined West African folkways with the cultural imperatives of their British-American masters to construct creole cultural forms. These creole cultural forms exhibited the two key features of creole languages identified above. They were, first of all, simplified rather than elaborate forms. Second, they tended to combine West African and British-American influences in a distinctively creole manner. While the "lexicon" or outer form of the cultural practice seems to have been derived from British-American culture, the "grammar" or inner form of that practice seems to have been derived from West Africa. "If slave clothing consisted of the garments issued by the masters," Joyner notes, "how those garments were worn and what their wearing meant to the slaves reflected cultural continuity with Africa."[22]

This discursus into linguistic and cultural theory should convey some sense of what will be meant here when Olcott's Buddhism is referred to as a "creolization" of the Protestantism of his youth and the Buddhism of his adulthood. Like linguistic and cultural creoles, Olcott's "creole" faith represented, first of all, a simplification of both Protestantism and Buddhism.

Introduction

Olcott's Buddhism was a nominal Buddhism, shorn of ostensibly peculiar beliefs and rituals that Olcott thought were extraneous to "real" Buddhism. Second, and perhaps more importantly, Olcott's creole faith combined Protestant and Buddhist elements in a distinctive way. While the lexicon of his faith was almost entirely Buddhist, its grammar was largely Protestant. If you think of the religious beliefs and behaviors of Olcott as a form of discourse, it will become apparent that at the more superficial lexical level, Olcott echoed his Asian Buddhist acquaintances both in words and in actions. At this level, Olcott was able to leap out of his American Protestant past, to utter the correct words, perform the appropriate actions, and thus to pass not only as a Buddhist but also, at various times, as a Hindu, a Muslim, a Jew, and even a Zoroastrian! But at the more enduring grammatical level of deep structural and unconscious assumptions, Olcott remained an American Protestant. Glimpse Olcott for a moment and he looks like a Buddhist apologist; but survey him more carefully and you will discern a Protestant missionary.

The point of this admonition to look at Olcott with a sort of double vision is not to reinforce the obvious truth that things are seldom what they seem but to underscore the fact that Olcott's life can teach us something more than the veracity of the now-popular thesis that American religion has for some time been astonishingly pluralistic. In fact, it is my contention that historians of American religion who are now attempting to supplant theses of Protestant hegemony with theses of the triumph of pluralism are not only misreading the historical evidence but also misunderstanding the process through which Americans have appropriated faiths foreign to their parents.[23] While it is undoubtedly true that Olcott and his Theosophical Society contributed to religious diversity in America by helping to transform Asian religious traditions into plausible religious options for many Americans, it is equally true that they accomplished this formidable task only by reshaping those religions in the direction of American Protestantism. Thus my contention that Olcott's life represents evidence not only for the pluralization of American religion in the late nineteenth century but also for the persistence in that same period of American Protestant influence.

In addition to arguing that Olcott's Buddhism was a creole faith that combined elements of the Buddhism of his adulthood and the American Protestantism of his youth, this book takes on one additional task: to explain how Asians themselves, and especially Asian Buddhists, responded to Olcott's attempts to "creolize" their faiths. To what extent did they acquiesce to his innovations? And to what extent did they resist them?

Exactly how successful Olcott was in transplanting his creole faith to

The White Buddhist

Asian soil is difficult to assess. Most obvious, however, are Olcott's successes. At the time of Olcott's arrival in Ceylon, there were only four Buddhist schools there, but at the time of his death in 1907 Buddhist schools numbered in the hundreds, and their pupils in the tens of thousands.[24] Moreover, before Olcott, no Sinhalese Buddhist had thought to reduce Buddhism to its beliefs and then to compress those beliefs into a simple question-and-answer format, as Olcott did, in his celebrated *The Buddhist Catechism* (1881). Shortly after its publication, Olcott's catechism became a standard textbook in the Buddhist schools he had established across the island. As children reared in Olcott's schools, and read in his catechism, grew up and achieved positions of power, Olcott's idiosyncratic Buddhism began to present a serious challenge to traditional Theravada Buddhism. Soon this new tradition, which scholars now refer to as "Protestant Buddhism,"[25] had become the religion of choice for the island's influential new middle class. In our century, many of the island's great leaders were educated in Olcott-founded Buddhist schools.[26]

Of course, not all Asians applauded Olcott's creolization of traditional Theravada Buddhism and liberal American Protestantism. Buddhist reformers, such as Ceylon's Anagarika Dharmapala, eventually rejected both Olcott's definitions of their faith and his attempts to subject them to "the civilizing process." Gradually they came to see Olcott not as some *homme universel* standing above and beyond national and religious loyalties but as a particular, even peculiar, product of a specific time and place. Toward the end of his life, Olcott's Hindu friends rejected him as too Buddhist, and his Buddhist allies as too Hindu. Some theosophists, meanwhile, determined he was not theosophical enough. In the end, Olcott's various quests for unity ended in failure. His Theosophical Society was rent in two, his "United Buddhist World" did not materialize, and his "United Brotherhood of Humanity" collapsed in a series of mutual recriminations.

Hindsight—and a dose of postmodern skepticism about unities, universals, and other grand schemes—reveals that what finally undermined Olcott's Asian errand was the very thing that initially made it successful: the creole nature of his religious faith. On numerous occasions, Olcott had informed his Asian audiences that he had severed his ties with the nation and with the religion of his birth. He had, in effect, gone native, transforming himself into "a Hindu in white skin" or, in the parlance of his Sinhalese admirers, "the White Buddhist." But Olcott did not magically eradicate his American Protestant past. Following his arrival in Asia, Olcott was received magnificently by Hindus and Buddhists alike as a champion of Asian religions and a critic of Christian missions. He was able to sustain alliances

Introduction

with Asian religious reformers, however, only so long as they were acquainted merely with his superficial beliefs and behaviors (the "lexicon" of
his faith). As soon as Olcott's Asian allies became aware of the enduring
structural assumptions that informed his thought and action (his "grammar"—to say nothing of what I will analyze as his theosophical "accent"),
they rejected his faith as foreign to their own.

To view Olcott's life, therefore, is not simply to see the pluralization of
American religion or the "Protestantization" and "Americanization" of the
religious traditions of Asia. It is also to view indigenous Asian attempts,
successful and otherwise, to resist those transformations. It is, moreover, to
glimpse some of the means whereby all people of faith in conditions of
cultural contact contest both the forms and the meanings of their religious
traditions.

In conclusion, readers should be forewarned that this book is a critical
work. That is not to say, however, that it represents yet another polemical
book on the theosophical movement. Inquirers interested in a vigorous defense of Olcott as a co-sufferer alongside Helena Blavatsky in the cause of
truth will find no comfort here, but neither will readers interested in a
denunciation of Olcott as Blavatsky's accomplice or dupe. I quite intention-
ally finesse questions regarding, for example, the genuineness of spiritual
phenomena attributed to Blavatsky and the reality of her beloved "Masters"
or "Mahatmas." Happily, readers interested in these subjects will not suffer
for a lack of relevant texts. Believers and skeptics alike have published a
seemingly endless stream of tracts and treatises on these matters, and I do
not see anything to be gained by adding my two cents.[27] My tendency
throughout, therefore, is to bracket any judgment not only of Blavatsky's
work as a medium but also of Olcott's various spiritual experiences. I do
not know what criteria might distinguish a genuine mesmeric healing from
a fake one. And even if I did, I do not pretend to occupy any privileged
seat from which I might objectively judge the relevant evidence. I endeavor
instead simply to interpret what those experiences might have meant to
Olcott himself and what significance they might have had on his life.

Despite my insistence on treating these matters "phenomenologically," I
do present a critical perspective on Olcott's life. My criticisms are aimed,
however, less at Olcott himself than at the liberal theories of religion he
expounds and at the liberal style of interreligious encounter that he exemplifies. These liberal theories and this liberal style were (and are), in my
view, at least vaguely colonial and imperialistic. According to Olcott, all
religions were one, but the one religion toward which all other religions
converged was Olcott's own creole faith, which was itself identical, in

Olcott's view, with "true" Buddhism, "genuine" Hinduism and, of course, theosophy rightly understood. And while Olcott extolled religious tolerance, he was exceedingly intolerant of people of faith (conservative Christians in particular) who did not share his liberal views. Olcott's encounter with the Asian "other" reduced, more often than not, to an encounter with his liberal American and Protestant "self."

Given my conviction that Olcott's Asian legacy was mixed, on the one hand, and Olcott's own interest in body "doubles," on the other, it might be appropriate to conclude this introduction with the observation that Olcott frustrates the biographer's quest for personal coherence by incarnating himself in Asia in two antithetical modes. Like Rudyard Kipling, in whose speech critics have discerned two mutually contradictory voices—a "masculine" discourse of imperial right and responsibility (the "saxophone") and a "feminine" discourse of cross-cultural empathy (the "oboe")—Olcott spoke in two distinct voices. Perhaps because Olcott's empathetic "oboe" is so readily heard and so easily celebrated by contemporary readers (especially liberal readers in the West), this book takes pains to enable the reader to tune a more critical ear to his imperial "saxophone." Thus this interpretation of Olcott as an American Protestant who hacks at his roots but never quite severs them—an American gentleman abroad who remained until his death as much Protestant as anti-Protestant, as much American as anti-American, as much missionary as anti-missionary.

It would be unfair both to Olcott and to his admirers, however, not to attend sympathetically to Olcott's "oboe" as well, and this book attempts to do just that. Olcott was undoubtedly at least as much a victim of colonialism as he was a perpetuator of it. And in seeking to shape Buddhism in his own image he was probably doing nothing more nefarious than what religious people have always done: creatively adapting his faith to his circumstances. During his lifetime, listeners attentive to the creative tones of Olcott's "oboe" constructed the Colonel as a revolutionary "King of Righteousness" who had come to deliver the Buddhists of the island of Ceylon from rule by Christian colonizers. And long after his death, less ardent but more effective reformers invoked Olcott's name in the successful struggle for an independent Sri Lanka. These interpretations of Olcott's life were embraced by large numbers of the island's inhabitants not simply because they were useful but also because they rang true.

Despite his inability to cut the perhaps unseverable ties that bound him to America and to Protestantism, Olcott did travel farther, both geographically and spiritually, into the heart of Asia than any of his American contemporaries. In Sri Lanka, Olcott assisted at the birth of a new religious tradition that scholars now refer to as "Protestant Buddhism." And in India he contributed, albeit more indirectly, to the Indian Renaissance. Though many of Olcott's programs and projects died with him, his Theosophical Society abides, as do his many Indian and Sri Lankan schools. And, thanks to the books, articles, letters, and diaries he left behind, so too does one of the grandest metanarratives of the modern period—a poignant reminder of what now seems like a very distant time and place.

One

Universal Reformer

To most Americans 1832 lacks the ring of, say, 1492 or 1776. But to the Buddhist community in Sri Lanka, the worldwide family of theosophists, and the Olcott clan in America, 1832 rang with significance. In the sacred time of millions of Sinhalese Buddhists, the year produced a being who was destined to become a Buddhist revivalist. In the hallowed history of the Theosophical Society, 1832 brought into the world a boy who would become its founder. And to the more immediate family of Henry Steel Olcott—his father, Henry Wyckoff Olcott, and his mother, Emily Steel Olcott—this was the year that the Lord Jesus Christ blessed their Orange, New Jersey, home with its firstborn son.

For those Americans who were graced with neither patriarch nor savior nor son in 1832, the year still offered its share of memorable events. The American people—or at least the majority of white freemen who went to the polls—reaffirmed their faith in President Andrew Jackson; and Charles Grandison Finney, the father of modern revivalism, engineered yet another revival, this time at the Chatham Street Theatre in New York City, not far from the Olcott family home.

Henry's parents shared their newfound parenthood, therefore, with the Age of Jackson and the Second Great Awakening; and their son inherited, along with his parents' genes, that curious amalgam of Jacksonian democracy and Protestant revivalism that Ralph Gabriel has described as "the American democratic faith."[1] Olcott would in adulthood pledge his allegiance to the Republican rather than the Democratic party, and to Buddhism rather than Christianity, but he would carry a combination of liberal Enlightenment and Protestant Christian influences with him, largely unwittingly, on his mid-life passage to Asia.

In 1832, however, that ritual passage lay far ahead. Olcott's more immediate task was to assist his country in a rite of passage of its own. At the time Olcott was born, America stood poised between rural and urban life, and between agricultural and industrial economies. The campaigns for women's rights, temperance, and the abolition of slavery were getting under way. Charles Lyell's *Principles of Geology* (1830–1832) had fired the opening salvo in the warfare between science and religion. And thanks to burgeoning immigration, the nation's Protestant-dominated past was gradually giving way to a religiously plural future.

Universal Reform

Americans responded to these intellectual and social challenges in a variety of ways. Between the end of the War of 1812 and the beginning of the Civil War, many, Olcott included, took up a career that had not existed in the previous century. They became reformers. Inspired by Enlightenment promises of freedom and equality, as well as Protestant hopes for individual perfection and a coming millennium, this new breed labored not to grow wheat or to operate machines but to improve individuals. The most famous and successful reform movement of the antebellum period was, of course, abolitionism. But reformers in Olcott's time typically championed a host of additional improvements, including temperance, Christian missions, women's rights, world peace, Sabbatarianism, humanitarianism, and health and educational reform. These reformers also latched on to a few causes that many now view as illiberal or irrational or both. Anti-Catholic nativism and laissez-faire economic theories, for example, were rife among reformers; and many believed that phrenology or spiritualism would produce a better world at least as quickly as the abolition of slavery.[2]

Although some of these reformers banded together into utopian communities that aimed at nothing less than the establishment of heaven (or, almost as frequently, ancient Rome) on earth,[3] others formed slightly less grandiose but ultimately more enduring voluntary associations that focused on specific problems and particular tasks. Many of these interdenominational organizations—the American Bible Society, the American Tract Society, the American Home Missionary Society, the American Sunday School Union—were devoted to Christian missions. But others, such as the American Temperance Society, the American Peace Society, and the American Antislavery Society, crusaded for causes that even the most committed rationalists could love. Together these voluntary associations comprised a "benevolent empire" dedicated to remaking the world by transforming individuals along a combination of Protestant and Enlightenment lines.

This "benevolent empire" did not enjoy absolute moral and spiritual authority in the antebellum period; many conducted their lives independent of its considerable influence. But it did enjoy hegemony in many areas and among many individuals in America. Nowhere is the hegemonic reach of this reforming empire more evident than in the rhetoric of its critics. Nathaniel Hawthorne thought the reformers' potent combination of religious enthusiasm and public power merited denunciation, which he delivered forcefully in novels such as *Blithedale Romance* (1852). But Orestes A. Brownson, a journalist who flirted with Universalism and Unitarianism before pledging his fidelity to the Roman Catholic Church, may have been the reform movement's most eloquent debunker. "Whole armies of real or pretended reformers swarm over the land," he complained in a speech in 1844. "They meet us in highways and byways; they come into our houses, into our sleeping chambers, and our kneading troughs. There is no escaping them, and they give us no rest by day or by night."[4] Brownson's denunciations were, of course, hyperbolic. There may have been "no escaping" reformers in the liberal Protestant circles of middle-class New England society in which Brownson ran, but the pulse of reform was far fainter among Catholics, in the South and the West, and among working-class Americans. For all its fame (and notoriety), reform remained a minority movement in antebellum America. Nonetheless, in a country still dominated by a Protestant establishment firmly rooted in New England soil and middle-class society, antebellum reform was a national impulse to be reckoned with.[5]

The antebellum reform spirit that Brownson derided differed significantly from the spirit that possessed reformers after the Civil War. That the Civil War precipitated an important shift in American reform was recognized by intellectuals in Olcott's time. Francis Parkman, the patrician historian who trekked the Oregon Trail in 1846, discerned a "new reform" in the postwar period.[6] Historians now highlight the differences between antebellum and postbellum reform by referring to the former impulse as "universal" and the latter as "progressive."[7] The differences between these two reform impulses are crucial to the telling of Olcott's story because Olcott's style of reform synthesized the two. He was one of a significant minority of nineteenth-century reformers who carried the ethos of antebellum reform into the postbellum period, transforming it along the way.

Historians have distinguished between "universal" and "progressive" reform in four related ways. First, universal reform was comprehensive. Andrew Jackson Davis, spiritualism's premiere philosopher, referred to a "Fraternity of Reforms" in the antebellum period. Thomas Wentworth Higginson, perhaps the most "universal" of all universal reformers, feminized Davis's metaphor, championing a "Sisterhood of Reforms" and noting that "one was expected to accept all, if any." Unlike later reformers who typically focused on one cause, antebellum reformers were obliged to reexamine *every* social institution and individual practice—"the institution of the State or the practice of shaving, the institution of the Church, or the eating of meat, the institution of marriage or the wearing of beards."[8]

A second, related characteristic of antebellum reform was its unbridled optimism. Unlike postwar reformers, who saw the road to progress as both long and treacherous, universal reformers perceived few obstacles on the rapid road to individual perfection and social improvement. Even the names of the utopian communities they founded—"Hopedale" and "New Harmony," for example—testified to these reformers' boundlessness. While progressives aimed simply to improve society as best they could, the goal of these universal reformers was nothing less than the kingdom of God on earth and the brotherhood and sisterhood of the human race.

Third, universal reform was individualistic and anti-institutional. Like the revivalists who stressed individual conversion rather than churchly rites, these reformers emphasized individual transformation rather than institutional modifications. Convinced that the best way to change society was to change individuals, they did not attempt, for the most part, to enlist in their crusades the coercive powers of government. This attitude differentiated them markedly from postwar reformers who saw government as an ally. Informed by the experience of the Civil War, these later reformers had witnessed firsthand the capacities of government to organize for change. In order to ensure that government live up to these capacities, they struggled to reform the political system itself, exposing corruption among city machines such as Boss Tweed's Tammany Hall and laboring to purify the civil service.[9]

Finally, universal reformers distinguished themselves from their postwar counterparts by the intensity of their religious commitments. Whereas later reformers drew on the authority of science more frequently than the authority of scripture, most antebellum reformers were religious enthusiasts. An abundance of antebellum reformers were northeastern Protestants; and reform burned hottest in areas previously ignited by revivals.

Despite their commitments to Protestantism, however, universal reformers contributed, albeit unwittingly, to the liberalization and democratization of American religion. Along with evangelical Protestant notions such as millennialism, voluntaryism, and perfectionism, antebellum reformers drew on liberal Enlightenment ideals such as reason and science, benevolence and human rights, equality and brotherhood, the inevitability of progress and the possibility of human perfectibility. As Finney had democratized Puritanism in his celebrated Second Great Awakening revivals, these universal reformers liberalized revivalism itself. Individual regeneration remained the goal, and the individual self retained the capacity to choose it. But the way to that goal was now education and moral uplift rather then conversion. Through the efforts of the universal reformers, the home and the schoolhouse supplemented the camp-meeting and the church as sites for individual regeneration, and the mother and the schoolmarm became, along with the Protestant preacher, arbiters of religious and moral transformation.

Comprehensive, optimistic, individualistic, and religious, universal reform articulated one of the grandest metanarratives of an age inundated with grandiose schemes. In the *grand récit* of the universal reformers, evangelical and liberal ideals alike played key roles. Thanks to the joint labors of preachers and schoolmarms, the best men and women of America were, through a host of interrelated reforms, propelling individuals, society, and indeed the whole world inexorably upward and onward toward a utopia approximating, on the one hand, the ancient Republic of Rome and, on the other, the future kingdom of God on earth.

As the following narrative of Olcott's young adulthood will demonstrate, Olcott was to become an energetic universal reformer. While in the United States, Olcott would enlist in reform movements as diverse as spiritualism, mesmerism, chastity, cremation, and agricultural reform. And he would eventually found a new reform movement, theosophy, after determining that the spiritualist movement was itself in need of improvement. But Olcott would freely mix elements of antebellum and postbellum reform even as he translated the American metanarrative of universal reform into an Asian idiom. In the United States, he would aim not only to reform individuals but also to uplift institutions. He would struggle to rationalize insurance law, to clean up the Army and Navy, and to rid Tammany Hall of corrupt politicians. And in Asia, he would work for nothing less than a fundamental refashioning of Buddhist and Hindu ideas and institutions. But even as he championed these seemingly "progressive" causes, Olcott would remain committed to what may have been the primary principle of "universal" reform, namely, the commitment to reforming individuals first.

For the time being, however, Olcott would concentrate on reforming Americans. He would embrace a multitude of reforms in the hope that transformed individuals would usher in a kingdom of moral and spiritual harmony in which the chaos of urbanization, immigration, and industrialization would yield to an orderly nation and a unified people. If, as newspaperman Horace Greeley wrote of the mid-nineteenth century, "not to have been a Reformer is not to have truly lived," then Olcott was most emphatically to be found among the living.[10]

From Presbyterianism to Spiritualism

Henry Olcott was the eldest of six children born to Henry Wyckoff and Emily Steel Olcott. At least in the adult memory of their firstborn son, the Olcott household was a happy one and its heads were pious Presbyterians. As such, they were members of an unofficial but nonetheless hegemonic Protestant establishment that lorded over the public religious life of the nation. The theology of that establishment was, according to Philip Schaff, a German-born church historian who visited the United States during Olcott's youth, "the reigning theology of the country."[11]

Although the Olcotts were faithful enough to baptize their son and to tithe to the church, we do not know whether they adhered strictly to the Calvinist orthodoxy of American Presbyterianism. We do know, however, that Olcott received an excellent biblical education, since as an adult he peppered his speeches with New Testament parables and quoted the Bible repeatedly and correctly. Olcott also must have received an excellent education in the sort of pithy moral maxims for which Ben Franklin was famous, since his adult writing is nearly as replete with aphorisms such as "Heaven helps those who help themselves," as it is with Bible verses.[12]

Olcott apparently also imbibed the major Calvinistic tenets of the "reigning theology," including the absolute sovereignty of God, the total depravity of humans, and God's predestination of individuals to either heaven or hell. In fact, Olcott was so thoroughly immersed in the worldview of conservative Presbyterian theology that he would throughout his adult life misidentify Calvin's legacy in American Puritanism and Presbyterianism with Christianity itself. While many who shared Olcott's distaste for conservative theologizing were making their way into liberal Protestant churches, Olcott was so steeped in conservative Presbyterian theology that he was unable to imagine, at least until very late in his life, a liberal Christianity shorn of Calvinist horrors. This inability to imagine a liberal Christianity would later fuel not only his praise of the ostensibly tolerant religious traditions of the East but also his adult disdain for the Christian tradition.

Olcott's odyssey from the orthodox verities of his Puritan and Presbyterian ancestry to the liberal truths of Buddhism apparently began quite early. Olcott reports that at the age of twelve he traveled to western New York state to witness the clairvoyant powers of Andrew Jackson Davis, the

"Poughkeepsie Seer" who would later serve as spiritualism's unofficial philosopher. There he supposedly watched Davis, himself a young man of seventeen, determine "from a lock of a sick man's hair held in his hand, . . . an accurate diagnosis of the disease, its cause and remedy."[13]

At some time during Olcott's youth, his family moved from Orange, New Jersey, to New York City. In 1847, at the age of fifteen, he enrolled at the University of the City of New York (now New York University).[14] After one year, however, he dropped out, joining many young men of his generation in heeding the call to "Go West" into America's wilderness. This manly adventure took him as far as northern Ohio, a bit short of the frontier. There Olcott encountered various forms of "ultraist" excitement that inhabited the popular landscape of the "Burned-Over District."[15] Olcott's youthful encounter with religious traditions far removed from the Presbyterianism of his youth—adventism, Mormonism, mesmerism, Swedenborgianism, and, most significantly, spiritualism—constituted his initiation into the multiplicity of "religious liberalism"[16] in mid-nineteenth-century America and set him on a road that would eventually lead him to embrace Buddhism.

Although the religious movements that scorched the frontier are rightly understood as discrete spiritual impulses, they had much in common. Perhaps most importantly, each was a liberal faith that stood against the sorts of Calvinist verities that Olcott had encountered in his Presbyterian home. Like liberal Protestantism, the most widely practiced and influential form of this diffuse liberal faith, each of these impulses tended to emphasize individual religious experience over corporate rituals, and good works ("deeds") over confessionalism ("creeds"). Each was drawn to Enlightenment values such as liberty, equality, and human brotherhood and sisterhood. Participants in these traditions also refused for the most part to discriminate between clergy and laypeople. They posited no external authorities mediating between themselves and God or Truth. Some even shunned distinctions between humans and God. Almost all participants in these liberal faiths displayed tendencies toward optimism and activism. They roundly rejected Calvinist constructions of human depravity and believed that through strenuous efforts human beings could improve not only their lots and the lives of their families but also society at large. Together these affinities inclined religious liberals toward commitments to both individual regeneration and social reform. Their traditions promised to all who would strenuously pursue it a coming new day.

Of all these liberal traditions, spiritualism commended itself most highly to Olcott. Spiritualists joined religious liberals of all stripes in conspiring to democratize the American religious landscape in mid-nineteenth-century America. But spiritualists distinguished themselves from other religious liberals in two controversial ways. First, spiritualists affirmed that spirits of the dead can and do communicate, through the agency of mediums, with the living; and second, they participated in rituals that formulated even as they expressed this belief.[17]

The genesis of American spiritualism is typically traced to March 31, 1848, when mysterious rappings first emanated from beneath the kitchen table of Margaret and Katherine Fox of Hydesville, New York. The successful transformation of that isolated event into a popular theatrical can be attributed in large measure to the largesse (or self-interest) of magazine and newspaper editors, most prominently Horace Greeley of the *New York Tribune*. Convinced that spiritualist séances made good copy and at least a modicum of good sense, Greeley and other editors helped to turn spiritualism into popular entertainment in antebellum America. Among the famous folk drawn into spiritualist circles were Harriet Beecher Stowe, William Lloyd Garrison, George Ripley, Lydia Maria Child, William Cullen Bryant, and James Fenimore Cooper. Perhaps because of the tendency of mediums, many of them women, to speak the language of women's rights, many early feminists, including Susan B. Anthony, Elizabeth Cady Stanton, Frances Willard, Victoria Woodhull, and Sarah and Angelina Grimké, were also attracted to the movement.

Despite its undeniable ability to capture the imaginations of white, middle-class reformers, spiritualism remained for the most part a popular pastime, spread more effectively by P. T. Barnum (who took the Fox sisters on tour) than by New York literati. Although historian Jon Butler has attempted to restrict spiritualism's clientele to "white, mostly Anglo-Saxon, middle- and upper-middle-class former Protestants," scholars more widely read in the movement have concluded that spiritualists cut a surprisingly long and wide swath across lines of region, class, ethnicity, and gender. Ann Braude has uncovered significant support for spiritualism among women, blacks, urban and rural laborers, Southerners and Catholics; Lewis O. Saum has found that the letters of ordinary Americans in the period immediately before the Civil War evinced "a large fascination" with mediums and their messages; and R. Laurence Moore has concluded that spiritualism was "a truly popular movement in nineteenth-century America." One factor that apparently commended spiritualism to everyday folks was its compatibility with the democratic dictates of the Age of Jackson. "Spiritualism is democratic," a mid-century adherent affirmed. "It is addressed to the common people, and we are all common people."[18]

Among the "common people" who attended mid-century spiritualist

The White Buddhist

séances was Henry Steel Olcott. Olcott's western march to manhood had taken him through northern Ohio—first to Cleveland, then to Elyria and finally to Amherst—where he had traded in his college books for farming tools. While working as an agricultural laborer, Olcott met relatives whom he would later describe as "my true [spiritual] godfathers."[19] The Steele brothers, well-to-do citizens of Amherst, Ohio, who had lent Olcott his middle name, had formed a spiritualist circle after attending a Cleveland demonstration of the Fox sisters' powers.[20]

True to its roots in universal reform, early spiritualism abhorred institutions. The spiritualist circle was, therefore, the closest the movement came to institutionalizing itself in its early years. Circles such as the one Olcott joined in Ohio typically followed the dictates of the new Victorian cult of domesticity.[21] The creed of this cult affirmed at least two verities: first, that the woman's domain was the private sphere of the home, while the man's domain was the public sphere of the workplace; and second, that women were the guardians of moral and spiritual virtues, which were to be exercised at home among the family. Like the domesticity cult, the spiritualist circle restricted its members to family (and, in some cases, close friends) and met in the sanctity of a member's home; its rites too were private rather than public. The Steeles' circle, though typical in most respects, diverged from the norm by including only men. Bereft of the gender acknowledged as expert in the spiritual and domestic domains, the circle met for eight months without enjoying a single spirit manifestation. Immediately after a female medium joined their ranks, however, the Steeles began to receive communications from spirits of the dead. Subsequently, three male members were empowered to perform the more "masculine" task of healing by the laying on of hands.

Through his participation in the Steeles' circle, Olcott was introduced to the wonders of spiritualism. He saw tables suspended in air, heard spirit-raps, and dodged objects hurled mysteriously around a séance room. He also participated in a series of spiritualist theatricals in which five or six mediums were empowered "to speak different languages, and to imitate the customs of different tribes and nations, showing the different stages of man's progression." Through these cosmopolitan dramas, Olcott was initiated into the liberal theory of progress in both the material and the spiritual spheres. Simultaneously he was awakened to the fact of cultural and religious diversity. At one séance, Olcott reportedly "acted the aboriginal or Indian character to perfection."[22]

Thanks to the efforts of his "spiritual grandfathers," Olcott became at the age of twenty a self-proclaimed "convert to spiritualism."[23] But coinciding with Olcott's conversion to spiritualism was an equally formative conversion to universal reform. While in Ohio in 1852, Olcott reports, he was reacquainted with Andrew Jackson Davis, who informed him that a "great field of Reform" was opening up in the United States and abroad for worldly-wise spiritualists who were willing to work as "missionaries to the infidel world."[24] These words inspired Olcott to make himself into just such a reformer, setting him on a course that would eventually lead him to India and Ceylon and impel him to embrace reforms as diverse as antislavery, women's rights, temperance, educational reform, vegetarianism, agricultural reform, cremation, and Buddhist revivalism.

For a time, however, Olcott was content to reform spiritualism itself by investigating its causes and effects. This he did by immersing himself in the study of psychology, hypnotism, psychometry, and mesmerism—disciplines that he hoped would explain rationally the mysterious abilities of his "spiritual grandfathers" to perform healings with their hands. During Olcott's young adulthood, these nascent disciplines had not yet split into their current respected (psychology), quasi-respected (hypnotism), and unrespected (mesmerism) wings. So Olcott was not dissuaded from mesmerism, which quickly became his favorite science of the mind.

Although spiritualism and mesmerism became intimately interconnected in the United States, mesmerism borrowed its name, as well as its healing techniques and metaphysical theories, from a European: the Austrian physician Franz Anton Mesmer. According to Mesmer, all human beings possessed a subtle bodily fluid called "animal magnetism," and sickness resulted when this fluid became imbalanced. The goal of the mesmeric healer, therefore, was to rebalance the patient's "animal magnetism." This aim was typically accomplished through a series of passes of the healer's harmonious arms over the disharmonious area of the patient.[25]

Olcott had barely begun his investigations of mesmerism when he discovered that he possessed the gift of mesmeric healing. In a later letter to a friend, Olcott recalled that he had "developed clairvoyance in my first Mesmeric subject and cured my second of an inflammatory rheumatism at a single setting." In this first experiment, Olcott "placed a woman in a state of trance during which a surgical operation was performed upon her without her being aware of it until after she was released from the mesmeric spell." Not until he began to practice mesmerism in earnest in Ceylon much later in his life did Olcott achieve renown as a spiritual healer, but at least one friend viewed his mesmeric skills as evidence of his spiritualist credentials. This friend described Olcott as a spiritualist virtuoso—a healing "medium."[26]

Olcott's initiation into spiritualism and other forms of liberal religion came to an end in 1853, when at the age of twenty-one he returned to New York. There he continued to pursue both spiritualism and agriculture, another interest he had cultivated during his sojourn at the frontier. These two concerns coalesced when he enrolled in a course in agricultural chemistry taught by Professor James J. Mapes, himself a spiritualist. Soon Olcott was working as an assistant editor for the *Working Farmer*, Mapes's monthly magazine devoted to experimental agriculture, and holding down a post as American correspondent to the London-based periodical of the corn trade, the *Mark Lane Express*. Olcott had found his first calling, as a big-city journalist.

Olcott's new career did not prevent him, however, from continuing to devote the bulk of his creative energies to spiritualism. In 1853 he became one of the founding members of the New York Conference of Spiritualists, a group that met regularly at Dodworth Hall on Broadway in an attempt to provide some organizational form and intellectual substance to the diffuse movement.[27] The organization aimed, according to its charter, not to promote but merely to investigate spiritualism. Its objectives were twofold: "first, to ascertain, if possible, whether there is a life awaiting us in the future; secondly, whether there is an intercommunication between this and the Spiritual sphere."[28]

Like other spiritualists in America, members of the New York Conference of Spiritualists were divided over whether spiritualism should be understood as a supplement or an alternative to Christianity. So when a group of freethinking members proposed a Sunday lecture series on spiritualist topics, Christian members of the group rose in spirited opposition. Sabbath gatherings, they argued, were irreverent and Sunday lecturers might cut into the authority of Protestant preachers. The stance Olcott took on this issue provides the earliest evidence we have of his tendency toward freethought. In this debate (which the Christian spiritualists lost), Olcott aligned himself with the victorious freethinkers. When a committee was created to organize the conference's new Sunday lecture series, Olcott's name was included in its ranks.

From 1853, when the Dodworth Hall group was founded, until 1856 when an alternative calling diverted his attention from the spiritualist movement, Olcott utilized his newfound skills as a journalist by authoring a dozen or more articles in the New York-based *Spiritual Telegraph*, the most popular spiritualist newspaper of the time. These articles, many of them written under the pseudonym "Amherst," provide a rough outline of the contours of Olcott's early spiritualist faith.[29]

"The Spiritualist's Faith"

Olcott's first contributions to the *Telegraph* were largely reportorial: accounts of a spiritualist's funeral, a prophet's dreams, or the spiritual experiences of a German nobleman.[30] Later articles, more analytical in tone, attempted to integrate the spiritualist worldview with the allied sciences of psychology, hypnotism, and mesmerism.[31] Finally, and most significantly, a series of articles on mediumship revealed Olcott not simply as a spiritualist but also as a reformer intent on transforming the spiritualist movement from within.

In an attempt to capture the attention (and respect) of both convinced spiritualists and intrigued skeptics, Olcott portrayed himself in his articles as a middle-of-the-road captain who would steer the ship of spiritualism between the dangers of excessive credulity on the one hand and excessive skepticism on the other. He echoed fellow spiritualists by arguing that most mediums were able to produce genuine spiritual manifestations, but he conceded to the movement's despisers that even the best of mediums weren't above an occasional trick or two. Distancing himself from spiritualists who tended to exalt mediums as superhuman and to accept as genuine virtually all claims of spirit manifestations, Olcott contended that both the spirits that populated the séance rooms and the mediums that hosted them were merely human, and as such were prone to error and, occasionally, fraud. This mediating position presumed, of course, both the existence and the accessibility of some standard that could separate genuine manifestations from false ones. And the standard Olcott proposed was pragmatic. "The test of genuineness in Spirit-manifestations," Olcott contended, "is their promise of usefulness."[32]

This pragmatic rule was one of the key themes of Olcott's early writing on spiritualism. It demonstrated Olcott's temperamental preference for order over anarchy (a preference he would *not* share, by the way, with Theosophical Society co-founder Helena Blavatsky) and became, in his hands, a powerful force for constructing order amid the spiritualists' chaos of competing mediums and multiplying manifestations. It also exemplified the depth of Olcott's roots in bourgeois American culture and liberal Protestantism.

Consider, for example, Olcott's argument against the practice of spirit-writing—the most popular manifestation of early spiritualism in which mediums transcribed communications from spirits of the dead. Though apparently inclined in intellectual matters to freethought, Olcott leaned, in constructing his argument, neither on the words of Voltaire nor the counsel of Paine but, like any good Protestant preacher, on the authority of the Bible. Citing Paul's counsel in 1 Corinthians 14:26–33 that speaking in tongues should be conducted in good order, in the presence of an interpreter, and for the purposes of edification, Olcott argued that spirit manifestations also ought to produce orderly and practical results. The object of spiritualism was, in his view, "to prove the existence of life beyond the grave, and not to establish a series of cheap magical soirees to amuse the million."[33]

Proofs of the soul's immortality could come, of course, in as many guises as there were costumes at the Steele circle dramas. But, as Olcott frequently lamented, the collection of rappings and roarings, spirit-writings, and table-tossings that was spiritualism in the 1850s did not yet amount to a coherent philosophy. Spiritualists had recruited notables such as New York State Supreme Court Judge John Edmonds and U.S. Senator Nathaniel P. Talmadge, but they had not yet produced a philosopher. Spiritualism was still awaiting, in Olcott's words, a "new Newton" who could "unfold the laws of gravity, attraction and repulsion, that govern the particles of the Spirit-world."[34]

Olcott was neither sufficiently vain nor sufficiently trained in science and philosophy to fancy himself the synthesizer spiritualism was awaiting. He was, after all, only twenty-three years old and still a student of the movement. But in the last article he published in the *Telegraph*, Olcott did attempt to sum up his personal faith. This strikingly ethnocentric creed is especially noteworthy given Olcott's later pronouncements regarding the equality of all religions.

Olcott propounded in "The Spiritualist's Faith" an evolutionary theory of the triumphant march of religion from "savagery" to "civilization" that anticipated the anthropological theories of the steady progress of "culture" later advanced by scholars such as Herbert Spencer and Edward Tylor.[35] Just as in the theories of Tylor and Spencer "savage" cultures yielded to "barbarism" and finally to "civilization," in Olcott's theory "nobler" religions blossomed in soil formed by the crumbling of "baser" faiths.[36] "Tribes who have no idea of a God or of an immortality," he argued, are "steeped in barbarism, low and degraded in the scale of human being." And Islam, while preferable to this tribalism, is still based on "gratification of lust" and "thirst for dominion." Only with the emergence of spiritualism do we witness, according to Olcott, a faith built on "reasoning, hopefulness, mirth, benevolence, spirituality, reverence and universal tolerance."

Alongside this theory of the evolution of religion from the "primitive" to the "civilized," Olcott propounded an analogous theory of progress in the material sphere that echoed the hopes of many Christian missionaries of his time. According to Olcott, houses would soon replace huts, steam engines supplant paddle canoes, and barbaric tyrants yield to just governments. "Progression!" he wrote, "progression is the eternal law of our existence." Everything was advancing in his view "from lowest to highest, from bad to good, from small to great" in a "ceaseless, silent and irresistible march . . . upward, onward, to something more perfect, more Divine!"

In this cosmic drama of self-improvement and social reform spiritualism was a key actor. By fostering "an upright, dignified, conscientious, happy and intellectual mind," spiritualism contributed to the "advancement and elevation of character," and thereby to "a cheerful home." But spiritualism did far more than promote individual happiness and bliss at the shrine of the domesticity cult. By demonstrating with absolute certainty "the fact of immortality," spiritualism would provide the greatest possible incentive for ethical action and thus for a harmonious society. In the end, spiritualism would ensure nothing less than the triumph of democracy over tyranny. Even the resolution of factional disputes between northerners and southerners into "common interests and a common destiny" would be accomplished by heeding messages from the spirit world!

What is intriguing about this metanarrative is how Olcott integrated both equality and hierarchy, both religious pluralism and racial condescension. Thanks to the eclecticism of the Steele circle, and the inclusivism of periodicals like the *Telegraph* (whose editors printed articles on "Turkish customs and superstitions" and "Hindoo philosophy"), Olcott's awakening to spiritualism was also an awakening to cultural and religious diversity. But Olcott's nascent religious pluralism was tinged with a large measure of racial condescension. In Olcott's writings, as in the evolutionary dramas of the Steele circle in northern Ohio, the "lower races" played distinctly subordinate roles. So did spiritualism's own "barbarians"—the uneducated and sometimes unmarried mediums who according to Olcott were more interested in "dreamy speculations" than "the obligations of family, society, morality and decency." The genteel Olcott saw himself as a minister to both groups; he aimed to uplift all of them from animality and ignorance into a more harmonious order of philosophical coherence, moral responsibility, and cultural refinement.

According to Olcott's metanarrative, some religions, some races, and some individuals were more advanced than others. But this hierarchy was contingent rather than necessary. The religions, races, and individuals who had achieved a more lofty status had done so through their own legitimate efforts. And those who had worked less strenuously had been equally justly left behind. All were equally capable of being elevated by the inexorable force of what was best, but only some religions, some races, and some individuals had fully utilized those capacities.

Olcott's scheme thus represented a theological analog to laissez-faire economic theory. For Olcott, as for laissez-faire theorists, the fact that the playing field was level (whether in religion or in economics) legitimized the unequal outcomes of the game. Social order resulted neither from an equality of outcomes (as in socialism) nor from some static hierarchy (as in classical economic theory) but from a hierarchical dynamism in which everything was being lifted up. The fact that some were being lifted up more quickly and to higher heights was legitimized by the fact that those who rose in the ranks were also the hardest working.

Along with laissez-faire economic theory, a number of additional influences may have been at work in Olcott's early articles on spiritualism. Andrew Jackson Davis, whom Olcott evoked in one article as "the Harmonial philosopher," is perhaps the most obvious influence. Olcott's doctrine of progression, for example, is clearly indebted to Davis's vision that the soul after death passes through six increasingly glorious spheres.[37] The influence of Unitarianism is also apparent. In fact, the oft-cited credo of Unitarianism—"the Fatherhood of God, the Brotherhood of Man, the Leadership of Jesus, Salvation by Character, and the Progress of Mankind Onward and Upward Forever"—provides a strikingly apt abstract of Olcott's "A Spiritualist's Faith."

Transcendentalism also appears to have inspired, however indirectly, Olcott's construction of spiritualism. Olcott's God—and he *did* posit a deity—was more like Emerson's Oversoul than Calvin's Jehovah. This "God of Love . . . whisper[ed] to the soul in every evening breeze, flash[ed] in every sparkling sunbeam, live[d] in every shivering leaf . . . and shine[d] with ineffable glory in each traveling planet!" The patriarch not only of Christianity but of all religions, this "great Father of all" knit all of humanity into "a great network of brotherly love." Emerson's influence was also evident in Olcott's exaltation of spirit over matter, in his reliance on a doctrine of correspondences (which Emerson himself had borrowed from Swedenborg), and in his emphasis on self-culture.

Finally, Olcott appears to have imbibed at least something of the spirit of the communitarianism of antebellum utopians such as Robert Owen,

John Humphrey Noyes, and Albert Brisbane. Just as each of these reformers was drawn to spiritualism, Olcott was apparently drawn to their romantic universalism. Along with these men Olcott evinced a desire to resolve particularity into unity. He too embraced the many by imagining them as the one. "As the great sea is made up of single drops," he wrote, "so the family of man is composed of separate races, nations, tribes, and individuals, each acting independently of the other, and yet all together going to make up a harmonious whole."[38]

Olcott's "spiritualist's faith," while unorthodox, was no infidelity. Like many liberal Protestants, Olcott leaned on the authority as well as the literary models of the Christian scriptures even as he pressed beyond the Calvinist orthodoxies of the past. And like them he appealed to Jesus as a spiritual and moral exemplar—a man of "kindly tolerance" possessed by a "spirit of love"—even as he rejected traditional understandings of the Trinity and the unique divinity of Christ. Olcott distinguished himself from other religious liberals, in fact, in little more than his insistence that spiritualism was the *summum bonum* of religious evolution.

By the mid-1850s Olcott had thus become an odd sort of religious outsider. Though he had pressed beyond the Bible-based Presbyterianism of his youth to embrace a freethinking form of spiritualism, his new faith displayed important continuities with the faiths of other religious liberals, including liberal Protestants. Along with Unitarians like Channing, transcendentalists like Emerson, and utopian reformers such as Brisbane, Olcott affirmed a faith that was optimistic, activistic, adaptationist, cosmopolitan, reform-minded, and committed to resolving particularities into unity.

Agricultural Reform and Cultivating Character

"Amherst's" contributions to the *Telegraph* ended abruptly in April of 1856. One month later the *Telegraph* published advertisements for "Olcott and Vail's Farm School." At least for a time, Olcott had jettisoned his journalistic career. He had become an agricultural entrepreneur.

Advertisements described Olcott's Westchester Farm School in Mount Vernon, New York, as a place "where young men are taught the practical application of such scientific truths as have a direct bearing on agriculture." And, as if to shoo away bookish sorts who might be unwilling or unable to haul their share of hay, the ads warned that "a portion of the day is devoted to labor on the farm."[39] Later in life, Olcott wistfully remembered the Westchester Farm as a place "so well kept . . . that the passengers by the New Haven Railway . . . would crowd to our side of the train to look at our field."[40] But gaping passengers didn't pay the bills, and Olcott and Vail's experiment became one of many casualties the economic Panic of 1857.

Olcott's venture in entrepreneurial capitalism was not a complete failure, however. Experiments Olcott conducted on the culture of sorghum provided the subject matter for his first book, *Sorgho and Imphee, The Chinese and African Sugar Canes* (1857), which went through seven editions.[41] And Olcott's day-to-day experience on the farm provided material for speaking engagements before the New England Horticultural Society, the Agricultural Committees of the Massachusetts, the New York, and Ohio legislatures, and (much later) assorted agricultural organizations in India and Japan. During these lectures Olcott discovered his public voice and the status that resulted from its exercise. He also demonstrated for the first time a willingness to readily shift the objects of his reform. As passionately as he had argued for the reform of spiritualism and as fervently as he would soon contend for the reform of Buddhism, Olcott pleaded in the mid-1850s for the reform of agriculture. His labors on behalf of agricultural reform earned him two medals of honor from the U.S. Agricultural Society; and when that society appointed a committee in January 1857 to judge the latest improvements in agricultural implements and machinery, Olcott was in its ranks.[42]

Olcott's agricultural and journalist careers coalesced in 1860 when he revised and edited a do-it-yourself manual entitled *How to Cultivate and Preserve Celery*.[43] Although this book is for the most part an uninspiring document, Olcott's preface, which might more aptly have been titled, "How to Cultivate and Preserve Character," is a fascinating example of nineteenth-century self-help literature. Olcott devotes more ink to Emerson's beloved self-culture than to celery-culture, and his saga of Theophilus Roessle (the author of the manual and the hero of Olcott's introduction) mirrors in its style and in many of its details the Rollo stories of Jacob Abbott and the later morality tales of Horatio Alger. Like Abbott and Alger, Olcott aims in his preface not to induce in a depraved reader a Puritan conversion experience but to urge a basically decent reader to improve his or her character by practicing Yankee virtues such as hard work, honesty, and frugality. Olcott demonstrates his closeness to Abbott by situating his lesson not in the dangerous cities of Alger but in the idyllic countryside of Rollo. He presses beyond Abbott (whose readers were already solidly middle-class), however, and toward Alger (who appealed to readers who, like Olcott, were only aspiring to bourgeois status), by making ambition a virtue and holding out to his readers the promise of social mobility.[44]

Olcott begins his narrative by observing, with the dispassion of a budding Social Darwinist, the tendency of every type of business to produce winners and losers. He then observes the equally strong inclination of the losers to "think themselves the victims of malign influences, and bewail their bad luck." A more impartial observer, Olcott notes, would see that "the successful man has conquered his fortune by being industrious, economical, observing . . . [and] by using foresight and good judgment." This general observation Olcott then applies to the specific practice of market gardening. Frequently, he notes, people attempt to wrest a living from the soil without bringing to their business either "industrious habits" or "common sense." "These, and their number is very great," he observes, "are the ones who fail, and bewail their luck, and grow poorer and poorer, and finally sink to the condition of hired laborers for their more clever neighbors."

Happily, Olcott's Theophilus Roessle was not such a man. A rugged German immigrant who arrived in Rochester in 1825 with a boyhood friend, young Theophilus soon lost both his bag (to robbers) and his only friend (to illness). "Penniless in a land of strangers," he walked the country in worn shoes, without a change of clothes, and unable to speak English. While searching for a job he passed a farmer who offered to pay him sixpence to watch his horse while he stopped to eat breakfast. Theophilus accepted this modest work cheerfully. Odd jobs—shoveling snow, cutting firewood, and working in a doctor's office—followed. Eventually Roessle worked his way into the agricultural business and, by "living with the strictest frugality," amassed a great fortune.[45]

This preface clearly marks Olcott as both a consumer and a producer of the self-help literature of his time. Like Abbott and Alger, Olcott rejected not only the predestination of Calvin but also the closed class structure of England, both of which seemed to him unsuited to a world in which enlightened agriculturalists could make themselves wealthy by producing bumper crops where one generation earlier God had apparently willed them not to grow. Olcott's encounter with Buddhist and Hindu texts would later introduce him to a doctrine that could rationalize the process by which the cosmos distributed "good" and "bad" luck. That encounter would provide him, moreover, with the opportunity of introducing Buddhist and Hindu children to the bourgeois values celebrated in the writings of both Abbott and Alger. But long before he had heard the word "karma," Olcott was convinced that hard work produced good luck as surely as laziness yielded bad fortune.

How Olcott rationalized the bad fortune of his Westchester Farm School we do not know. But he did not respond by abandoning either his optimism or his commitment to laissez-faire economic theory. When, in the midst of a severe economic depression, Horace Greeley offered him a job at the *New York Tribune*, Olcott eagerly accepted. He was back in the business of journalism.

The *Tribune*

When Olcott joined the *Tribune* there was no shortage of big news. The failure of the New York branch of the Ohio Life Insurance and Trust Company had set off a spiral of foreclosures, bankruptcies, and unemployment that we now remember as the Panic of 1857, northerners were swelling the ranks of the newly formed Republican party, and the South was rehearsing for secession. *Tribune* writers, of course, covered those events like good Republicans, denouncing southern secessionists as traitors and bankers as immoral money-grubbers.[46]

Because the *Tribune* published most of its articles without bylines, it is difficult to document exactly which, if any, of these subjects Olcott investigated during his three-year tenure on Greeley's payroll. His previous journalist experience was with farming papers, such as the *Working Farmer* and the *Mark Lane Express*, and his official title at the *Tribune* was associate agricultural editor, so he probably devoted much of his time to agricultural subjects.[47] But he did cover other topics, including the hanging of abolitionist John Brown, who was sentenced to die on December 2, 1859, in Charlestown, Virginia, following his rebels' raid on the federal arsenal at Harper's Ferry. In one of his many reports on the execution, which he witnessed, Olcott marked himself as an antislavery reformer, if not an abolitionist. He was, he wrote, "greatly impressed with the dignity of [Brown's] bearing." A martyr, Brown had in Olcott's view unswervingly served "a purpose which to him was holy and noble."[48]

In a later retelling of his adventures in Charlestown, Olcott revealed that during his time with the *Tribune* he was not only a Republican but also a Freemason. Because of the *Tribune*'s notorious republicanism, Olcott related, he had to attend the execution incognito. When some witnesses to the hanging discovered his Yankee roots and thus surmised his antislavery sympathies, Olcott had to enlist the aid of a fellow Freemason in order to secure safe passage out of town.[49]

While at the *Tribune*, Olcott met Mary Eplee Morgan, the daughter of Episcopal minister Richard Morgan of New Rochelle. The couple married on April 26, 1860, and had their first child, Richard Morgan Olcott, in January of 1861. Unfortunately, Olcott cultivated expertly the Victorian virtue of unexpressiveness, which historians have recognized as one of the marks of mid-century manliness, so little is known about the state of his exceedingly private relationship with his wife and children. Whether his unorthodox theological views caused him trouble in his dealings with his wife or his ecclesiastical father-in-law is not known. What is clear is that in the decade that followed his marriage Olcott tabled his spiritualist concerns. At least for a time, his family life was stable. When the Civil War broke out in 1861, he and his wife were expecting their second child.

The Civil War and Civil Service Reform

Like many young men of his time, Olcott responded to the start of the Civil War by volunteering for military service. He became a signals officer in the Union Army and "passed at the front the first year of the war, joining the Burnside expedition at Annapolis, participating in the capture of Roanoke Island, the battle of Newbern, the siege and capture of Fort Macon, the battles on the Rappahannock during Pope's retreat and other military operations."[50] If he could have written the conclusion to his battlefield career (as he wrote this at least partially embellished summary of its beginning), his narrative might well have ended with him sticking a sword into the wretched soul of some sinful slaver. But dysentery overtook him and he spent the rest of his tour of duty convalescing in a military hospital. There he lay until November of 1862, when Secretary of War Edwin M. Stanton appointed him special commissioner of the War Department. Stanton was apparently alerted to Olcott's talents as an investigative reporter by Charles A. Dana, who worked with Olcott at the *Tribune* and served as assistant secretary of war under Stanton. Olcott was entrusted with a two-week task that turned into a three-year assignment.

Olcott's job was to examine papers relating to allegations of fraud against Solomon Kohnstamm, a military supplier suspected of bilking the northern army out of $25,000.[51] There is no need to detail Olcott's investigations here, but by all accounts he did his job well, collecting evidence sufficient to convince a jury to sentence Kohnstamm to ten years at notorious Sing Sing prison for committing over $300,000 worth of fraud.[52] While investigating Kohnstamm, Olcott unearthed a much wider pattern of corruption, which he later described melodramatically in an article on "The War's Carnival of Fraud." If only for its resplendent language, the text would deserve some extended attention, but it is also significant for revealing Olcott's Republican leanings and his tilt in the direction of the more progressive cause of civil service reform:

If it was the golden hour of patriotism, so was it equally that of greed, and, as money was poured by the million, by the frugal, into the lap of the government, so was there a yellow Pactolus diverted by myriad streamlets into the pockets of scoundrels and robbers. . . . Our sailors were sent to sea in ships built of green timber, which were fitted with engines good only for the junkshop, and greased with "sperm" oil derived from mossbunkers and the fat of dead horses. For one pound of necessary metals, one yard of fabric, one gallon of liquid, the price of two was paid. Our soldiers were given guns that would not shoot, powder that would only half explode, shoes of which the soles were filled with shavings, hats that dissolved often in a month's showers, and clothing made of old cloth, ground up and fabricated over again.[53]

For all his hard work battling this "yellow Pactolus" Olcott was amply rewarded, both by Secretary Stanton, who extended his commission, and by Secretary of the Navy Gideon Welles, who later hired him to uproot fraud in naval yards. Olcott apparently accomplished his army and navy tasks dutifully. He initiated within the army improvements such as the "reformation of standards for army-supply contracts, the suspension of contractors' vouchers and certificates, new regulations for the procurement of supplies, new methods of inspection, transportation, and chartering." And in naval yards along the eastern seaboard, he instituted a number of changes in both accounting and bookkeeping.[54]

By uprooting fraud and rationalizing accounting procedures, Olcott claimed, he had saved the government millions of dollars. Whether this figure is correct is not known. What is certain is that in performing his work Olcott was moving toward a synthesis of the paradigms of "universal" and "progressive" reform. In championing these changes in army and navy procedures, Olcott was enlisting himself in the campaign for civil service reform that would occupy so many Americans in decades to come. Olcott differentiated himself from other civil service reformers, however, by continuing to pursue not one but a myriad of reforms and by persevering in his hope that his reform efforts would result not simply in better institutions but also in uplifted individuals—not only in contained improvements but also in grand and glorious transformations. Through his work with the army and navy, Olcott argued, he had checked the "demoralization of the people, and the sapping of ancient virtues" and thus contributed significantly to the moral purification of the nation.[55]

Olcott's contributions to army and navy reform came to an abrupt end on April 14, 1865, when President Abraham Lincoln was shot and killed at Ford's Theater by John Wilkes Booth. Two days later Olcott sent a telegram

to Secretary of War Stanton offering to the inquest his investigatory expertise. Satisfied, no doubt, that Olcott possessed considerable skills in the
typically progressive profession that would soon be known as "muckrak-
ing," Stanton responded affirmatively. "I desire your services," he wrote,
"Come to Washington at once."[56] Upon his arrival in Washington, Olcott
was installed as a special commissioner in the Bureau of Military Justice
and charged with investigating allegations of an assassination conspiracy.
Olcott's most memorable role in this inquiry was his interrogation of Mary
Surratt, whose son, John H. Surratt, was suspected of being Booth's co-con-
spirator. Despite the fact that neither Olcott nor his co-investigators uncovered coherent evidence of a conspiracy, Mrs. Surratt was convicted and
hanged.[57]

Reforming the Law and Public Morals

In October of 1865, six months after Lincoln's assassination, Olcott re-
signed his military commissions and turned to quintessentially progressive
employment: the practice of law. Admitted to the New York Bar in 1868, he
opened the law offices of F. C. Bowman and H. S. Olcott on 7 Beekman
Street in New York City and soon became a specialist in insurance law. Char-
acteristically, he also became a legal reformer.

Appointed in the early 1870s as secretary of the National Insurance Convention of the United States, Olcott used his office to promote a series of
popular benevolences and business reforms. In 1871, for example, he organized a public collection of books for a polar expedition and petitioned
readers of the *Times* to contribute money for a flag memorializing the bravery of New York police.[58] During that same year he co-authored a tract calling for "a more enlightened policy in the regulation of the great and
beneficent scheme of insurance."[59] Then, following the Chicago fire of 1871
and the Boston fire of 1872, Olcott compiled on behalf of the Continental
Insurance Company of the State of New York a pamphlet proposing reforms
in fire insurance law. Like his previous pamphlet, which had proposed regulations regarding capital investment, limitations of risk, advertising restrictions, and the standardization of mortality tables, *The Safety Fund Law of the
State of New York, in Relation to Fire Insurance: Its Advantages Explained* sought
to rationalize the state's insurance industry.

Thus by the early 1870s Olcott had proven that he was, as he had
claimed, "a radical anti-Tammany Republican."[60] In addition to uprooting
government and business fraud in the army and navy, he had worked to
standardize accounting procedures throughout the War Department, to ra-

tionalize insurance law, to bolster the morale of New York City's police, to bring the assassin of a beloved president to justice, and to undermine the nefarious influence of a city boss.

But despite his commitments to reforming the civil service, Olcott had not yet abandoned his earlier posture of "universal reform." In the summer of 1872, Olcott piled one more reform item onto his already crowded plate: the issue of chastity. In his new capacity as ad interim drama editor for the *New York Sun*, Olcott published approximately twenty-five articles, ranging from accounts of Johann Strauss's first New York appearance to a story about "The Man Who Eats Fire and Swallows Swords"—an appropriate mix for an age that was only beginning to construct a wide divide between "high" and "low" culture. In this series of reviews, however, Olcott did far more than dispassionately evaluate dramatic performances.

Laying bare his genteel sensibilities, Olcott waged war in his moralistic reviews against the sins of the stage, even as he titillated his audiences with details of its illicit delights.[61] He denounced as "immoral in sentiment" an English-language adaptation of Dumas's "La Princesse Georges." The title, he complained, ought to be changed to "Adultery Made Easy; or, A Warning Against Matrimony."[62] Later Olcott pleaded for an end to "those monstrous productions of British and American parentage, in which the fun consists of wretched puns, the display of half-naked women, and the playing of female parts by men and vice versa." "It is time," Olcott argued prudishly, "that somebody should protest in plain language against this leprosy of the state that . . . has done so much to poison the whole public mind."[63] Olcott's moral indignation reached its rhetorical climax in a review of entertainer Lester Wallack's "The Stars of the Stage." According to Olcott, Wallack's "nude ballet" violated not only genteel probity but divine commandments. "Wallack still pins his fortunes to the skirts ([though] they are hardly long enough to be called so) of the 'British blondes' and, like the children of Israel in their time of backsliding, elevates the calf for our adoration," he wrote. "If this one is not, like the other, golden, it at least coins gold for its owner and exhibitor, while it commands the homage of as great a crowd of idolaters."[64]

As these *Sun* reviews indicate, Olcott had severed neither his roots in liberal Protestantism nor his connections to antebellum reform. In fact, he had become by 1872 a most universal sort of universal reformer even as he had earned accolades as the "most progressive American of the Americans."[65] In his first forty years Olcott had embraced reforms as diverse as spiritualism, mesmerism, agricultural reform, antislavery, civil service reform, legal reform, and chastity. If American society was an Augean stable, then Olcott was its Hercules, cleansing the mess with the rivers of moral decency. But among the many reforms that Olcott embraced were causes that smacked more of "progressive" than of "universal" reform. Olcott's attempts to standardize government bookkeeping and to rationalize insurance laws would typically have been shunned by universal reformers, who distinguished themselves from the reformers of the Progressive Era by their marked indifference to government. Olcott's efforts to reform the military and the insurance industry also tilted away from universal and toward progressive reform insofar as their purpose was decidedly more modest than the wholesale transformation of the world.

Along with many other reformers of his generation, Olcott was caught between these two eras of reform. He was participating, in short, in what Robert Wiebe has described as a "search for order" and John Higham as a transition from "boundlessness" to "consolidation." Although these historians differ about the dates and the details of this transition, they agree that the United States underwent during Olcott's adulthood a broad cultural shift "from diffusion to concentration, from spontaneity to order."[66] This centripetal tendency manifested itself in a host of new large-scale institutions (professional associations, political parties, corporations, denominational bureaucracies, private universities, public libraries and museums), a new cadre of elites (the new middle class), a new set of bureaucratic values ("continuity and regularity, functionality and rationality, administration and management"), and a new style of reform.[67]

Like many members of his generation, Olcott faced this transition with great ambivalence. No longer a Protestant agriculturalist but not yet a secular bureaucrat, Olcott found himself between the boundless optimism of universal reform and the more consolidated calculations of what Jon Butler has described as "regulated, systemized, professional reformism."[68] Olcott resolved this tension, at least provisionally, by merging the lofty goals of prewar reform with the pragmatic techniques of reform in the postwar period. While pursuing sweeping reforms, he would be sure to chart realistic passages to attainable ends. And while pursuing less grandiose improvements, he would be sure to do so with an exceedingly lofty purpose in mind. Whether in America or in Asia, he would continue to seek his utopias, but he would do so in an orderly and calculated fashion.

Two

From Spiritualism
to Theosophy

By the time spring yielded to summer in 1874, Olcott's marriage had endured fourteen years and produced two healthy children. His law practice,
serving clients such as the New York Stock Exchange, the United States
Treasury, the City of New York, and the Panama Railway Company, was
booming. And his skills as a writer had combined with his connections at
the *Tribune* to earn him membership in the Lotos Club, a prestigious men's
social organization catering to Manhattan's artistic and literary elite.[1]

Now on the cusp of middle-age, Olcott had navigated a passage that
America itself had endured. He had transplanted himself from agricultural
life in a village to industrial life in a city. In the process, he had become a
bona fide member of the new middle class. Olcott's social location can,
however, be more precisely mapped. He was, after all, a resident not just of
any American metropolis but of New York City, and the trade that first
earned him middle-class status was journalism. Olcott was, therefore, a
member of a bourgeois New York City subculture that historian Thomas
Bender has identified as the "metropolitan gentry."[2]

Unlike an earlier (and loftier) patrician gentry that looked for its intellectual models to the Edinburgh of David Hume, this gentry yearned, according to Bender, for Matthew Arnold's Paris. More cosmopolitan than
their patrician predecessors, many members of this social class, Olcott included, were conversant in French. They indulged their literary interests
and met their economic needs by reading and writing for organs such as
Harper's Monthly, *Century*, *Atlantic Monthly*, and *North American Review*. Many,
again like Olcott, wrote for newspapers like the *New York Tribune*. Unlike
earlier patrician elites, these writers and reformers achieved their social
status through self-cultivation and hard work rather than means or breed-
ing; they thus comprised the first generation of New York intellectuals who
fed, clothed, and housed themselves exclusively by vending their ideas.

Perhaps because of their standing between the old patrician gentry and
the new middle class, members of the metropolitan gentry vacillated between commitments to equality and fears of social chaos. Their keyword
was "culture" and their core problematic was, according to Bender, "the

tension between democracy and standards."[3] Many, Olcott included, described themselves as radical Republicans, but their social and political theories were qualified significantly by a near-obsession with order, which was threatened in their view by the supposedly inferior (and potentially anarchic) subcultures of the urban and immigrant masses. Members assuaged their fears of social chaos and satisfied their obsession with order by working feverishly to instill "culture" in immigrants, blacks, and laborers through various forms of education and character-building. By "uplifting" the ostensibly barbarous masses to their supposedly superior level of "civilization," members of the metropolitan gentry pursued a typically liberal aim: to create out of the diversity of America's many subcultures one unifying "culture." In this way they participated in what historian Richard Bushman has described as "the refinement of America."[4]

The metropolitan gentry identified by Bender shared important characteristics with the "genteel reformers" described in more general studies by Stow Persons, John Tomisch, and others. Their style was didactic and moralistic; they too were "committed to the mission of teaching men how to behave."[5] But Bender's elites were not quite as highbrow as these "genteel reformers." According to Bender an amalgamation of Emerson's unabashedly American "self-culture" and Arnold's Francophilic "culture," their culture was both more democratic than that of the patrician gentry and less democratic than the culture celebrated, for example, in Walt Whitman's *Democratic Vistas*. And their culture, though supposedly radically distinct from and superior to the subcultures of immigrants, blacks, and laborers, was at least theoretically accessible not merely to the high-born or well-bred, but to clever men and women of all races and stations in life.

Around the time of Olcott's birth, Emerson had written that every society "wants to be officered by a best class, who shall be masters instructed in all the great arts of life; shall be wise, temperate, brave, public men, adorned with dignity and accomplishments."[6] Thanks to his connections at the *Tribune*, his membership in the Lotos Club, and his partnership at his law practice, Olcott had by his middle years maneuvered his way into that "best class." In his attempts to "uplift" first American spiritualism and, later, Buddhism and Hinduism, Olcott would be acting as an "officer" of this refined class of men.

People from the Other World

Olcott's public successes as a lawyer, journalist, and Lotos Club member apparently stood in the mid-1870s in marked contrast to his private failures as a husband. Like Dumas's raunchy production of "La Princesse Georges," his family life was becoming "A Warning Against Matrimony." The details of the disintegration of his relationship with his wife are sketchy, but Olcott's neglect of his marriage is clear. Tellingly, Olcott responded to these difficulties (which would soon result in a divorce) by repressing rather than addressing them. If he had devoted even half of his vast energies to reforming his family life, he might well have saved his marriage. But instead of casting about for a solution to his private problems he chose to plunge one more time headlong into a public reform. And the cause that caught his imagination was, once again, spiritualism.

Olcott's account of his return to the spiritualist crusade reads like a Puritan conversion narrative. In Olcott's telling, however, the saint is redeemed not from sin to salvation but from the boredom of bureaucracy to the joys of ferment or, to use Higham's terms, from "consolidation" to "boundlessness":

> One day, in the month of July, 1874, I was sitting in my law-office thinking over a heavy case . . . when it occurred to me that for years I had paid no attention to the Spiritualist movement. . . . I went around the corner to a dealer's and bought a copy of the *Banner of Light*. In it I read an account of certain incredible phenomena . . . which were said to be occurring at a farm-house in the township of Chittenden, in the State of Vermont, several hundred miles distant from New York. I saw at once that, if it were true that visitors could see, even touch and converse with, deceased relatives who had found means to reconstruct their bodies and clothing so as to be temporarily solid, visible, and tangible, this was the most important fact in modern physical science. I determined to go and see for myself.[7]

The farmhouse Olcott determined to go see was the homestead of the Eddy family, and the phenomena were the materialization of spirits (at the behest of five Eddy children) in séance cabinets. Olcott went to the homestead and in the *New York Sun* published an account of his adventures. After reading his story, an editor at the *New York Daily Graphic* commissioned him to return to Chittenden to conduct a thorough "scientific" investigation and to report his findings in a series of biweekly letters.[8]

In these letters, republished in book form in 1875 as *People from the Other World*, Olcott portrayed himself as an impartial, scientific investigator. Like other men (and almost all of spiritualism's investigators *were* men) charged with determining the genuineness of the phenomena of spiritualism, he dutifully measured the dimensions of cabinets, scrutinized rafters and crawl spaces, weighed apparitions, and bound and gagged mediums. Following his investigations, Olcott lamented that the alleged materializations had not taken place under test conditions but judged them genuine nonetheless. He remained agnostic, however, about the etiology of the materializations, refusing to sanction the spiritualists' contention that the phenomena had been caused by spirits of the dead. But as much as he struggled to maintain a posture of scientific detachment and reserved professionalism, Olcott could not fully conceal his personal attachment to spiritualism. Near the end of his book Olcott the universal reformer came to light as he prophesied a glorious day when the spirits of the dead would combat crime by testifying against their murderers in courtrooms across America![9]

Olcott's Janus-faced reporting frustrated numerous reviewers. Daniel David Home, recognized in both England and America as one of spiritualism's most accomplished mediums, denounced Olcott as a "pseudo-investigator" and his book as a fanciful romance "ten times more meaningless than the gospel of Mormon." Its style, he wrote, is "beneath criticism" and its reasoning, "beneath contempt." Home was especially frustrated by Olcott's unwillingness either to decry the Eddy manifestations as fraudulent or to pronounce them unequivocally as genuine. This "utter disregard for consistency" stemmed, in Home's view, not from journalistic objectivity but from Olcott's desire to milk the story for all it was worth.[10]

Some readers, of course, disagreed with Home's assessment. Among those who applauded Olcott's effort was Alfred R. Wallace, the British biologist and spiritualist sympathizer to whom Olcott dedicated *People from the Other World*. Wallace praised Olcott's "fair and impartial spirit" as well as the book's "great literary merits."[11]

Helena Petrovna Blavatsky

Another reader who appreciated Olcott's book was a recent Russian immigrant named Helena Petrovna Blavatsky (1831–1891). A mysterious woman described by her contemporaries as both large in girth and great in spirit, Blavatsky was born Helene Hahn von Rottenstein at Ekaterinoslav in the Ukraine in 1831. Her father was an officer in the Russian army and her mother, who died when Blavatsky was only seventeen, was a novelist of some renown. While still a teenager, Helena married Nikifor Blavatsky, vice-governor of the Yerivan province in Armenia. But she left her husband soon thereafter, fleeing for Constantinople and a life of adventure.

A host of Blavatsky biographies have failed to establish how the enigmatic aristocrat spent her next twenty-five years.[12] Blavatsky claimed she passed this secret time as a pilgrim, traveling the world, sitting at the feet of gurus, and being initiated into ancient mysteries in, among other places,

Tibet. Clearly Blavatsky did travel widely in Europe, the Middle East, and perhaps North America. On the way she learned enough about spiritualism to conduct séances during occasional trips to her family's Russian home.

While in Cairo in 1871 and 1872, Blavatsky attempted to launch a society devoted to the investigation of spiritual phenomena. But she lacked the organizational skills to sustain the following her charisma attracted, and her "Société Spirité" flopped. She moved to Paris and then, in July of 1873, to New York where she occupied a room in a boardinghouse for indigent women. Gradually she scratched out a name for herself, although her notoriety—as a rough-talking, chain-smoking Bohemian who ate too much and slept too little—exceeded her fame. While in New York, Blavatsky read Olcott's *Daily Graphic* letters and determined to take herself to Chittenden. One suspects she was looking for a publicist to propagate her eclectic esotericism and for a kindred spirit blessed with organizational talents she clearly lacked. She found both in Colonel Olcott.

The meeting of "H.S.O." and "H.P.B."—as they soon referred to themselves—is now thoroughly entrenched in theosophical lore. Blavatsky pulled out a cigarette; Olcott offered her a light. "Our acquaintance began in smoke," Olcott later recalled, "but it stirred up a great and permanent fire."[13] Soon Olcott and Blavatsky discovered that they shared an interest in spiritualism, an elite disdain for its popular manifestations, and a commitment to reforming it from above. They also shared an interest in one another.

Among the traits that attracted Olcott to Blavatsky was her Bohemian bearing. She sported a bright red Garibaldian shirt and spoke familiarly about exotic places and faraway folk. Before Blavatsky's arrival in Chittenden, the cast of disembodied spirits that paraded nightly across the Eddy family's darkened stage was confined largely to Anglo-Saxons and American Indians. But now the cast expanded marvelously to include "a Georgian servant boy from the Caucasus; a Mussulman merchant from Tiflis; a Russian peasant girl . . . a Kourdish cavalier armed with scimitar, pistols, and lance [and] a hideously ugly and devilish-looking negro sorcerer from Africa."[14] The cosmopolitan Blavatsky was awakening Olcott and American spiritualism to the world.

Whether the sparks that flew between Olcott and Blavatsky ever ignited anything other than platonic affection remains a topic of debate. At least according to Olcott, he and Blavatsky were "chums," not lovers. The chemistry that undoubtedly flowed between them was, he insisted, "the attraction of soul to soul, not that of sex to sex."[15] One reason that Olcott and Blavatsky remained "twins" rather than mates may have been that Blavatsky did not fit Victorian stereotypes of the feminine. Together with her admirers, Blavatsky dealt with the obvious dissonance between her assertive self and the passive Victorian woman by portraying herself as an androgyne. She dressed in men's clothing and instructed her close friends (Olcott included) to call her "Jack." Olcott obliged, and soon he was describing her in his diary as a "she-male." Blavatsky did make some concessions, however, to Victorian female virtues by describing herself as subject to male "Masters" in faraway places and by eventually seeing that Olcott served as the president of the Theosophical Society.[16]

Not everyone accepted this imaginative construction of Blavatsky as an androgyne. Mary Olcott, for one, saw Blavatsky as an all-too-female rival. However ambiguous, the relationship between her husband and his Russian friend soon proved too much for her to bear. She charged Olcott with committing adultery with a prostitute and divorced him on December 28, 1874.[17] Blavatsky, who had previously divorced her first husband after only two months of marriage, celebrated Olcott's new-found bachelorhood in her own inimitable style, by marrying Philadelphia businessman Michael Betanelly on April 3, 1875. But Olcott, who judged her second marriage "a freak of madness," continued to devote most of his leisure time to conversations with Blavatsky (who did not take her second husband's name).[18]

In the months that followed her return with Olcott to New York in November of 1874, Blavatsky gradually initiated her newfound friend into her esoteric philosophy and her occult powers. She also introduced him to the Near East, where, she informed him, she had encountered a race of spiritually advanced beings called "adepts." Furthermore, she herself had been initiated into the mysteries of the ancient Near East by "Masters" or "Mahatmas."[19] Members of a secret occult brotherhood who had been entrusted throughout the ages with the task of conserving and propagating the ancient wisdom, these "Masters" had sent her to America and charged her with combating both the skepticism of materialists and the philosophical naïveté of spiritualists. This she would do by affirming (contra the materialists) the reality of spiritual phenomena while advancing (contra the spiritualists) an alternative theory regarding their sources.

Despite protestations in print to the contrary, Olcott was clearly attracted to the spiritualists' claim that spiritual phenomena originated with spirits of the dead who used living mediums as passive vehicles for their messages. But Blavatsky rejected this thesis, advancing a novel theory of her own. Spiritual phenomena resulted, she informed Olcott, not from the passivity of mediums but from the activity of "adepts" who utilized their knowledge of occult laws to manipulate occult forces. Blavatsky's charisma soon won

Olcott over. He vowed to use his administrative skills and journalistic connections to spread her neo-spiritualist gospel far and wide.

Reforming Spiritualism

In the spring and summer of 1875 Olcott began in earnest to market Blavatsky's message of spiritualist reform. He approached E. Gerry Brown, editor of the Boston-based *Spiritual Scientist*, about turning that economically troubled spiritualist paper into the unofficial organ of Blavatsky's ideas. Olcott offered Brown financial assistance and aid in recruiting writers in return for his support. Brown assented, and the transaction was consummated on April 29, 1875, when the *Spiritual Scientist* published an article announcing the existence of a secret society of Egyptian adepts.

Cryptically signed by the "Committee of Seven, Brotherhood of Luxor" but actually written by Olcott, this article chastised other spiritualist periodicals for devoting so much space to cataloging phenomena and so little to developing a philosophy to explain them. Citing the examples of London's *Spiritualist* and Paris' *Revue Spirite*, the piece noted the need for a similar American periodical that would "devote more space to the discussion of principles, the teaching of philosophy, and the display of conservative critical ability, than to the mere publication of the thousand and one minor occurences [*sic*] of private and public circles." It then announced that the *Spiritual Scientist* had been selected to fulfill this important mission.[20]

Over the next few months, in articles in the *Spiritual Scientist* and the *Tribune* and in lectures across the city, Olcott articulated and defended this critique of spiritualism and a plan for its reform. Significantly, he prefaced his controversial theses by tipping his cap not to Andrew Jackson Davis or Franz Anton Mesmer but to his earliest Puritan ancestor, a gentleman who according to Olcott had followed his conscience across rough oceans and savage wilderness. "If this hard-headed old Puritan left me no other inheritances," he remarked, "he at least bequeathed to me the sacred example of being true to one's convictions." Olcott then vowed to follow his ancestor's example by professing what he believed "at any cost" and enduring whatever hardships and persecutions would follow.[21] Clearly Olcott was inviting trouble.

The critique of spiritualism devised by Blavatsky and Olcott was quintessentially reformist. It amounted to a two-fold argument that the spiritualist movement was morally backward and philosophically naive. In the moral argument there was little new. Two decades earlier, in the *Spiritual Telegraph*, Olcott had marked himself as a genteel spiritualist by condemning unthinking spiritualists as barbarians. Now he denounced mediums as "whiskey-drinking and immoral men and women" who committed "a vast amount of fraud." He deplored the "puerile, absurd, and often repulsive character" of many spiritualist tricks as well as "the disgusting fallacies of free-love, affinity, and individual sovereignty" to which spiritualism had given birth. No longer willing to remain associated with such immorality, Olcott cut his ties with the movement: "I repudiate all connection with American Spiritualism in its present form, and refuse to be classified by my critics along with the free-lovers, pantarchists, socialists, and other theorists who have fastened upon a sublime and pure faith as barnacles upon a ship's bottom."[22]

The moral argument advanced by Olcott contained little that was new, but the philosophical argument was novel. Previously Olcott had denounced spiritualists for devoting so much time to ogling spiritual phenomena and so little to explaining them. He had prophesied the coming of a "new Newton" who would "deduce from the fall of one of these Sodom-apples of the circle the law of spirit-intercourse, and demonstrate with mathematical certainty the immortality of man's soul."[23] But he had avoided specifying either the dates of that second coming or the details of the spiritualist's analog to gravity. Now, however, emboldened by Blavatsky's charisma and informed by her esotericism, Olcott advanced a novel theory regarding the origins of spiritual phenomena.

True spirit manifestations were caused, according to Olcott, not by *mediums* passively channeling disembodied spirits of the dead (as he and other spiritualists had previously believed) but by *adepts,* who because of their initiation into the mysteries of the ancient Near East were able to actively manipulate occult forces in accordance with occult laws. Olcott distinguished between these two groups of religious virtuosi by arguing that mediums were passive and worked in the dark while adepts were active and worked in full light. Mediums, Olcott noted, frequently slipped into a trance state and preferred a darkened room. They functioned, as their appellation implies, as inert conduits through which information was transmitted between the dead and the living. Adepts, on the other hand, shunned both trance states and poorly lit rooms. Not unlike magicians, they drew on a vast storehouse of esoteric knowledge to fashion seemingly miraculous effects. They produced messages from the world beyond the living not by becoming possessed by the spirits of the dead but by tapping into what Olcott would later describe as the "Akasha," a secret and eternal record of past thoughts and events.

Along with these adepts, Olcott postulated the existence of "elementary spirits," beings who according to Olcott occupied a link in the great chain of being somewhere higher than animals and lower than humans. These "elementary spirits" were able to materialize in human form. Rather than the disembodied spirits of the dead who were typically credited with instigating spiritual phenomena, these were the entities that spoke to mediums and appeared mysteriously in séance cabinets.[24]

What commended these theories to Olcott was the fact that they supposedly explained the conundrum of the coexistence of genuine and fraudulent mediumship. One of the major theoretical problems for more gentrified American spiritualists like Olcott was how to explain the existence of both genuine spirit manifestations (which they affirmed) and fraudulent spirit manifestations (which they could not reasonably deny). A related problem was how to explain the lofty powers of mediums as well as their apparent tendency to slip, at least on occasion, into behaviors that violated Victorian propriety. Blavatsky's theory responded persuasively, in Olcott's view, to each of these concerns.

Olcott's promotion of this theory amounted to nothing less than an attempt to effect a paradigm shift from spiritualism to what would be called theosophy—from a tradition of mediums (predominantly female) passively channeling spirits of the dead in the darkness, to a tradition of adepts (predominantly male or, in Blavatsky's case, ostensibly androgynous) working in full light, cajoling "elementary spirits," and actively manipulating occult forces in accordance with occult laws. While Blavatsky stressed the philosophical benefits of the shift from spiritualism to what would be called theosophy, Olcott underscored its moral virtues. Incorporating broader cultural assumptions regarding the dangerous passivity of women and the willful activity of men, he reasoned that since mediums worked in the dark and had to be passive in order to be successful, they were "feeble to resist [the] evil" that inevitably lurked in the night. Adepts, on the other hand, were occupationally active and worked without cabinets and in full light. More adroit than mediums at evading "the imps of darkness," they tended, like modern-day Boy Scouts, to be "chaste, temperate, conscientious and brave."[25] The existence of elementary spirits only extended the explanatory powers of this theory. Since elementary spirits were subhuman, they tended at least as much toward evil as toward good and thus harbored no compunctions about luring ever-impressionable (and usually female) mediums into free-love and fakery.

What is striking about this synthesis is its close affinities with contemporaneous forms of religious liberalism. Olcott, Blavatsky, and others who would come to be called theosophists would clearly cultivate their outsider status (and thus their group identity) by insisting that the world was populated by "adepts" and "elementary spirits" and governed by "occult laws" but their affinities with liberal religious culture are at least as striking as their departures from it.[26] In the great religious disputes of the day, Olcott and Blavatsky consistently would align themselves with other religious liberals by opposing *both* conservative Catholics and Protestant evangelicals (who rejected evolution, lauded missions, and affirmed miracles like the Atonement and Biblical inspiration), *and* radical freethinkers and materialists (who rejected religion altogether). Not unlike other forms of religious liberalism, theosophy would represent itself as forging a middle path between these two extremes.

For the time being, however, Olcott's presentation of Blavatsky's agenda for spiritualism's reform would earn the disdain rather than the praise of other liberal religionists. More specifically, it inspired an undoubtedly anticipated uproar in the spiritualist press. Among the spiritualists who resented being labeled an immoral ignoramus was Mary Fenn Davis (the wife of Andrew Jackson Davis and an important spiritualist in her own right) who responded to Olcott's attack with a pamphlet warning her co-religionists against "retrogression." Olcott and Blavatsky were in her view attempting to steer the ship of spiritualism out of the sunlight of modernity and into "the darkness of Egypt and the Middle Ages." Another spiritualist advised Olcott and Blavatsky to pack up their society and move to the Orient. "There, amid the ignorance and superstition of enslaved millions," he wrote presciently, "your institution may for a while longer be tolerated. It will be a signal failure in free and enlightened America."[27] Olcott's decidedly nongenteel response to this furor proved that Blavatsky's brash style was rubbing off. In a letter to the *Banner of Light* he called his critics "asses."[28]

Regardless of what one thinks of Olcott's self-described crusade "to purify American Spiritualism from the dirt of free love," one must wonder about the motivations underlying Olcott's reforming zeal. The man clearly was as committed to correcting the moral shortcomings of spiritualism as Blavatsky was to correcting its metaphysical mistakes. But at the same time he was by his own admission far more worldly than the run-of-the-mill Christian gentleman. Now well into middle-age, Olcott was, at least publicly, a model of Victorian manners—a champion of moral improvement in politics, the military, and even the arts. In private, however, he was by his own account "a worldly man . . . a man of clubs, drinking parties, mistresses, a man absorbed in all sorts of worldly . . . undertakings and speculations." His wife had divorced him for adultery, he was sharing an apartment with a Russian occultist, and he was a well-known tippler at the Lotos Club. Gradually, Olcott and Blavatsky were coming to resemble the stereotypes of the "Confidence Man" and "Painted Lady" that so bedeviled middle-class Americans of their time.[29] Olcott's paean to personal equilibrium may well have been based, therefore, at least in part on his own experience of domestic chaos. His condemnations of spiritualist "free love," like his criticisms of Wallack's bawdy musical, may have been, at least in part, judgments of himself. The same man who in public pleaded with New York's producers to lower their actresses hemlines was by his own admission worshipping the female calf in private. Olcott's sermons against spiritualist sin may have constituted, therefore, not only a prolegomenon for theosophy but also an individual vow. Olcott would compensate for his misdeeds not by praying to an atoning God for forgiveness (as had his Puritan forebears) but by acting vigorously in the world, by practicing the more liberal but still identifiably Protestant religion that, in his words, "subordinates profession to practice, and writes over the doors of its sanctuary the legend, 'Deeds, not words.' "[30]

The Theosophical Society

While Olcott was spreading this neo-spiritualist gospel in spiritualist periodicals and the New York press, Blavatsky was lording over a European-style salon in her Manhattan apartment. There gawkers and sympathizers alike affirmed their genteel status by engaging in parlor theatricals and discussing an array of subjects as vast and controversial as Blavatsky herself: "the Phallic element in religions; the soul of flowers; recent wonders among the mediums; history; Italian character; the strangeness of travel; chemistry; poetry; Nature's duality; Romanism; Gravitation; the Carbonari; jugglery; Crooke's new discoveries about the force of light; the literature of magic."[31]

It was out of such eclectic discussions that the Theosophical Society was born. During one particularly lively salon gathering, Olcott rose to propose the formation of a voluntary association devoted to the scientific investigation of "spirit phenomena, mesmerism, Od Force, psychometry, the magnet, occultism and practical magic." According to one observer, "His plan was to organise a society of Occultists and begin at once to collect a library; and to diffuse information concerning those secret laws of Nature which were so familiar to the Chaldeans and Egyptians, but are totally unknown by our modern world of science." Olcott's proposal met with unanimous assent. The next evening this new society was duly organized with all the pomp and circumstance Victorian fastidiousness required. Tellingly, almost all of the sixteen founding members—Blavatsky was the notable exception—came from New York City's metropolitan gentry. Lawyers, doctors, and journalists were all represented among the founders, and this sort of educated, professional person would remain throughout Olcott's lifetime the main constituency of the society.[32] Soon these reformers had settled on a name (the Theosophical Society), a corresponding secretary (Blavatsky), and a president (Olcott).

The Theosophical Society was actually Olcott's second attempt to institutionalize Blavatsky's charisma. The first—a "Miracle Club," announced in the *New York Daily Graphic* on May 4, 1875, and the *Spiritual Scientist* on May 20 of the same year—was handicapped by the inability of Olcott and Blavatsky to agree on its object. Olcott saw the club as a scientific body dedicated to investigating spirit manifestations "without a cabinet and in the light." Blavatsky, on the other hand, envisioned the organization as an occasion to spread her esoteric philosophy while securing her martyrdom.[33]

But sometime in the summer of 1875 the soon-to-be "Theosophical Twins" apparently came to a meeting of the minds. At a September 26, 1875 meeting of spiritualists, Olcott formally announced the organization of his new society. Its object was grand: "to seek a knowledge of God and the higher spirits." And its quintessentially modern telos—"a new epoch for Science and Religion"—was even grander. The society, Olcott proclaimed, would provide a "neutral ground" on which scientists and people of faith could stand side by side. "To the church it offers proof that the soul is immortal, at once final and irresistible; to science, those mathematical demonstrations of new forces and an unseen universe the lack of which has hitherto sent its votaries adrift in that current whose vortex sucks them into Infidelity, Darkness, and Despair," he announced. "To the Universe, [it] restores an appreciable First Cause, and it floods the sky of the philosophical student with the dawn of an Eternal Day of Knowledge."[34]

Curiously, the society began with no clear summary of theosophical beliefs. On issues such as the genuineness of spiritual phenomena, for example, the society was officially "non-committal."[35] Its only discernible dogma was the paradoxical liberal shibboleth of nondogmatism. "Whatever may be the private opinions of its members, *the Society has no dogmas to enforce, no creed to disseminate,*" its preamble read, "Its only axiom is the omnipotence of truth, its only creed a profession of unqualified devotion to its discovery and propagation."[36]

From the start, however, Olcott had some difficulty living up to this liberal promise of religious neutrality. Long before he met Blavatsky, Olcott had joined other religious liberals in criticizing as capricious orthodox Christian doctrines such as human depravity, divine sovereignty, and the substitutionary atonement. But his parries at the church had been jabs rather than roundhouse punches; they were directed at certain Christian doctrines rather than the Christian tradition itself. Now, however, Olcott began, under the influence of Blavatsky's more strident (and more European) anticlericalism, to portray the church as spiritualism's foremost foe. He called on his listeners to join the war on Christianity. "If you do not organise to crush your irreconcilable enemy the Church," he prophesied in a speech to a group of spiritualists, "she *has* organised, and will crush *you*."[37]

First Presidential Address

This theme of the warfare between true religion (i.e., theosophy) and false religion (i.e., Christianity) spilled over into Olcott's First Presidential Address, which he delivered at Mott Memorial Hall on Madison Avenue on November 17, 1875. John William Draper, a professor at the University of the City of New York while Olcott was a student there, lent to Olcott's lecture the grand theme of the cosmic battle between the good forces of science and the evil forces of religion, even as Draper's famous *History of the Conflict between Religion and Science* provided the epigram for Olcott's printed speech. Following Draper, Olcott now described the Theosophical Society's mission in military terms, as a two-flank war against both false science and false religion. Modern science, Olcott claimed, was arrogant, materialistic and atheistic. But the Christian religion was equally problematic: the Protestant's Bible wouldn't bear the "test of reason"; and the Catholic Church was conspiring, through schemes to "romanize" America's schools, to import its "ecclesiastical despotism" into the United States. Finally, spiritualists, who might otherwise offer a way out of the errors of science and religion, were debasing themselves with "tricky mediums, lying spirits, and revolting social theories." Olcott capped his address by likening the theosophist's "holy cause" to the favorite campaign of universal reformers: abolitionism. The Theosophical Society would do for truth what William Lloyd Garrison had done for justice. Theosophists too would face "abuse, misrepresentation, and every vile assault." But in the end they would also "surmount every obstacle, vanquish every foe, and attain what we are in all in search of, the peace of mind which comes of absolute knowledge."[38]

Given the Theosophical Society's impending tilt toward Asia, it is striking that Olcott's quintessentially modern metanarrative did not incorporate any references to Oriental wisdom. Echoing Blavatsky's interests in the esoteric saints of occultisms past, Olcott referred in his first Presidential Address to Albertus Magnus, Alfarabi, Roger Bacon, Cagliostro, Pico della Mirandola, Robert Fludd, Paracelsus, Cornelius Agrippa, and Henry More, as well as the Chaldeans, Kabalists, Egyptians, hermeticists, Alchemists, and Rosicrucians. By placing himself and his fellow theosophists in an esoteric line going back thousands of years, Olcott simultaneously invented and legitimized a theosophical tradition.[39] Tellingly, however, Olcott's list of references extended no farther than the Near East (from whence came Blavatsky's revered "Masters").

Early theosophical documents reveal that, at least in the beginning, both Olcott and Blavatsky understood the Theosophical Society not as an organization devoted to propagating Asian wisdom but as an organization committed to the moral and philosophical "uplift" of spiritualism. Part scientific body and part social reform agency, Olcott's organization shared more with the American Anti-Slavery Society and the American Academy of Arts and Sciences than it did, for example, with India's reform-minded and Unitarian-influenced Brahmo Samaj. Theosophists, whom Olcott described in quasi-biblical terms as "investigators, of earnest purpose and unbiassed [sic] mind, who study all things, prove all things . . . seek, inquire, reject nothing without cause, accept nothing without proof," would proceed scientifically and inductively.[40] First, they would study and catalog spiritual phenomena. Then they would conduct and discuss spiritualist experiments of their own. Finally they would induce hitherto-undiscovered laws of the mechanics of the spirit. As a result of these investigations and inductions, both the naturalistic science of John Tyndall and Thomas Huxley and the theological dogmas of Protestant preachers and Catholic popes would yield to the one sublime and ancient law that governs all true science and religion. The final outcome of these scientific advances would be nothing less than a grand combination of individual moral perfection and social harmony—a theosophical world enjoying a new epoch of Truth, Justice, and Virtue.

Two Theosophies

This account should make clear that from the beginning that Olcott and Blavatsky played two very different roles in the theosophical movement. In simplest terms, Blavatsky was its philosopher while Olcott was its ethicist. If spiritualism lacked a coherent, unifying philosophy, then it was Blavatsky's job to provide it; and if whiskey-drinkers, free-lovers, and socialists had overtaken the spiritualist movement, then it was up to Olcott to restore moral order. But the two reformers also operated in two decidedly different arenas. Influenced no doubt by the Victorian ideology that separated men and women into "separate spheres" of the home and the workplace,[41] Olcott utilized his oratorical skills and journalistic connections to disseminate a more exoteric theosophy in the public sphere while Blavatsky relied on her personal charisma to spread a more esoteric theosophy in the privacy of her Manhattan salon.

Although Olcott and Blavatsky agreed on maintaining at least the appearance of confining one another to these "separate spheres," they disagreed in their definitions of theosophy itself. The two worked hard throughout their theosophical careers to maintain the image of a united front, but there was considerable (and ultimately irreconcilable) tension between the two from the start regarding both the form of their organization and its aims. Given the differences, both in style and in substance, between the genteel Olcott and the aristocratic Blavatsky, it may be helpful to think of not one but two theosophies existing side-by-side from the start.

Blavatsky distinguished herself from Olcott on at least three key points. First, Blavatsky's vision for the Theosophical Society was far more esoteric. While Olcott promoted the society as a relatively open, public body devoted to empirical investigations and scientific induction of the laws of occult science, Blavatsky saw it as a smaller, private body, open only to a chosen few—an American lodge of an international esoteric order that included, for example, the mysterious "Brotherhood of Luxor" in Egypt. The society was devoted, in her view, not to the *discovery* of occult laws through scientific methods (a la Olcott) but to the "*unveiling*," through esoteric channels, of occult laws already known, if only to a few.

Second, Blavatsky's cosmos was more hierarchical and less democratic. Although Olcott undoubtedly saw the individual as engaged in a lifelong struggle to improve ethically and spiritually, it was Blavatsky who articulated the grand metaphysical scheme that depicted each person as comprised of seven interpenetrating bodies, each of which was subdivided into "higher" and "lower" sheaths. These seven bodies were themselves arrayed from the "lowest" physical body to the "highest" spiritual body. The individual's life was depicted, then, as a grand cosmic drama in which one was working to uplift one's essence from body to astral body to soul to spirit—away from the groveling animals and up toward the "Masters" who had united their spirits with the imperishable and indescribable Absolute. This scheme allowed for multiple discriminations even among elites and left Blavatsky and perhaps a small number of other adepts at the top of the cosmic scale.

The third major difference between Olcott and Blavatsky was her relative indifference to his social reform agenda. If in Hindu terms Olcott pursued *karma yoga* or the discipline of action, Blavatsky pursued *jnana yoga*, the discipline of wisdom. Blavatsky soft-pedaled Olcott's activist agenda for at least two reasons. First, she was in her personal life an unapologetic Bohemian who enjoyed smoking and drinking as much as she enjoyed cursing. Second, for Blavatsky the religious drama was individual rather than social. One labored to uplift *oneself,* not to uplift *others.* Olcott's repeated insistence that the cultivation of "entirely truthful, pure, temperate, self-helpful" theosophists would result in utopian social transformations was conspicuously absent from Blavatsky's early work.[42]

The difference between Blavatsky's secret society and Olcott's scientific society for social reform was, in short, the difference between Russian aristocracy and metropolitan gentility. Though Olcott and Blavatsky agreed that spiritualism was in need of reform, that it was worth reforming, and that it should be reformed from above by elites like themselves, the shapes their reforms took differed significantly. Blavatsky aimed to lord over the Theosophical Society like a czar, diffusing through secret rituals the ancient wisdom she claimed to have received from her "Masters" through occult initiations. Olcott, on the other hand, aimed to govern the society like the president of a federation of sovereign states and independent citizens. And while Blavatsky planned to initiate only a small coterie of trusted friends who would guard the secrecy of her ancient truths, Olcott hoped to publish theosophy's discoveries widely and thus to gather into the society a broad array of clever ladies and gentlemen. Finally, though Blavatsky was as interested as Olcott in uplifting bad science and bad theology into the higher philosophical synthesis of the ancient wisdom, she was less interested in individual moral uplift and collective social transformation. Both reformers disdained the supposedly "vulgar" masses and saw western society headed toward catastrophe, but only Olcott worked to uplift the masses and to save society. Blavatsky, on the other hand, was content to cultivate the intelligences of a select few, then to sit back and watch her prophesies of social ruin come true.

Early theosophy amounted, therefore, to two parallel attempts to reform the spiritualist tradition: Olcott's effort to "gentrify" spiritualism and Blavatsky's effort to "aristocratize" it. More than an example of "harmonial religion" or an "alternative spirituality tradition," theosophy was in its infancy an outgrowth of spiritualism.[43] If, as R. Laurence Moore has argued, spiritualism "took the message of liberalism down the social scale,"[44] then theosophy represented an attempt to ratchet it back up. Most of the liberal elements in spiritualism—its critique of Calvinist predestination in the name of individual liberty, its anticlericalism and emphasis on vernacular preaching by the laity, its antidogmatism and exaltation of individual conscience, its attempt to improve the role of women in society, and, finally, its hope of fashioning something akin to the kingdom of God on earth—

survived in the theosophies of both Olcott and Blavatsky. What did not survive the transmigration were certain supposed spiritualist crudities— the preoccupation with spirits of the dead, tendencies toward communal- ism and free love, seemingly excessive reliance on female spiritual interme- diaries, etc.—that would not appeal to genteel and aristocratic markets.

A Theosophical Rite

Though Olcott and Blavatsky differed in their interpretations of theoso- phy, they worked together throughout 1875 to keep their ideas in the pa- pers and on the lips of fashionable New York elites. This objective they ac- complished famously by turning the death of one of their most highbrow converts into a great controversy.

Baron Joseph Henry Louis Charles de Palm, who according to one acer- bic but insightful journalist was destined to become "principally famous as a corpse," arrived in New York in the winter of 1875 and joined the Theo- sophical Society shortly thereafter.[45] After befriending Olcott, he fell ill and moved into a room in Olcott's apartment, where he received medical care from a physician and theosophical instruction from Olcott and Blavatsky. Unfortunately, neither course of treatment resolved his sickness into health, and the baron died at Roosevelt Hospital on May 20, 1876.

Before his death, de Palm had asked Olcott to arrange a funeral rite befitting his theosophical faith. He had requested, more specifically, that Olcott rather than a clergyman should officiate at his last rites and that the funeral should be performed "in a fashion that would illustrate the [Near] Eastern notions of death and immortality."[46] In accordance with these wishes, the entertainment that came to be known as the baron's "pagan funeral" was held on Sunday, May 28, 1876, at the Masonic Temple of the free religionist preacher, Reverend O. B. Frothingham.

During the week before the funeral, city papers gave the story consider- able, if not consistently flattering, attention. The *World*, for example, satiri- cally promised a procession consisting of: "Colonel Olcott as high priest, wearing a leopard skin and carrying a roll of papyrus . . . [an] Egyptian mummy-case, borne upon a sledge drawn by four oxen . . . [a] colored boy carrying three Abyssinian geese (Philadelphia chickens) to place upon the bier . . . slaves in mourning gowns, carrying the offerings and libations, to consist of early potatoes, asparagus, roast beef, French pancakes, bock-beer, and New Jersey cider." The critic also promised that mourners would be treated to an ancient Egyptian dirge sung in a distinctively New York style:

Isis and Nepthys, beginning and end;
One more victim to Amenti we send.
Pay we the fare, and let us not tarry,
Cross the Styx by the Roosevelt Street ferry.[47]

Thanks to an obliging press, the baron's funeral was a cause célèbre long before the opening hymn was sung.

On the morning of the funeral, police attempted to control the unruly crowd that had gathered outside the temple. When the doors were opened the 2000-person hall filled to capacity. According to the *Times*, which featured the story on its front page, the hall was unadorned except for the altar, which supported an incense burner "emblematic of the worship of fire" and a wooden cross wrapped by a serpent, symbolizing "the evolution of matter."[48] In the midst of these symbols lay a silver and ebony casket topped with seven candles—five white, one red, and one green. On the stage behind the coffin sat Colonel Olcott with an entourage of theosophical dignitaries, each of them frocked in a black gown and carrying green leaves said to signify "good will and peace toward men."

The service, which adroitly conflated religious ritual with mass entertainment, began with a prayer to the "Eternal Soul of souls." Then came a theosophical credo, which included praise for "the Divine light" which is "one and universal" and an affirmation that just as the body is "the temporary envelope of the soul" so is death an illusion substantiated by the ubiquity of change. The statement concluded with an Emersonian proclamation that harmony is maintained through a delicate equilibrium of life and death, light and shadow, good and evil, spirit and matter: "Harmony is in equilibrium, and equilibrium subsists by the analogy of contraries."

The harmony of the funeral itself was interrupted briefly when an angry gentleman—responding to Olcott's seemingly innocuous metaphysical profession that "There is but one first cause"—stood up and shouted, "That's a lie!" The man, who happened to be the father of the organist, marched down the aisle, tapped his daughter on the shoulder and escorted her out of the hall. As the audience started to stir from its solemnity, Olcott stepped forward. Dramatically placing his hand upon the baron's coffin, he intoned, "We are in the presence of death!" Thus calming the crowd, Olcott was able to proceed with his eulogy.

Eulogy, however, is probably not the correct term, since Olcott's oration was devoted more to the birth of the Theosophical Society than to the death of Baron de Palm. In keeping with theosophy's origins in spiritualism, Olcott began his sermon by noting that the Theosophical Society had been established "to study the history of ancient myths and symbols, relig-ions and science, the psychological powers of man, and his relations with all the laws of nature." He then defined theosophy over against Christianity. But in the process, he made theosophy sound like an at least vaguely Chris-tian faith—a strange combination of Protestant liberalism, William H. Channing's associationism and Ralph W. Emerson's transcendentalism.

Like Channing, Emerson, and other liberal religionists, Olcott rejected once-and-for-all biblical revelation. His theosophy, based on "experiment and self-development," demanded only that each seek one's own revelation. As such, it was more empirical and more democratic than orthodox Chris-tianity. Olcott also joined the transcendentalists in rejecting the Atonement on moral grounds. Theosophy, he remarked, "offers no compromises to the licentious, the glutton, the greedy, the idler, the seeker after worldly advan-tage. It is no fair weather religion. It believes in no death-bed repentances. It issues no post-mortem fire insurance policies. It calls things by their right names; and a ruffian standing upon the top of a gallows is in its eyes a ruffian still, though he have said twenty *confiteors*, and twice as many *credos*." In Olcott's cosmos—as in Emerson's—"the law of compensation" pre-vailed: no crime went unpunished and no good deed unrewarded. Olcott illustrated this "law of cause and effect" with one of his few references to Baron de Palm. If the deceased was "just, upright, pure, temperate, spiri-tual-minded," Olcott argued, then he will enjoy immortal life. But if he was "a sensualist, usurer, an oppressor, a corrupter," then no one can forgive him, since to cancel the debts of the sinner is to plunge the cosmos into chaos.[49] On this stern note Olcott's oration ended. Because of the abrupt departure of the organist, the orphic hymn that was to close the ceremonies was foregone. So the funeral ended with a whimper rather than a bang, and Baron de Palm's body was carted away, if only provisionally, to a vault in a Lutheran cemetery. Soon his body would become the first to be cre-mated in modern America.[50]

The next day all the major New York newspapers reviewed Olcott's per-formance as they would have reviewed a new Lester Wallack play. A ritual expert from the *Tribune* judged the service "random and prosaic" and dis-missed the Theosophical Society as "a bit of medieval Cabbalism ingrafted upon modern Spiritualism, and so awkwardly that the two kinds of bark are not united." He labeled the ceremony a "dire disappointment" and con-veyed his pity on the corpse.[51]

But despite the critical reviews, the rite did serve its two main purposes: ushering the baron's body out of the world, and (perhaps more impor-tantly) ushering theosophy in. As surely as Olcott's first Presidential Address announced the birth of theosophy in speech, this event demonstrated the-osophy's arrival in ritual action. The fact that the drama was held in the Masonic Temple of free religionist O. B. Frothingham symbolized theosophy's early association with both freemasonry and radical religion. And its clearly anti-Christian yet equally obviously sentimental character manifested theosophy's ambiguous relationship with the late Victorian culture out of which it emerged. The theosophists' antagonism toward Christianity signaled their distance from late Victorian religious norms, but their ritual simultaneously participated vigorously in both the "theatricality" and "sentimental ritual" of mourning that a number of historians have identified as marks of that culture.[52]

Olcott's persona as the "High Priest" of the rite announced, moreover, his new status as the eminently public president of the Theosophical Society as surely as Blavatsky's near-invisibility symbolized her relegation to theosophy's private sphere. Finally, the ritual also served to sacralize (at least for theosophists) both the ancient Near East and modern America, even as it conflated those regions. The repeated references in liturgical language, ritual dress, and sacred objects to Egypt continued the process of the invention of a theosophical tradition by enacting the emerging myth of that tradition's origination in the ancient Near East. The insistence that the captain of New York City's Roosevelt Street Ferry could transport the souls of the dead to their place of rest as efficaciously as could the mythical Charon, meanwhile, constructed New York City and, by extension, America itself as an eminently sacred (and theosophical) space.

Unveiling Isis

Publicity surrounding the founding of the Theosophical Society and the funeral of Baron de Palm kept theosophy alive through the end of 1876.[53] But by the beginning of 1877 the Theosophical Society was, by Olcott's admission, "comparatively inactive"; like Blavatsky's ill-fated "Société Spirité" and Olcott's equally short-lived "Miracle Club," it had become "a dead letter."[54] Although the Theosophical Society had not legally dissolved, time had separated the curious from the committed, and the group seriously concerned with investigating occult laws and reforming spiritualism had proven to be far smaller than the group of gawkers and hangers-on curious about when Blavatsky would pull the next spiritual rabbit out of her occult hat.

Faced with the near certainty that an unaltered Theosophical Society would meet an early death, Olcott and Blavatsky cast about for a new direction for their organization. And the direction they turned was east. Olcott and Blavatsky had previously looked to the Orient for spiritual inspiration, but their gaze had gone no farther than the Near East. In the year that followed Baron de Palm's death, however, the "Theosophical Twins" discovered the literature of ancient India. Olcott and Blavatsky made this critical discovery while researching her magnum opus, *Isis Unveiled* (1877), and it was upon publishing the book, which claimed to trace all modern western knowledge to ancient Oriental sources, that they announced their discovery to the world.

When it appeared in September of 1877, *Isis* was a financial if not a literary success. A first edition of one thousand copies sold out in ten days,[55] but critics differed on the book's literary merits. The *New York Herald* praised *Isis* as "one of the most remarkable productions of the century" but the *Sun* denounced it as "discarded rubbish" and the *Springfield Republican* as "a large dish of hash." The *Tribune*, persisting with the alimentary metaphors, called Blavatsky's erudition "crude and undigested."[56]

At least to the uninitiated, *Isis* is a hodgepodge—an awkward mix of evolutionary theory, occult doctrines, freethought, freemasonry, anti-Catholic nativism, and Buddhist and Hindu teachings. But from the midst of this mélange emerge two important themes that would subsequently shape theosophy: hatred of Christianity (especially Catholicism) and devotion to an ancient Asian wisdom tradition on which all the world's religions (with the possible exception of Christianity) are constructed and toward which all converge. *Isis* argues that all religions came from "one primitive source," teach "one eternal truth," and tend toward one common goal. It locates the *Ursprung* of this universal religion not in the Near East (as the titular reference to the Egyptian fertility goddess Isis would suggest) but in the Far East. "Pre-Vedic Brahmanism and Buddhism are the double source from which all religions sprang," Blavatsky writes, "Nirvana is the ocean to which all tend."[57]

If in *Isis* all religions are true, some religions are less true than others and least truthful of all is Christianity, especially in its Catholic form. Blavatsky begins her argument against Christianity with the familiar freethought contention that the tradition was derivative rather than unique. Biblical teachings and Christian rituals, she argues, are but crude copies of more ancient practices.[58] She then advances a moral argument against Christianity's "murderous fanaticism." Above all the anticlerical Blavatsky denounces Catholics: the Vatican, "whose despotic pretensions have become hateful to the greater portion of enlightened Christendom," and the conspiratorial

Jesuits who "have done more moral harm in this world than all the fiendish armies of the mythical Satan."[59]

The publication of *Isis* represented the first step by both Blavatsky, who wrote the manuscript, and Olcott, who edited it, in the direction of Asia. The event thus signaled a shift in the sacred center of the theosophical cosmos, away from Egypt and toward India, the birthplace of Hinduism and Buddhism. The book also provides evidence of a critical contradiction inherent in theosophy, which proclaimed as its chief dogma the unity of all religions yet clearly preferred some religions (the religions of Asia) over others (Christianity). The fact that Blavatsky justified this apparent inconsistency by noting that Buddhism and Hinduism championed religious tolerance while Christianity denounced it only complicated the difficulties, since both Blavatsky and Olcott demonstrated an obvious inability to tolerate conservative Christians, especially Christian missionaries.

A Visit from the Masters

If the villains of *Isis* were the Christians, its heroes were the religious virtuosi that Blavatsky called "Masters" or "Mahatmas." Olcott's faith in these adepts solidified in May of 1875 when he received a letter signed by one "Tuitit Bey" of the Egyptian Brotherhood of Luxor. This epistle included four elements that would characterize the Masters' subsequent communications to Olcott: cryptic admonitions to "TRY"; orders to dispel all doubt (about either Blavatsky or the Masters); commands to come to the aid of Blavatsky; and promises of future rewards for such fidelity. "He who seeks us finds *us*. TRY. Rest thy mind—banish all foul doubt," the letter began. "Sister Helen is a valiant, trustworthy servant. Open thy Spirit to conviction, have faith and she will lead thee to the Golden Gate of truth."[60] Subsequent letters from "Serapis Bey," another member of the Egyptian brotherhood, exhorted Olcott to be friendly and merciful to Blavatsky, not to leave her, to comfort and forgive her, to write her daily, and even to provide her with money. Again, Olcott was promised—in language strikingly reminiscent of the King James Version of the Bible—that his hard work would be amply compensated:

> Try to help the poor broken-hearted woman and *success* will crown your noble efforts. Sow healthy grains and choose your soil and the future will reward you by unexpected harvests. . . . Do not forsake her cause . . . *Try*. Seek and ye will find. Ask and it will be given ye. . . . Watch over

her, Brother mine—forgive her outburstings of passion, be patient, merciful, and charity bestowed on another will return to thee a hundred-fold.[61]

Although these mysterious messages did serve to dispel Olcott's "black doubt" and "mistrust" regarding his chum and her Masters, they did not fully satisfy his skepticism. Ever the empiricist, Olcott held out for more compelling evidence.

One evening, after he and Blavatsky had put *Isis* to bed for the night, Olcott retired to his room, sat in his favorite chair, and began to read. What ensued he later described as "the most momentous" event of his life.[62] While reading, Olcott glimpsed out of the corner of his eye a whitish gleam. Turning toward the light, he saw an immense Hindu man clad in white, his long black hair tumbling from underneath a turban, and his black beard parted at the chin and twisted up and over the ears "in the Rajput fashion":

> His eyes were alive with soul-fire; eyes which were at once benignant
> and piercing in glance; the eyes of a mentor and a judge, but softened
> by the love of a father who gazes on a son needing counsel and guid-
> ance. He was so grand a man, so imbued with the majesty of moral
> strength, so luminously spiritual, so evidently above average humanity,
> that I felt abashed in his presence, and bowed my head and bent my
> knee as one does before a god or a god-like personage.[63]

Laying his hand on Olcott's head, this god-like personage then explained that he had come to help him through his current crisis so that he could get on with the "great work . . . to be done for humanity." He further promised Olcott that the tie between Blavatsky and him would be strained but never broken.

Olcott later recalled that doubt crept again into his thoughts. "What if this be but hallucination; what if H.P.B. has cast a hypnotic glamour over me?" he asked. "I wish I had some tangible object to prove to me that he has really been here; something that I might handle after he is gone!" Suddenly, as if reading Olcott's mind, the Mahatma unraveled the turban from his head and laid it on a table, leaving Olcott with "tangible and enduring proof" that he had received a visitation from "one of the Elder Brothers of Humanity, one of the Masters of our dull pupil-race." This resolved Olcott's doubts about Blavatsky and her Masters into an unshakable faith. "From that moment I had a motive to live for, an end to strive after," Olcott later wrote. "However others less fortunate may doubt, I KNOW."[64]

In this theophany, Blavatsky's Masters displaced the Steele brothers as Olcott's spiritual godfathers, even as Indian gurus supplanted Egyptian adepts in his theosophical pantheon. Soon Olcott would refer to his Indian guru as "my dear Father," just as he had undoubtedly prayed to "God the Father" in his Presbyterian youth. Like Emerson's "representative men," these adepts now functioned in Olcott's cosmos as the bearers of culture and civilization, the uplifters of humankind. And like Arnold's "men of culture," they had a "passion for diffusing, for making prevail, for carrying from one end of the society to the other, the best knowledge, the best ideas of their time."[65] For Olcott these "best ideas" now issued not from Egypt (from whence his previous Masters had come) but from his new holy land of India. And that holy land, he would soon decide, was reaching out to greet him.

Three

An Errand to Asia

Among historians of theosophy and theosophists alike there is a widespread misconception that Olcott and Blavatsky founded the Theosophical Society with the express intent of pursuing its oft-cited "three objects":

> (1) to form the nucleus of the Universal Brotherhood of Humanity, without distinction of race, creed, sex, caste or colour; (2) to encourage the study of comparative religion, philosophy and science; (3) to investigate the unexplained laws of Nature and the powers latent in man.[1]

Although it is the case that Olcott and other theosophists eventually came to identify theosophy with spanning the divide between East and West, their society was founded to promote the reform of American spiritualism, not the study of Asian religions. Olcott and Blavatsky aimed in the early years of the Theosophical Society simply to discover through scientific investigations the occult laws governing spiritual phenomena. References to Asian religious traditions and to a panreligious universal brotherhood were conspicuously absent from the early writings of Olcott and Blavatsky and from formal statements of the nascent society. Only after the Theosophical Society failed to fulfill this original objective did Olcott and Blavatsky begin to cast a collective glance to the East. The society's co-founders did not begin to teach the doctrine of reincarnation, for example, until after they arrived in India.[2] And it was not until the early 1880s that Olcott and Blavatsky first articulated their newly fashioned society's "three objects." It is important to distinguish, therefore, between early theosophy (as scientific spiritualism) and later theosophy (as Asian wisdom).

Hints that Olcott and Blavatsky were beginning to effect a transition from early to later theosophy appeared as early as Blavatsky's withdrawal from public view in 1877 to work on her *Isis* manuscript. But it was a historic correspondence with Asian religious reformers that convinced Olcott and Blavatsky that they possessed significant numbers of allies among Asian intellectuals and that the future of theosophy lay outside the United States.

Although the theme of most of this correspondence was the celebration of commonalities, its undertone was a not-so-successful attempt to eradicate differences. One reason this attempt was not successful was the fact that

Olcott and his Asian correspondents employed different unification strategies. The Asians sought to bridge barriers between themselves and the theosophists either by trying to convert Olcott and Blavatsky to their respective faiths or by convincing themselves that the theosophists were already converts. Olcott and Blavatsky, meanwhile, attempted a more subtle transformation, seeking to impose on the manifold Buddhisms and Hinduisms of Asia their theosophical framework. By imaginatively reconstructing all religions, both East and West, in light of their theosophical perspective, they hoped to reduce religious differences to ephemera that paled in comparison to the commonalities that supposedly pervaded all the religions of the world. Lurking behind the shared theosophical rhetoric of "unity achieved," therefore was a strategy of "unity constructed" through the eradication of difference. Even before the theosophists departed for Asia, tensions existed in the unities they hoped to construct with their newfound friends. A close examination of the extant letters reveals significant fault lines between the emerging "creole" faith of Olcott and the more traditional faiths of his correspondents.

East-West Correspondence

Olcott's Asian correspondence began in 1877 when an acquaintance who had recently returned from India arrived one evening at the New York apartment Olcott was now sharing with Blavatsky. The visitor, while examining a photograph of two Indian men who had accompanied Olcott on a trip to England in 1870, recognized one of the men as a friend named Moolji Thackersey. Olcott obtained Thackersey's address and wrote to him, outlining a new version of the history of the Theosophical Society and inviting him to join. In this letter Olcott claimed, probably for the first time, that the mission of the Theosophical Society was not to reform spiritualism but to import Asian wisdom to the United States. Thackersey responded to Olcott's letter by eagerly accepting membership. This response encouraged Olcott, who was soon engaged in a lively correspondence with Hindu and Buddhist religious reformers across South Asia.

In this correspondence Olcott reinvented the early history of the Theosophical Society and recast its aims. Scuttling the earlier, failed emphasis on investigating and reforming spiritualism, Olcott now claimed that the Theosophical Society began with two closely related objectives in mind: to promote Asian religious traditions in America and to discredit Christianity in Asia. In letters to a Hindu from Calcutta, for example, Olcott contended that the Theosophical Society was organized "to promote the study of the

esoteric religious philosophies of the East" and to expose the moral bank-
ruptcy of Christianity. Clearly influenced by freethought, Olcott's inflammatory letter portrayed the Christian tradition in the worst possible light:

> Christianity has nearly run its course, the Popist half is lapsing into Fet-
> ishism, the Protestant into Nihilism. . . . Vice and crime increase daily un-
> der the festering influence of the dogma of the Atonement; the white
> races are becoming sensualized and brutalized; society is honeycombed
> with drunkenness, hypocrisy, sexual sin, breach of trust, fraudulent com-
> mercial usage. Meanwhile, millions are lavished upon gorgeous
> churches, the pay of the clergy increases, vast sums are spent to send
> missionaries to lie to the *Heathen* about the practical benefits of Christi-
> anity, the court calendars are burdened with cases of seduction, rape,
> adultery, by church members and often pastors; there are poisonings, ar-
> sons, forgeries, and every other crime of the Decalogue, by the same
> classes of persons.[3]

One "chief object" of the Theosophical Society, Olcott added, was to publish these grim facts in non-Christian lands. When the "Heathen" learn the
truth about Christianity, he argued, they will repudiate that "bastard creed"
of the missionaries and return to "the pure faiths of their fathers." Olcott
then asked for his new friend to send a "truly pious Hindu scholar" to the
United States. If such a pundit were to come, Olcott claimed, he could
"sweep the country" with Oriental wisdom.[4]

The Christian-bashing here is curious. Although Olcott had publicly
identified himself as a non-Christian decades earlier, he had never before
resorted to such anti-Christian invective. So the fact that he used this language in the mid-1870s cries out for some sort of explanation. Unfortunately Olcott never explicates, either in his unpublished diary or in his written *corpus*, why he came to see Christianity as an enemy. But at least three
sources for his ardent anti-Christian sentiment can be plausibly deduced.

The first such source is Blavatsky herself. Unlike Olcott, Blavatsky had
traveled widely in Europe, where she was exposed, especially in Catholic
countries such as France and Italy, to a more virulent strain of infidelity
than Olcott had seen in America.[5] In fact, Blavatsky was so riled about
Christianity that she would, according to Olcott, get "hot and angry" whenever Roman Catholicism was mentioned.[6] And she clearly initiated Olcott
into this more radical infidelity while the two of them were working on her
bitterly anticlerical *Isis Unveiled*. Olcott's letter and much of his subsequent
writing on Christianity reflect the more militantly anti-Christian position
that Blavatsky had imbibed in Europe.

A second source for Olcott's shift to a more stridently anti-Christian position is the historical context in which that position developed. In the period after the Civil War, the United States embarked on an era that historian James Turner has identified as "Modern Unbelief." "In 1850, the intellectual ground of belief in God had seemed like bedrock," Turner has argued, "by 1870, it felt more like gelatin."[7] Accompanying this demise in the viability of time-honored justifications for the Christian faith was a new boldness in staking out arguments for various forms of atheism and agnosticism and against traditional Christianity. Olcott, who entered middle age as his country entered this era of "Modern Unbelief," was clearly influenced by this aspect of the temper of his times.

A final source of Olcott's newly heated anti-Christian rhetoric is the East-West correspondence itself. Olcott was well aware that the Asians with whom he was corresponding were engaged with Christian missionaries in a battle far more fierce than the warfare between science and religion that he had conjured up a few years earlier in his First Presidential Address. He knew, therefore, that his Christian-bashing would be welcomed among his Hindu correspondents. Later, a missionary critic would describe theosophy as "a strange mixture of Brahmanism, Buddhism, Mysticism, and Spiritualism" and contend that "the only bond of union between their motley followers is a common dislike of the Christian religion."[8] While dislike of Christianity was certainly not the only force keeping theosophists together, it was an important one nonetheless. Olcott was at the time he entered into this correspondence casting about for a new direction to take his society—searching, in short, for a more marketable theosophy. And what he was learning was that praising Asian religions and damning Christianity were two sides of the same, eminently salable coin.

Convinced no doubt of the viability among India's Hindus of this two-pronged strategy—anti-Christian propaganda in the East and pro-Asian propaganda in the West—Olcott commenced a similar correspondence with Buddhist reformers in Ceylon, and thus became part of a broader American discussion of Buddhism carried forward by academics, travelers, Christian critics, and other Buddhist sympathizers.[9] In the summer of 1877, he sent a letter to a prominent Sinhalese monk that underscored the wide divide between Oriental wisdom and "the common enemy—Christianity." Look to the West, he wrote, and you will find "a sensual clergy; a demoralizing theology; a forged book; the substitution of faith for merit; of words for deeds." But look to the East, and you will encounter "the way to purification, illumination, power, beautitude [sic]."[10] Olcott then asked this

Buddhist correspondent (as he had asked his Hindu friend earlier) to send an emissary to "sweep the country" with Asian wisdom:

> Fathers, brothers, the Western world is dying of brutal sensuality and ignorance; come and help; rescue it. Come as missionaries, as teachers, as disputants, preachers. Come prepared to be hated, opposed, threatened, perhaps maltreated. Come expecting nothing but determined to accomplish everything.[11]

Although this later letter mirrored his earlier one in many important respects, something distinguished it from the first: a startling confession of Buddhist faith. But even this short confession—"We the leaders of the Theosophical Society believe in the Incomprehensible Principle and the Divine Philosophy taught by Sakya Muni. With all my heart and soul I accept and profess the philosophy and try to act up to the precepts of Gautama Buddha"[12]—was by no means orthodox. From the beginning, Olcott's creole faith made room both for "soul" and "divinity," two concepts utterly foreign to traditional Theravada Buddhism.

Olcott followed this profession of his Buddhist faith with an appropriate confession (one he would soon retract) of his ignorance of the tradition. He then vowed, probably for the first time, to combat his ignorance by traveling to Asia to study under the direction of Asian teachers. "I am so ignorant . . . that I do not dare to set myself up as a teacher," he wrote. "I cannot say that I understand the sublime doctrine of Sakya Muni. I see myself at the feet of his disciples as one of the humblest though most sincere disciples." Olcott then announced his determination to travel to Asia and to "set myself to studying" the hoary truths of the Buddhist tradition under the direction of learned monks.[13]

Olcott apparently revealed his newfound Buddhist interests to friends at home as well as to acquaintances abroad, because soon the word was out in New York that Olcott had embraced Buddhism. "You are not a Spiritualist," a *Banner of Light* editor complained in a December 1877 letter to Olcott, "but a Buddhist."[14] And so he was. But the faith Olcott now confessed was an odd sort of Buddhism. Long before he departed for Asia with the express intent of sitting as an ignorant disciple at the feet of monks and gurus there, Olcott had constructed for himself a relatively fixed image of "Buddhism." And this image bore at least as much resemblance to Blavatsky's theosophy and liberal Protestantism as it did to the Buddhism of Theravada monks. In fact, the only ostensibly Buddhist principle to which Olcott appealed in his letter to the Sinhalese monk was also theosophy's central dogma and one of the key affirmations of liberal Protestantism:

"that we should respect every man's faith, holding our own, nevertheless, in chief affection."

More than a monastic way of life or a system of lay beliefs and practices, Buddhism was for Olcott, at least in the beginning, a liberal antidote to Christian sectarianism. Olcott denied Christianity and affirmed Buddhism because the former was in his view intolerant and the latter, tolerant. He preferred Buddhism over Christianity, in short, because he was a religious liberal for whom religious tolerance was something akin to dogma. "If we form a league against Christianity," Olcott explained, that is because it "sets itself up to be the one true religion, bears the curse of the eternal damnation against all who deny its supremacy, and by cunning and violence aims to subdue and corrupt the whole earth."[15] From the start, Olcott's Buddhism was a creolized subspecies of religious liberalism.

Resisting Olcott's Heterodoxy

Responses to Olcott's entreaties were at first largely appreciative. A number of his Asian correspondents accepted membership in the Theosophical Society and soon a theosophical branch was established in Bombay. At least from across the oceans, Olcott initially appeared to many Buddhists and Hindus as one of their own. But Olcott's heterodoxy was apparently not entirely lost on his Asian interlocutors.

Hikkaduve Sumangala, a leading Sinhalese monk, responded negatively (and presciently) to Olcott's plan to publish a series of English translations of Buddhist sutras on the grounds that it was "a matter next to impossibility" to translate Buddhist philosophy into English while retaining its "energy, sweetness and propriety."[16] Swami Dayanand Saraswati, the future leader of an important Indian reform society called the Arya Samaj, responded more positively to a similar plan to translate Hindu scriptures. But perhaps because of his awareness of the possibility (if not the probability) of cross-cultural and interreligious misunderstanding, he took pains to articulate his worldview with some care. In what was surely one of the earliest attempts by a Hindu to explain Hinduism in writing to a westerner, he described God in an April 21, 1878, letter as:

> that Lord of the Universe, who deserves all endless praise, who is omnipotent and all-pervading, who stands as a mine of all good qualities, namely, truth, knowledge, all-joy, justice, and mercy; who is infinite, undivided, unborn, immutable, without destruction; who is the prime cause of creation, protection, and destruction; who is naturally accompanied by true qualities and actions; who is unerring and all-learned.[17]

Saraswati then attempted to convert Olcott to his faith. Since "God is one
. . . men cannot but have one religion," he reasoned, and this "true religion"
consists "in the worship of, and obedience to, the Supreme Governor . . .
in accordance with the Vedic views" (emphasis mine). Other religions,
Saraswati concluded, only "serve the selfish motives of mean-minded and
ignorant persons."[18] Saraswati then followed up this letter with a July 26,
1878, missive that supported these views with extensive quotations from
the Vedas, denounced at least some spiritual phenomena as "trickery and
vileness," and concluded with a hymn of praise to the Almighty.[19]

These illiberal manifestos must have disappointed Olcott. A few months
earlier Olcott had expressed, in a letter to the president of the Arya Samaj,
his preference for "an Eternal, Boundless, Incomprehensible Divine Essence" of the kind that might have moved in the heart of Emerson over the
sort of personal God, "capable of being moved by supplications and propi-
tiated by promises," that ruled the Calvinists.[20] But now Saraswati seemed
to be embracing a far less impersonal deity than Olcott's divine principle.
Moreover, Saraswati's back-to-the-Vedas orthodoxy clearly conflicted both
with Olcott's liberal commitment to the equality of all religions and with
his spiritualist interests.

Rather than confronting Saraswati or Sumangala, Olcott apparently responded to these disagreements with a sort of denial. In May of 1878 the
leaders of the Theosophical Society voted to affirm institutionally the unity
that Olcott and leaders of the Arya Samaj were ostensibly constructing intellectually. On that day they officially merged with the Arya Samaj, renam-
ing their ecumenical organization "The Theosophical Society of the Arya
Samaj." Olcott remained troubled, however, by mounting evidence that the
merged societies were proceeding on different theological planes. In the
spring of 1878 Olcott attempted to circumvent "any possible misconception" by sending a pamphlet outlining the views of the Theosophical Society to a representative of the Arya Samaj and an explanatory public letter
to the *Indian Spectator* (his first to an Asian periodical).[21] In the letter Olcott
celebrated the union of the Theosophical Society and the Arya Samaj and
anointed Saraswati the "supreme religious Teacher, Guide and Ruler" of
this new amalgamation. But he simultaneously distanced himself from both
Saraswati and the Arya Samaj by referring often to Buddhism and by arguing that Buddhist truths antedated the Swami's beloved Vedas!

In the *Indian Spectator*, Olcott once again defined Buddhism in peculiar
terms: as "the religion of Bodh or Buddh (Wisdom)—in short, Wisdom-
Religion." "It is this Wisdom-Religion which the Theosophical Society ac-
cepts and propagates," Olcott explained, "and it was only upon finding its
doctrines in the teachings of Saraswati that the Theosophical Society was

moved to affiliate with the Arya Samaj." "You see then," he concluded, "that we are neither Buddhists in the popular sense, nor Brahmanists as commonly understood. . . . The Theosophical Society prays and works for the establishment of a Universal Brotherhood of races."[22]

Even a cursory reading of this strange passage reveals that Olcott's affirmation of Buddhism and his allegiance to the Arya Samaj were far from unequivocal; already he was constructing a creole faith and speaking of that faith with a decidedly theosophical accent. Saraswati saw the Vedas as the *Urreligion* and traditional Buddhists viewed their sutras as authoritative. But Olcott collapsed both into Blavatsky's "Wisdom-Religion." What Olcott was accepting, therefore, was not the tradition of the Buddhists but a "Buddhism" of his own invention—a Buddhist lexicon informed by a Protestant grammar and spoken with a theosophical accent. Moreover, the organization with which his Theosophical Society was merging was not the Arya Samaj of the Arya Samajis but an "Arya Samaj" of his own imagining. Olcott, therefore, was not merely carving out some middle ground for himself; he was assuming that his imaginative constructions of both Buddhism and Hinduism were more authoritative than the ideas of the Buddhist monk and the Hindu swami.

Olcott's theosophy thus shared with missionary Christianity an assimilative impulse characteristic of other colonial ideologies. Olcott distinguished himself from missionaries in India by refusing both to recognize differences between religious traditions and to construct hierarchies of superiority and inferiority based on those differences. He explicitly opposed, for example, the missionary project of bringing Buddhists and Hindus into the Christian faith. But Olcott's ideology of the equality of religions mirrored the missionary's ideology of religious difference in one crucial respect: it too refused to recognize the Buddhists and Hindus of India as full human subjects. Because of his refusal to accept the differences between himself and his Asian correspondents, Olcott came to understand these Oriental "others" almost exclusively as reflections of his Occidental "self." Thus Olcott's seemingly empathetic embrace of both Buddhism and Hinduism shared with missionary Christianity and British colonialism an imperial thrust. He was demanding, in short, that his Asian correspondents become "anonymous theosophists"—adherents of a new ideology that was not self-consciously their own.

Like his contemporaries in the Society for the Propagation of the Gospel who believed that every knee should bow to Jesus Christ and the Queen of England, Olcott was convinced that all the world could and would come to share his faith. By spanning (and thereby controlling) within his grasp the Babel of sectarian ideologies, Olcott would weave a sacred canopy under which all religions and races could coexist in a harmonious "Universal Brotherhood." The fact that his particular faith was but one among many never occurred to Olcott, however, who remained unaware of the parochialism of his universal vision. Long before his departure for India, Olcott was mistaking his contribution to the sacred canopy for the sacred canopy itself.

Preparing the Way

Through his Asian correspondence and his work on *Isis*, Olcott's love of Asian wisdom gradually deepened into a desire to visit the land that was tugging at his heart. His initial plan mirrored the paths that would be taken in the next century by thousands of Americans attracted to the Orient. He would travel with Blavatsky to India and/or Ceylon to study under local religious experts; then, after a period of training, he would return to the United States to share with modern Americans the ancient wisdom he had learned during his sojourn in the East. Olcott initially viewed this plan as nothing more than a possibility, but the globetrotting Blavatsky soon became obsessed with the idea. Her conviction, however, could not shake Olcott's ambivalence. "An insatiable longing possessed me to come to the land of the Rishis and the Buddhas, the Sacred Land among lands," he later wrote. But "I could not see my way clear to breaking the ties of circumstance which bound me to America."[23]

Among the ties binding Olcott to America were financial obligations to his family. Apparently Mary Olcott was concerned that her ex-husband would not fulfill those obligations, because she fought valiantly to keep Olcott close to home. Frequent references in Olcott's diary to "Kali"—the bloodthirsty Hindu goddess whose name Olcott and Blavatsky uncharitably adopted to refer to his ex-wife—indicate that during the months before his departure the Olcotts were engaged in some sort of litigation, probably regarding alimony or child support.[24] By all indications, however, Olcott was willing to meet the payments of $1500 per year (not an inconsiderable sum at the time) that a judge in his divorce case had instructed him to make.

Olcott attempted to secure a source of income in India by starting an "Indo-American Trading Co." modeled after the East India Company of the British. Blavatsky melodramatically dubbed this scheme Olcott's "great final stake." The venture, in which Olcott would function as a broker of merchandise rather than culture, was, at least initially, surprisingly successful. By October of 1878 Olcott had used his Lotos Club connections to persuade thirteen of "the best men of N.Y." to back him in is effort to amass a "Syndicate" of businesses interested in supporting East-West trade, and by December at least one company had contributed $500 in seed capital.[25]

In addition to seeking financing for his trading company, Olcott worked to secure political support. In fact, he pursued his contacts with diplomats so vigorously that Blavatsky joked that Olcott harbored "hopes of making his entree into Bombay with the Govt. seal stamped upon his backside." Taking the task more seriously, Olcott tapped a Lotos Club contact to secure through Secretary of State William Evarts "a commission to report to Government upon the practicability of extending the commercial interests of our country in Asia." On December 13, 1878, Olcott received a special diplomatic passport from the State Department, along with a letter of recommendation from President Rutherford B. Hayes himself. Circumstances that a few months earlier were conspiring to keep him in New York now seemed to be beckoning him East.[26]

Olcott remained tied, however, to his own symbolic construction of his homeland. Around the time of his departure for India, Olcott accepted a commission from the Union Mutual Life Insurance Company to compile a pamphlet entitled *A Budget of American History*.[27] Four years earlier Olcott had wrestled with his Puritan roots while authoring a genealogy of the Olcott clan. Now he sat down on the eve of his departure for Asia to summarize his views of America itself.

Olcott's *American History* is, given its publication date of 1881, shockingly pluralistic. Unlike contemporaries who began their American sagas with Columbus or the Puritans,[28] Olcott began with the Eskimos and Aztecs. He shunned, moreover, the popular Protestant view that the United States was a country providentially set apart, affirming instead the more cosmopolitan view "that the continents of Asia and America were once united by an isthmus . . . our continent was peopled from Asia." Olcott supported this theory by engaging in a bit of comparative religion. There were, he argued, striking commonalities in beliefs and practice among Aztecs and native Americans on the one hand and the people of Egypt and the Far East on the other. Like the Natchez, he noted, the Parsees worship the sun and keep a sacred fire perpetually burning; young Chippewas, like Hindu and Siamese ascetics, retire to the forest and fast in an attempt to conjure up their protecting spirits; and the shrines of the Zunis are engraved with "the egg of Brahma and of Phtha, the parallel zigzag lines, the twin columns, the crescent moon, and other symbols of Eastern creeds." All these commonalities pointed, according to Olcott, to "a unity of religious thought" between Asia and the Americas.

In the *Heilsgeschichte* of Olcott's *American History*, the main motif was not a New Israel but a New (yet ordered) Babel. America was not the place where Protestant Christianity would triumph but the stage on which all the world's religions were destined to meet. Thus Columbus, who, according to Olcott, upon arriving in America "kissed the earth; and, planting the sacred cross, . . . thanked God for his success," shared the spotlight in Olcott's pluralistic drama with a host of other heroes who also overcame great obstacles in order to establish their faiths here. It was the pagan Vikings, after all, who discovered America; and the religion of the Buddha "was brought here by missionaries at a very early epoch."

As this tract attests, Olcott's ties to his homeland ran as deep as his religious interests ran wide. Through Blavatsky's energetic coaching, Olcott was gradually coming to view India as a holy land, but he continued to revere America as an equally sacred center. The Indus Valley may have been the birthplace of religion and the cradle of culture, but America was civilization's crowning achievement—the place where the concept of religious liberty was most thoroughly entrenched and where religious pluralism was most prominently on display.

Thus bound by commitments to household and homeland, Olcott remained ambivalent about the prospect of emigrating East. In an attempt to resolve his doubts, he recalled the inexplicable visit of the turbaned adept from India to his New York apartment, an event he later recalled as "the chief among the causes of my abandonment of the world and my coming out to my Indian home."[29] This recollection served to reinforce a sense of his Asian destiny but he longed nonetheless for more compelling and immediate evidence of the propriety of his impending move. Such evidence materialized in the form of a winter of 1878 epistle from one of Olcott's Egyptian Masters. Olcott's diary records the substance of the message: "*Orders* from Serapis to complete all by the first days of December. . . . *Have to go.*"[30] Whether this commandment resulted from the conjurings of an impatient Blavatsky, from Olcott's own desire to resolve his ambivalence, or from one of the Masters themselves, is not clear. What is clear is that from this point on there is no further evidence of Olcott looking back.

Rite of Passage

Late in the evening on December 17, 1878, Olcott and Blavatsky boarded the steamship *Canada* to begin an errand to Asia that Olcott clearly viewed as analogous to his Puritan ancestors' errand to the New World. The joint determination of theosophy's co-founders to leave New York amounted to an abandonment of their earlier vision of the Theosophical Society as a scientific body devoted to investigating spiritual phenomena and discovering occult laws. The membership list of the Theosophical Society had included notables such as inventor Thomas Edison and Abner Doubleday, the Civil War hero once falsely hailed as the inventor of baseball. But the organization had failed to sustain a sizable following. Perhaps Asia would be different from New York City. Perhaps the seeds of a new voluntary association devoted to gathering under the banner of the ancient wisdom of Asia a nonsectarian "Universal Brotherhood of Humanity" would blossom when transplanted in India. Perhaps Olcott, who could advance at least as well (if not better) than Blavatsky this new pro-Asian, anti-Christian agenda, would blossom too. Such were the hopes that Olcott harbored as he bade farewell to America's sacred soil.

Along with a phonograph he had obtained during a recent visit to Edison's home, Olcott packed in his trunk a few key assumptions. He assumed, first of all, that it was possible to construct a "nonsectarian" religious organization that could stand above the fray of the world's religions. A second assumption provided the rationale for the first: that people of all the world's religions could unite because in the last analysis they all shared the same worldview. The essence of Hinduism, Buddhism, and even true Christianity was, according to Olcott, one and the same. Following Blavatsky, Olcott traced this common essence back to ancient theosophical sources and called it "Wisdom-Religion."

Of course these assumptions were not entirely novel. During America's Second Great Awakening in the early nineteenth century, two leaders within Olcott's Presbyterian denomination had convinced groups of followers to shun denominational labels and to call themselves neither Baptists nor Methodists nor Presbyterians but, simply, "Christians." Certain that sectarian distinctions only detracted from their mission of calling Americans back to Christ, Barton Stone and Thomas Campbell had preached a simple gospel that downplayed denominational differences in both doctrines and rituals. They had rooted their model for Christian unity in the example of the primitive church, which in their view was bereft of sectarian squabbling. And they had attempted to construct their "Christian" unity not on creeds but on experience—the shared experience of conversion.[31]

Olcott's desire to bring together all the world's religions mirrored in a number of ways the hopes of Campbell and Stone to unify the Christian denominations. Olcott and his "Christian" counterparts disdained religious sectarianism, and sought to construct not a new sect but an organization that would stand above other sectarian structures. Each attempted to legitimize their unities through a rhetoric of "restoring" a largely invented "primitive" tradition. Each tried, moreover, to minimize doctrinal differences by invoking a simple faith of few theological essentials. Finally, and perhaps most significantly, Olcott and the "Christians" failed in their quest for unity even as they succeeded in establishing their alternative religious associations. The "Christians" of Campbell and Stone would eventually form the "Disciples of Christ," which was destined not to end denominational bickering but to add to it. Olcott's "Theosophical Society" would meet a similarly ironic fate.

Unaware that his nonsectarianism was itself a sectarian position, Olcott excluded from his "Universal Brotherhood of Humanity" anyone who believed that his or her religious tradition was more venerable, more true, or more virtuous than Blavatsky's *Urreligion*. Such people—and Christian missionaries were chief among them—Olcott dismissed as "sectarians," damning them to wherever intolerant folks go.[32] On the eve of his departure for Asia, Olcott was ebullient about the prospects of bringing Asians into what he saw as a theosophical synthesis of East and West. But he did not foresee how difficult it would be to incorporate Hindus and Buddhists into his theosophical and at least vaguely Protestant system. Soon Olcott would be accused by Hindus of being a Buddhist and by Buddhists of being a Hindu. Adhering to both (indeed all) religious traditions would prove to be daunting indeed.

On the day that Olcott and Blavatsky set sail, Blavatsky scribbled in large letters across the top of Olcott's diary, "CONSUMMATUM EST." Given her vow of chastity and Olcott's quasi-monastic description of his passage to Asia as "my abandonment of the world," Blavatsky presumably was not talking about her relationship with Olcott.[33] But she was astute in using the language of ritual process. What she and her "twin" were consummating was their long flirtation with the mysteries of the Orient. Soon she and Olcott would enter the dangerous border-zone between their former lives, as members of the Russian aristocracy and New York City's metropolitan gentry, and their future lives as Indophilic Buddhists. Their rite of passage to Asia was under way.

On Sacred Soil

Olcott and Blavatsky departed from New York on December 17, 1878, and, after a brief stopover in London, reached Bombay on February 16, 1879. Upon arriving in his new holy land, Olcott recapitulated the drama that according to Olcott's own *Budget of American History* Columbus had performed upon reaching the Americas. "The first thing I did on touching land," Olcott later recalled, "was to stoop down and kiss the granite step; my instinctive act of pooja! For here we were at last on sacred soil."[34] Through this act of worship, Olcott transformed India into sacred space, the day of his arrival into sacred time, and (most curiously) himself into something akin to Asia's Columbus. Like Columbus and the Puritans who followed in his wake, Olcott too would take it as his sacred duty to found among Indians a "New World."

The arrival of Olcott and Blavatsky in Bombay was duly and, for the most part, happily noted in the Anglo-Indian press. The *Allahabad Pioneer* welcomed the Theosophical Society as "a beneficent agency in promoting good feeling between the two races in this country." Its editor, Alfred Percy Sinnett, a British gentleman who would soon become one of the Theosophical Society's most influential converts, saw a wide divide between the selfish interests of previous émigrés and the altruistic motivations of Olcott and Blavatsky. "Hitherto the motives which have brought Europeans to India have been simple and easily defined. They have come to govern, to make money, or to convert the people to Christianity," he noted. "The Theosophists, on the other hand, have come because they are filled with loving enthusiasm for Indian religious philosophy and psychological science. They come neither to rule nor to dogmatize, but to learn."[35]

This was, of course, the theosophical line. While still in New York, Olcott had underscored his ignorance of the Buddhist and Hindu traditions. He and Blavatsky would come to Asia, he had promised his Asian correspondents, not as puffed-up teachers but as humble students. They desired nothing more than to sit at the feet of Asian gurus and to learn what the Orient had to teach.[36] Unlike the administrators, adventurers, and priests who preceded them, they had come neither to govern, to profit, nor to convert. And after they had learned sufficiently, they would return home. Almost immediately upon their arrival in Bombay, however, Olcott and Blavatsky diverged from their promised path. Neither India nor the Indians would measure up to Olcott's idealized images of them. They would require decades of teaching. And who better to "uplift" and "refine" them than Olcott himself?

"The Theosophical Society and Its Aims"

Less than a month after his arrival in Bombay, Olcott delivered his first Indian lecture. The title of the address was "The Theosophical Society and its Aims," but Olcott's primary subject was reforming India.[37] More specifically, Olcott argued, in a typically primitivist and restorationist vein, for a modern revitalization of "Aryavarta" or ancient India. But curiously, Olcott's hope for this regeneration depended in large measure on modern India's ability to become more like the United States. Before his departure for India, Olcott had stressed America's need for Asian truths. Now he supplemented that thesis with the contention that Asia was in need of American know-how. His argument for an East-West synthesis ran something like this: only if modern India can imbibe the technological and commercial spirit of America will it be able to prosper materially; and only if it prospers materially will it be able to revive the moral and spiritual example of ancient India; thus, just as surely as the morally decadent West needed the inspiration of the spiritually superior East, so impoverished India required the example of the economically superior United States.

In his first Asian address, Olcott revealed his roots in universal reform by arguing that the resuscitation of an anesthetized India depended on its adoption of a number of improvements. High on Olcott's list of reforms was a revision of the caste system in the direction of American ideals of social mobility. "If India is to be regenerated," Olcott contended, "it must be by Hindus who can rise above their castes and every other reactionary influence." India's reawakening also depended on the adoption of America's work ethic. Noting the subcontinent's nearly inexhaustible wealth of natural resources, Olcott argued that Indians could amass "fabulous national wealth" if only they could mobilize their immense human resources. "All that is lacking," Olcott contended, "is a share of that energy and foresight which in two centuries and a half have transformed the United States from a howling wilderness into a scene of busy prosperity." In order to tap into this tremendous supply of human energy, Olcott continued, India must also reform her educational system by focusing on technical skills rather than liberal learning. Anticipating a call that Booker T. Washington would soon make for technical education for African Americans, Olcott argued that India's elites must supplant their fruitless pursuit of unproductive university degrees with programs that will train engineers, geologists, carpenters, and manufacturers in "the management of practical affairs." Technical education "such as we have in America," Olcott argued, is "the great and crying want of modern India today."[38]

The metaphor that ran throughout Olcott's inaugural address was of India as "a mighty Nation like a giant benumbed with sloth." This metaphor implied both a condemnation of India's modern stupor and a prophesy that it would soon awaken to its ancient glory. But Olcott was not addressing India per se as much as he was addressing its emerging middle class. It was this class, after all, that was most in need of a work ethic and technical education. And it was the ranks of this class that would swell should caste reform be implemented. Not surprisingly, Olcott would draw most of his Asian followers from this segment of Indian society.

Toward the end of his speech, Olcott prophesied not only the resurrection of Aryavarta's primitive soul but also the restoration of modern India's economic prosperity. The children of India, he wrote, will rediscover both the wisdom of ancient Aryavarta and the hard work necessary in the modern world. "The youth of India will shake off their sloth, and be worthy of their sires," he wrote. "From every ruined temple, from every sculptured corridor cut in the heart of the mountains, from every secret Vihara where the custodians of the sacred Science keep alive the torch of primitive wisdom, comes a whispering voice, saying: 'Children, your Mother is not dead, but only sleepeth.' "[39]

Olcott laid bare in this lecture the twin yet conflicting nationalist agendas that would contend for his allegiance throughout the rest of his life. India was now his sacred soil, the country of his adoption. But America was the country of his birth, and remained an object of his affection. Olcott mediated this conflict, not unlike his fellow Victorians mediated the conflict of gender, by dividing the globe into two separate spheres, each with its own responsibilities. Like the American female, the Orient was allotted the private sphere of religion and morality. In matters of truth and virtue it was superior. But in matters of science, technology, and commerce the Occident ruled as surely as did the male in America's public sphere. What was needed, according to Olcott's ever-unitive vision, was a marriage of the two, a union of the feminine and spiritual East with the masculine and technological West.

This synthesis permitted Olcott to have it both ways. He would love America *and* leave it; adopt Asia *and* reform it. Although Asians were now his spiritual kinfolk, he would not cut the ties that bound him to his Puritan ancestors. On the contrary, he would celebrate his Protestant past by finding imaginative correspondences between that past and his Asian present. "Just as I have left my home, and business, and friends, to come to India to worship the Parabrahm of primitive religions," he proclaimed, "so, in 1635, one of my ancestors left his home in England to seek in the wilderness of America that freedom to worship the Jewish Jehovah which he could not have at home."[40] At least in his own mind, Olcott's errand to Asia was an extension of his Puritan predecessors' errand into the savage American wilderness. These Indians too would need to be civilized.

The Theosophical Society and the Arya Samaj

Olcott drew on the theory of the separate spheres of the feminine Orient and the masculine Occident in another lecture, which he delivered shortly after his first meeting with Swami Dayanand Saraswati of the Arya Samaj. In "The Joint Labours of the Arya Samaj and its American Sister, the Theosophical Society," Olcott praised Saraswati (again, in Protestant terms) as "the Luther of Modern India," and his society as the "twin sister" of the

Theosophical Society. He then articulated publicly the same vision of the separate missions of the two societies that he had previously spelled out in private letters. Just as the sphere for the work of the Arya Samaj was in the East, the sphere for theosophical activity, Olcott promised, was in the West. Olcott's mission in India, he announced, was not to reform Hindus but "to get you Eastern people to help us reform Europe and America." Yet Olcott belied this avowed division of labor by admitting to his Indian audience that "it is part of our duty to make you better acquainted with our country," meaning the United States. And why? Because it was "one of the richest, most active, and wonderful [countries] in the whole world." Olcott then went on to describe America's technological marvels: its trains and steamboats, telephones and telegraphs, light bulbs and dumbwaiters. Above all, Olcott praised America's public schools, "where a capital education is imparted, free of all cost, to the children of the poor and rich."[41] Along with these hymns of praise to the United States, Olcott hummed a few more subtle choruses, also aimed at reforming India in America's image. Taking up the women's rights theme that crowded the pages of American spiritualist papers in the 1850s, Olcott denounced the "unnatural" practice of child marriage as a "monstrosity." Women in ancient India were both well-respected and well-educated, Olcott argued. "India will never revive her ancient glory, until [the] Indian woman is rescued from ignorance and servitude."[42]

Although Olcott explicitly denied in this speech any personal mission to India, he propagated nonetheless a program for the nation's practical reform. His arguments for women's rights, universal education, and agricultural reform, combined with calls for caste reform, technical education, and hard work in his earlier speech, constituted an ambitious attempt to "uplift" Indian culture by refashioning it along American Protestant lines. Despite Olcott's claims to the contrary, the Theosophical Society was destined to wield its primary influence not in the West but in the East. India may have been spiritually superior to the United States, and Americans certainly had much to learn from the Hindus' Vedas and the Buddhists' Tripitaka. But in the physical sphere at least, Olcott argued, "America [was] giving light to India."[43]

Business Matters

Olcott's refrain regarding the prosperity of the West is a bit surprising for someone who left a lucrative law career in New York City and frequently lamented the acquisitiveness of British India. But it is not altogether unexpected for a man who was struggling to make ends meet. Thanks to the hospitality of the maharajahs and swamis whom Olcott and Blavatsky met during their initial tour of India, and the kindness of Sinnett and other members of India's English-speaking middle class, the "Theosophical Twins" managed to survive their first year overseas. But money was a near-constant worry. In fact, Olcott's diary for 1879 contains more references to finances than to any other topic, theosophy included. During that first year abroad Olcott made numerous attempts to transplant his "Syndicate" to India's sacred soil. He negotiated with leather traders, mill owners and even tiger-skin brokers about exporting their products to America; and he corresponded with American businessmen about importing such wares. At one point Olcott entered into an agreement with a Bombay businessman to organize a firm called "H.P. & Co."

Unfortunately, none of these business schemes yielded much, so Olcott made one last effort to profit from his unofficial status as "United States Commissioner to the East Indies."[44] In an April 30, 1880, appeal to Secretary of State William Evarts, Olcott outlined his rather dim view of the prospects for improved U.S.–India trade. "I have been doing as much as I could to establish commercial relations between the merchants of the two countries," Olcott wrote. "I have also caused the forwarding of orders for American goods and shipments of Indian products to American firms."[45] But these efforts had produced, according to Olcott, "unostentatious results"; they had done little to offset "the deep-rooted habits of conservatism" that prevailed among India's bourgeoisie, who according to Olcott preferred the safety of public servanthood over the entrepreneur's risk. At the end of his letter, Olcott suggested that he might be able to produce better results if the State Department could find the means to remunerate him for his work. "My regret is that my relations with the Department are not on such a basis of personal compensation," he hinted, "as to warrant my giving more time to the matter." Unfortunately for Olcott, there is no evidence that Evarts ever overturned his previous stipulation that Olcott's work be performed "without expense to the United States."[46]

In the absence of steady work, Olcott turned to his old stock-in-trade, freelance writing. Like Blavatsky, who peddled her travelogues to Russian periodicals,[47] Olcott sold a series of articles to the *New York Sun*. Months before his departure for India, Olcott had written an uncharacteristically undiplomatic article castigating the British Raj for holding "an unwilling people in bondage," and prophesying a native uprising more violent than the bloody Sepoy Rebellion of 1857.[48] But after some time in India, a more prudent Olcott was both more critical of the Indian masses and more appreciative of British elites. He massaged his American readers' prejudices with articles on "snake charmers" and "serpent worship" in India. And in keeping with the dictates of late-Victorian manliness, he lamented the "emasculation" of the Indian people—a trait he attributed to child marriage, vegetarianism and, oddly enough, the invasion of the presumably more effeminate Muslims. About the British colonization of India he now had only good things to say. Western-style education (and female education especially) he praised as "the cornerstone of national greatness," and he applauded the railroad for bringing together previously separated castes.[49] In these *Sun* travelogues, Olcott failed on occasion to discuss theosophy, but he never neglected the subject of U.S.–India trade. "Poor as they are, the Hindoos still buy enormously of British manufactures," he wrote in one letter. "A customer, this, not to be despised."[50]

Although worries about money filled Olcott's mind during his first year in India, cash flow was not his only anxiety. While on a tour of northern India, Olcott and Blavatsky discovered, as Olcott recorded in his diary for April 29, 1879, "that a handsome Englishman whom we had mysteriously met at every point where we had stopped on this journey was a Government spy!"[51] It is unclear exactly why the British thought it necessary to follow the theosophical leaders.[52] They may well have been wary of the Russian-born Blavatsky. But it is equally plausible that Olcott's earlier anti-Raj sentiments had raised colonial administrators' concerns. Apparently those administrators were not aware how thoroughly Olcott had repudiated his earlier views about the Sepoy Rebellion and the legitimacy of British rule in India. Influenced no doubt by his correspondences with Indian religious reformers, he had, even before arriving in India, become both more critical of the Indian masses and more appreciative of British elites. Convinced that his earlier pronouncements about the injustice and rapacity of British rule and the possibility (and desirability) of another mutiny had been naive, Olcott recorded in his diary for January 25, 1879, that "another mutiny is impossible . . . owing to increased intelligence among natives and better appreciation of a conservative just rule." Moreover, even if a mutiny were to occur and succeed, Olcott concluded, the Indian people would inherit a situation much worse than their present lot. Olcott's rationale for this conjecture is jarring, given his professed belief in the superiority of Asian civilizations. Westerners were, in his view, better not only at making machines but also at maintaining order. Indians, he concluded, in language that sounded more like a stereotypical Protestant missionary than an enlightened theosophist, "are not fit to rule India."[53]

Between May and June of 1879, Olcott complained about the espionage to British and American authorities, no doubt informing them about his new views regarding the beneficence of British rule [54] Eventually, through the intervention of B. F. Farnham, the American consul to Bombay, Olcott was able to arrange an interview on the matter with Governor of India Sir Richard Temple. During that interview, Temple was apparently persuaded that the theosophists' mission was something less than the overthrow of British rule in India. He issued an order terminating the surveillance.[55]

Though short-lived, this British spying episode was significant because it was out of these circumstances of suspicion that the myth of the apolitical Theosophical Society was born. From this point on, Olcott studiously avoided any language about British rule that was even potentially incendiary.

The *Theosophist*

During the summer of 1879, while Olcott was attempting to control the damage to his society caused by the spy controversy, his own prospects for prosperity went from bad to worse. On July 22, he received a letter from his friend and future theosophical adversary W. Q. Judge informing him that he had been bilked out of a $10,000 fee in an Albany insurance case and that his investment in a Venezuelan silver mine had gone sour. Cut off from these anticipated revenues, Olcott and Blavatsky devised a plan for raising needed funds from sources a bit closer to their adopted home.

Since their arrival in India, the correspondence of Olcott and Blavatsky had grown from massive to unmanageable. In an attempt to reduce the letter-writing, to lessen their financial difficulties, and to promote their new vision for the Theosophical Society, they decided to publish a monthly magazine "devoted to Oriental philosophy, art, literature and occultism."[56] The journal was to be distributed, at Olcott's insistence, in accordance with the "American plan" of payment in advance. Numerous friends counseled him against this plan, arguing that Indians, who traditionally were able to subscribe to magazines on credit, would resist the innovation. But Olcott stood firm and the *Theosophist* made its debut on October 1, 1879, with no debtors on its books.

The first number, officially "conducted" by Blavatsky but largely edited by Olcott, introduced its readers to theosophy ("the archaic Wisdom-Religion") and to the Theosophical Society (a "Universal Brotherhood of Humanity"). It promised to publish a number of articles by Buddhist, Hindu, and Zoroastrian teachers, who were described as "the only competent interpreters" of their religious traditions.[57]

Above all else it underscored the notion of theosophy as an apolitical, nonsectarian philosophy. Refuting charges (rooted no doubt in Blavatsky's Russian heritage) that the organization was a "political cabal" peopled by "spies of an autocratic Czar," one anonymous article maintained that the Theosophical Society was "unconcerned about politics" and cared little "about the outward human management of the material world."[58] This emphasis on the apolitical and philosophical nature of the society was outdone only by an emphasis on its nonsectarian, nondogmatic stance. One article cited numerous inspirations for this liberal vision, including Ammonius Saccas who maintained that various nations are "the children of one mother," and the old Buddhist axiom, "Honour thine own faith, and do not slander that of others." But it was the United States itself, the "Mother Land" of Olcott's organization, that provided the model for the Theosophical Society's nonsectarianism. Like the U.S., which afforded "absolute equality to all religions in its laws," the Theosophical Society was according to Olcott a "Republic of Conscience."[59]

This nonsectarian spirit manifested itself in future editions of the *Theosophist*, which included articles by leading Sinhalese Buddhist monks and a serial biography of Swami Dayanand Saraswati. One early number, featuring articles by representatives of the Hindu, Buddhist, Islamic, and Zoroastrian communities, prompted a self-congratulatory editorial note comparing theosophical pluralism with American Protestant ecumenism: "Did any magazine ever exhibit a more perfect and fraternal 'Evangelical Alliance' than this?"[60]

There was, however, one glaring exception to the *Theosophist*'s pluralism. Into its eclectic and cosmopolitan stew, consisting of articles like "Magnetism in Ancient China," "The Gesture-speech of the American Indian," and "The Jain View of Om," Olcott and Blavatsky stirred a near-equal measure of anti-Christian vitriol. One editorial note after another pounded away at the "profitless because hopeless" missionary enterprise. About the use of the legendary "missionary whip," for example, one annotation asked derisively, "What heathen could resist such persuasive arguments?"[61]

Apparently Blavatsky's more strident and more European anticlericalism was wearing off on Olcott, who was no doubt also learning that Christian-bashing solidified his growing reputation as a champion of traditional Indian religion and culture. Olcott exceeded all previous anti-Christian backbiting (and all but the most incendiary American freethought rhetoric) in an article responding to a reader's query on the adeptship of Jesus:

> There is no adequate proof to my mind either that Jesus was the Son of God, that he said or did the things ascribed to him, that either one of the four gospels is anything better than a literary fabrication, or that

Jesus ever lived. . . . [Christianity] is a bad religion and fosters every sin and vice against which its ethical code inveighs.[62]

Given Olcott's earlier statements regarding the incompatibility of Christianity and civilization, this strange mix of pluralistic esotericism and rabidly anti-Christian rhetoric should not be surprising. What was unexpected, for a magazine dedicated to ancient wisdom, was an extraordinary emphasis on the magic of modern western technology. Alongside translations of classic Indian texts, the first volume of the *Theosophist* contained glowing notes on Edison's telephone and "Gary's Magnetic Motor," articles on improvements in Indian agriculture and the development of the telegraph, even an "Official Report upon a Scorpion Poison Antidote."

Apparently the *Theosophist*'s mix of East and West, primitivism and science, esotericism and freethought hit the mark, at least among its target audience of India's English-speaking anti-missionary-yet-vaguely-pro-Western middle class. The magazine was favorably reviewed in the *Amrita Bazar Patrika* of Calcutta, Bombay's *Indian Spectator,* and the *Allahabad Pioneer*. It was also promoted, in a backhanded way, by the missionary press, whose unrelenting hostility to the Theosophical Society as "a hot-bed of anti-Christianism"[63] did little damage to their image as embattled outsiders and champions of the restoration of Indian culture to its primitive greatness. After only six months the *Theosophist* was turning a profit.

With the success of the *Theosophist*, however, came a number of failures. By the time of Olcott's first Indian anniversary in February of 1880, the "Syndicate" on which he had staked his financial well-being had died a slow death; an Aryan Temperance Society he had established on November 23, 1879, had come to an equally inauspicious, if more sudden, end; and the citizens of Bombay were mimicking the citizens of New York in benignly ignoring their resident theosophists. Finally, because of their early abandonment of their attempt to learn Hindi, Olcott and Blavatsky could address their theosophical gospel only to British civil servants and to English-speaking Indian elites.

But despite these setbacks, the star over the heads of Olcott and Blavatsky was clearly rising. Blavatsky's shamanic powers had earned her popular support from Madras to Darjeeling; Olcott, as the more genteel and decidedly more male theosophical leader, had worked his way into the good graces of Anglo-Indian high society; and a growing number of Indian and British elites were hitching their wagons to the theosophical star. On December 21, 1879, the Literary Society of Benares Pandits elected Olcott an honorary member of their society. "Although he is born in a foreign land," one member concluded, "yet he is assuredly a native of India."[64]

Such statements were, of course, music to Olcott's ears. Having left his homeland in the prime of life, he had established for himself a new home in India. Now this new "native" was, like the hero Arjuna in the *Bhagavad Gita* epic, ready to do battle on his next field of dharma. Sinhalese Buddhists who had been receiving the good graces of Olcott and Blavatsky through the mail were anxiously awaiting their arrival in the flesh.

Four

The Sinhalese
Buddhist Revival

When Olcott and Madame Blavatsky departed India on May 7, 1880, for their first tour of Ceylon, both Buddhism and British rule were charged topics on the island. Since ancient times, the Buddhist practices of monks and the governmental duties of kings had been closely linked there. The Sangha, or order of monks, was prohibited from engaging in worldly affairs so it had to rely on a succession of kings to maintain its temples and enforce monastic discipline. In return, the kings were provided with crucial ideological justification for their rule.

With the arrival of the Portuguese in 1505, state patronage of Buddhism ended and Catholicism became the island's established religion. Reformed Protestantism supplanted Roman Catholicism as the established faith when the Dutch ousted the Portuguese in 1656, but the state's policy of hostility to Buddhism persisted. Only in the Kandyan highlands, where a Buddhist kingdom endured throughout the Portuguese and Dutch periods, was the traditional symbiosis of monarchy and Sangha maintained. In 1796 the British forced the Dutch out of the island's lowlands, but not until 1815 were they able to oust the last Kandyan ruler from his highland kingdom. In the exit treaty or "Convention of 1815," the British agreed not to establish Anglican Christianity. But the agreement went much farther. In keeping with a more general policy of noninterference in the religious and cultural affairs of their colonial subjects, the British promulgated a celebrated "Fifth Clause" to the convention stating, "The Religion of Boodhoo professed by the Chiefs and Inhabitants of these Provinces is declared inviolable, and its rites, Ministers and Places of Worship are to be maintained and protected."[1]

In the early 1830s, however, Christian missionaries in both India and Ceylon began a campaign to overturn British policies of noninterference in religious matters. Soon they had convinced colonial administrators that a new "Christianization" policy would ensure social order more effectively than the old policy of religious neutrality. Freed from previous constraints by this policy change, Christian missionaries in Ceylon launched a highly successful evangelization campaign. Drawing on technological improvements and organizational practices popularized by revivalists in both Great Britain and the United States, these missionaries utilized the printing press and a network of voluntary associations to print and distribute Bibles, catechisms, prayer books, and a host of anti-Buddhist tracts.

These efforts were so successful that by the time Olcott and Blavatsky arrived in Ceylon in 1880, Christianity was the *de facto* religious establishment of the island colony. Of over 1200 government-sponsored schools in Ceylon, only four were Buddhist. Despite an 1868 bill mandating civil registration, most births, marriages, and deaths on the island were registered by Christian clergy in accordance with Christian rituals, and an English-language education was an unofficial but nonetheless necessary prerequisite for advancement into the new middle class. Perhaps most ominously for the island's religious majority, missionary schools had largely supplanted traditional modes of religious education offered by Buddhist monks in Buddhist temples, and even governmental classrooms were providing Christian instruction. Whatever remained of traditional Buddhist hegemony was further undermined when instructors turned from teaching Christ to teaching civilization. Gradually but persistently the sons (and, to a much lesser extent, the daughters) of Ceylon's Buddhist majority imbibed the bourgeois values not-so-cryptically encoded in the scientific textbooks and Victorian readers of British educators. It was not without cause, therefore, that Anglican officials in Ceylon reported in the decade before Olcott's arrival that the history of the church on the island was "an almost continuous record of advancement and progress" and that "by the testimony of all Buddhism is effete; its hold on the people is as slight as it is possible to be."[2]

Sinhalese Buddhists responded to the evangelization and "civilization" of their island with a Buddhist revival that rivaled in scope and intensity the earlier Protestant revivals of George Whitefield and Charles Finney in America. Anglican bishop R. S. Copleston attested to the success of this Buddhist resistance when he admitted in 1879 that "Buddhism as a whole is not conquered, or near it. It remains in the fullest sense the religion of the mass of the Sinhalese. . . . There is little doubt that Buddhism is far more vigorous in Ceylon than it was a hundred and fifty years ago."[3] Copleston then added that the impetus behind this revival was being provided by "the Secretary of an obscure Society" who had been corresponding with several Buddhist monks, "hailing them as brothers in the march of intellect."[4]

Buddhist Converts

This "obscure society" was, of course, the Theosophical Society and both its corresponding secretary (Blavatsky) and its president (Olcott) were to

Olcott in Indian dress—a "Hindu in White Skin," circa 1883. By permission of The Theosophical Society in America.

Olcott standing next to Hikkaduve Sumangala, the influential monk scholar of Ceylon who gave Olcott's *Buddhist Catechism* his stamp of approval. Source: C. V. Agarwal, *The Buddhist and Theosophical Movements.*

Stamp issued in Ceylon (now Sri Lanka) in 1967 to commemorate the many contributions of Colonel Olcott to the Sinhalese Buddhist Revival.

The "White Buddhist" as an older man, years after his arrival in India in 1879. By permission of the Theosophical Publishing House.

Portrait of Helena Petrovna Blavatsky, shot in New York City, probably in 1874, the year she met Olcott. Taken by a "spirit photographer," the photograph purportedly contains a cloud-like image of Blavatsky's enigmatic spirit in the upper left-hand corner. Source: estate of Eugene Rollin Corson, *Some Unpublished Letters of Helena Petrovna Blavatsky* (London: Rider). Used by permission.

Olcott and Blavatsky, the "Theosophical Twins." By permission of The Theosophical Society in America.

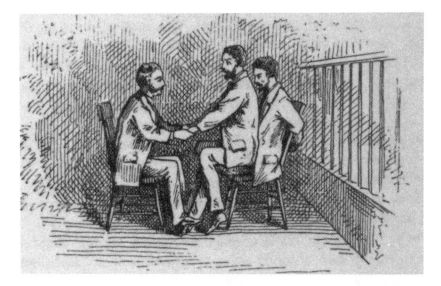

Olcott as investigator of spiritual phenomena at the Eddy homestead. Here Olcott (on the left) puts his feet on the toes of medium Horatio Eddy (whose hands were tied to a chair), while a volunteer from the audience sits on Mr. Eddy's lap. Source: Olcott, *People fron the Other World.* By permission of Charles E. Tuttle Publishing Company, Inc.

Weighing and measuring a spirit at the Eddy homestead. Prompted by the scientifically minded Olcott, a volunteer finds that "Honto," a popular Indian squaw spirit, stands over five feet tall yet weights only 58 pounds! Source: Olcott, *People from the Other World.* By permission of Charles E. Tuttle Publishing Company, Inc.

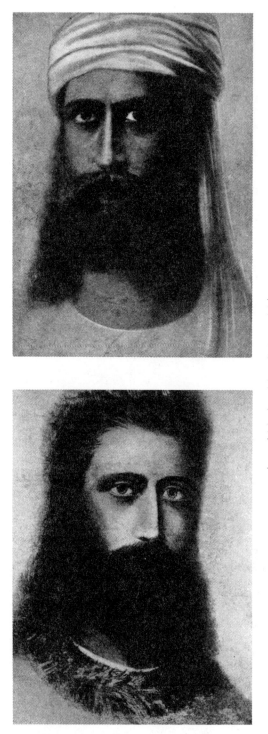

Artist renderings of Morya and Koot Hoomi, the two Mahatmas ("Great Souls") most intimately tied to the fortunes of the Theosophical Society. The existence of these occult Masters from the East and the genuineness of their "Mahatma Letters" were hotly debated in Olcott's time. Source: Harold Edward Hare and William Loftus Hare, *Who Wrote the Mahatma Letters?* (London: Williams and Norgate, 1936).

Olcott with representative Buddhist monks in Ceylon in 1880, the year he became the first American formally to convert to Buddhism overseas. By permission of The Theosophical Society in America.

Anagarika Dharmapala, the Sinhalese Buddhist reformer and one-time theosophist who initially worked with Olcott but later denounced him as insufficiently Buddhist. This photograph was taken around the time Dharmapala traveled to Chicago to represent Theravada Buddhists at the World's Parliament of Religions in 1893. By permission of The Theosophical Society in America.

Olcott (center) and Future Theosophical Leaders in London. Annie Besant (on the left) would emerge after Olcott's death in 1907 as the second president of the Theosophical Society while Olcott's longtime friend William Q. Judge (on the right) would lead a splinter group out of the original society, becoming the first president of the newly formed Theosophical Society in America. Olcott, *Old Diary Leaves*. By permission of the Theosophical Publishing House.

play a major role in the revival's growth. But the revival was not entirely the theosophists' doing. It had begun, in fact, at least a decade before Olcott's first letter to Ceylon's Buddhists, with an indigenous reaction to the missionary advance. Isolated Buddhist opposition to the "Christianization" of Ceylon started as early as the 1820s, but it was not until 1862 when the Sinhalese started their own Lamkopakara Press at Galle that the Buddhist resistance became organized. In that year the "silver-tongued orator" Mohottivatte Gunananda, an activist monk whom Olcott would later describe as "more wrangler than ascetic," organized the Sarvajna Sasanabhivrddhidayaka Dharma Samagama or the Society for the Propagation of Buddhism. That same year yet another Sinhalese press (purchased, ironically, from the missionaries themselves) began to issue a series of printed responses to anti-Buddhist pamphlets.[5] A tract war ensued, then a series of public debates, which began at Baddegama in 1865 and culminated in a famous exchange between Mohottivatte and Wesleyan clergyman David DeSilva at Panadura in 1873.[6] These battles, conducted in the press and on the podium, prompted the first phase of the Sinhalese Buddhist revival. The arrival of Olcott and Blavatsky would inaugurate, therefore, not the revival itself (as Copleston intimated) but the revival's second and most successful phase.

Olcott and Blavatsky arrived in Colombo on May 16, 1880. Apparently, their reputations, like their letters, had preceded them, since they received what Olcott later described as a royal welcome:

> A huge crowd awaited us and rent the air with their united shout of "Sadhu! Sadhu." A white cloth was spread for us from the jetty steps to the road where carriages were ready, and a thousand flags were frantically waved in welcome.[7]

Shortly after this reception the theosophists endeared themselves even more to their hosts by becoming the first European-Americans to formally embrace Buddhism. While still in New York, both Olcott and Blavatsky had pledged their allegiance to the Buddhist tradition,[8] but on May 25 at the Wijananda Monastery in Galle, Olcott and Blavatsky made that pledge official. Each knelt before a huge image of the Buddha and "took Pansil" by reciting in broken Pali the Three Refuges and the Five Precepts of Theravada Buddhism. By promising to rely on the Buddha, the Dhamma ("Teachings") and the Sangha ("Monastic Community"), and by vowing to adhere to the five moral rules incumbent upon Buddhist laypeople, Olcott and Blavatsky publicly and formally became lay Buddhists.

In his study of American Buddhism, historian Thomas Tweed has argued that Americans turned to Buddhism in the nineteenth century because it was somehow exotic but not utterly foreign. It thus provided an avenue for dissent without necessitating a wholesale break from what he calls the "consensus" of "Victorian culture." Tweed documents this thesis exhaustively, noting, on the one hand, how Americans inclined toward Buddhism dissented from their peers politically, economically, socially, culturally, and religiously and, on the other hand, how those same Americans retained "cultural continuity" with their country's religious mainstream. In the end, however, Tweed contends that his Americans' "turn to Buddhism can be understood as gradual and more or less complete shifts of frameworks of meaning or universes of discourse."[9]

This analysis certainly helps to illuminate the ambivalence Olcott displayed toward his Puritan and Protestant heritage. But it overestimates in my view Olcott's cognitive shift. Neither in Ceylon at this moment of his official "conversion" nor on the day in America when he first realized he was a Buddhist did Olcott undergo a "more or less complete" shift in his framework of meaning. What shifted for Olcott was merely the "lexicon" of his faith. The structural framework out of which he spoke his Buddhist words—what has been described here as his "grammar"—remained Protestant, and his "accent" remained decidedly theosophical.

In a later account of his conversion to Buddhism, Olcott underscored the difference between a "regular Buddhist" and "a debased modern Buddhist sectarian." Olcott, of course, understood himself as a "regular" rather than a "debased modern" Buddhist, but it was he who was the innovator. "If Buddhism contained a single dogma that we were compelled to accept, we would not have taken the pansil nor remained Buddhists ten minutes," he explained. "Our Buddhism was that of the Master-Adept Gautama Buddha, which was identically the Wisdom Religion of the Aryan Upanishads, and the soul of all the ancient world-faiths."[10] As this clarification attests, Olcott's Buddhism was unquestionably heterodox. Even on the day of his conversion to Buddhism, Olcott was discriminating between the false Buddhism of the Sinhalese people, which was in his view modern, debased, sectarian, and creedal, and his ostensibly true Buddhism—ancient, pure, nonsectarian, and nondogmatic.

Spreading the Faith

Olcott, of course, did not keep this creole faith to himself. He spread it across Ceylon in two ways. First, he popularized his ideas through a series of lectures; and, second, he gave those ideas institutional form by founding a series of schools and voluntary associations. In lectures he delivered in Colombo and Kandy in June of 1880, Olcott outlined in greater detail the contours of his creole Buddhism.[11] He denied, for example, missionary contentions that Buddhism was "a grossly materialistic, a nihilistic, a negative, a vile-breeding religion." But he spent more time distinguishing his Buddhism from the "ignorant superstitions" and sectarian squabbling of many Sinhalese Buddhists than he did distancing it from Christian stereotypes. Olcott claimed that his faith—unlike the vulgar rites of less refined Buddhists, which were in his view "totally at variance with Buddha's precepts"— was rooted in the person and the teachings of Gautama Buddha. But Olcott's ostensibly ancient Buddha sounded strikingly modern and western. A "religious reformer," the Buddha was not only the best but also the most genteel of men. He exceeded all others, Olcott wrote, "in wisdom, zeal, humanity, purity of life and thought; in ardour for the good of mankind; in provocation to good deeds, to toleration, charity and gentleness." The doctrines of this "heroic prince of Kapilavastu," Olcott intimated, were as genteel as his character. In addition to "benevolence," "gratitude," and "tolerance," Olcott wrote, the Buddha taught lessons that sounded both liberal and Protestant—"lessons of a common tie of brotherhood among all men" and "lessons of manly self-reliance."[12]

Although Olcott devoted much of his first tour of Ceylon to lecturing, he also found time to establish voluntary associations. During his first visit to the island, he founded seven lay branches and one monastic branch of the Buddhist Theosophical Society (or B.T.S.) Once again, Olcott was explicit about modeling his Asian work after Christian examples. In reasoning about one of his branch societies, Olcott wrote, "As the Christians have their Society for the diffusion of Christian knowledge, so this should be a society for the diffusion of Buddhistic knowledge."[13]

Olcott also founded, again on Christian models, Buddhist secondary schools and Sunday schools affiliated with the B.T.S., thus initiating what would become a long and successful campaign for western-style Buddhist education in Ceylon. Olcott's first school had an immediate impact on the Christian educational institutions on which it was modeled. According to Olcott it recruited, in addition to 90 students gathered from nearby Buddhist temples, 108 students from Wesleyan schools, 62 from Roman Catholic institutions, and 27 from schools sponsored by the Anglicans' Society for the Propagation of the Gospel.

Thanks to these efforts, Olcott and Blavatsky left Ceylon in July of 1880 as folk heroes. They had met a number of high-ranking monks, chief among them Hikkaduve Sumangala, who would soon become Olcott's most faithful Sinhalese ally. And they had been honored with a tour of Kandy's venerated Temple of the Tooth, the most sacred Buddhist site on the island. Equally important, Olcott and Blavatsky had been embraced by a large number of Sinhalese laypeople. As the first white champions of the Buddhist tradition in Ceylon, Olcott and Blavatsky passed "from triumph to triumph."[14]

Ceylon's missionaries used less flattering words to describe the activities of their newest antagonists, but their reports only corroborated Olcott's analysis of the tour. The *Ceylon Examiner,* for example, reported that the theosophists' arrival "created no little sensation among the ignorant Buddhists of this place, who seem to look upon them with awe and reverence as if they were demi-gods come down from the supposed blissful abode of Nirwana [*sic*]." The *Church Missionary Gleaner* also noted that the theosophists' visit issued in immediate and discernible results. "The opposition of the Buddhists," he concluded, "has been more active than in former years, their zeal having been provoked by the visit to Ceylon of two persons from America calling themselves Theosophists. . . . Thousands flocked to see a white man, and particularly a white woman, who had become Buddhists."[15]

The success of this first tour prompted Olcott to reevaluate his relationship with Blavatsky, his role in the Theosophical Society, and his view of his Asian mission. Olcott had planned upon his arrival in India in 1879 to spend some time learning about Hinduism and Buddhism from eastern experts. After an educational period in Asia, he would return to America, where he would devote the rest of his life to promoting theosophy and building up the Theosophical Society. Such a life he would live in the shadow of Helena Blavatsky. But the celebrity status that Olcott achieved during his first Ceylon tour led him to reevaluate his plans. Gradually he was coming to see himself more as a teacher than as a student. He was also coming to view India as his home. But perhaps most important, he was beginning to emerge from behind Blavatsky's formidable shadow. For the first time since his initial encounter with Blavatsky, Olcott achieved during his first Ceylon tour some independence from her domineering personality and theosophical agenda. Though Blavatsky was feted by elites and fawned upon by the nation's miracle-hungry populace, her status as a woman in a clearly androcentric culture prevented her from enjoying the access to monks that Olcott enjoyed. Moreover, because the tour itself highlighted Olcott's oratorical skills (exercised in the public realm of men) rather than Blavatsky's parlor-room charisma (wielded in the private world of women), Olcott garnered as much influence, if not as much fame, as his traveling companion. Before their departure the Sinhalese people were praising Blavatsky, but they were also hailing Olcott as one of their own—"The White Buddhist."

Over the next few years Olcott would continue to mediate theosophical quarrels, to edit issues of the *Theosophist*, to defuse charges of theosophical politicking, and to establish new Theosophical Society branches, but in the wake of his triumph in Ceylon these matters no longer merited the bulk of Olcott's considerable energies. As Olcott settled into Asia, his focus gradually shifted more and more toward Buddhism.

Second Ceylon Tour

Shortly after his return to India in July of 1880, Olcott manifested once again his roots in the didacticism of genteel reform when he determined that educational reform should be the cornerstone of the new Buddhist revival and the "benevolent empire" he was building there. Convinced that the island's Buddhists exhibited a "dense popular ignorance" of the moral and spiritual principles of his own tradition, he committed himself to cultivating in them Buddhist truths and virtues.[16] He decided to establish a "National Education Fund" to finance Buddhist schools for Sinhalese boys and girls, and he vowed to return to Ceylon to raise money for its coffers. When Olcott first broached this scheme to Blavatsky, she assured him not only of her own support but also of the support of the Mahatmas. But she soon changed her mind, demanding that Olcott cancel the tour and remain at Bombay. When Olcott refused, Blavatsky exploded, locking herself in her bedroom for a week. During her self-imposed exile, Blavatsky sent her ex-chum a bitter note warning that the Masters, who now also disapproved of the tour, would abandon both the Theosophical Society and its president if he persisted in his disobedience. But in an unprecedented exhibition of independence, Olcott held his ground. Reminding Blavatsky that the Mahatmas had initially approved of his plan, a newly skeptical and independent Olcott stated that he "did not believe them to be such vacillating and whimsical creatures," and that he would go to Ceylon even if meant that he would never see another Master again.[17]

Olcott set sail for Ceylon on April 23, 1881, and arrived four days later in the southern port of Galle. Together with Mohottivatte Gunananda, the activist monk who had spearheaded the first phase of the Sinhalese Buddhist revival, he crisscrossed the western province for eight months in a bullock cart of his own design. Villagers flocked, according to Olcott, to witness the mechanical wonders of this device, whose lockers for furniture and books, canvas roof to keep out rain, and cushioned central compartment with removable planks that could seat eight for dinner or sleep four, all testified to Olcott's Yankee ingenuity. When not impressing the Sinhalese with his cleverness and hard work, Olcott looked the part of the anti-Christian missionary. He sold merit cards and solicited subscriptions to support his National Education Fund, wrote and distributed anti-Christian and pro-Buddhist tracts, and secured support for his educational reforms from representatives of the island's three monastic sects, the Siyam, Amarapura, and Ramanna Nikayas.

Forty-seven "begging lectures" provided a focus for Olcott's tour. In constructing these talks, Olcott turned once again to Christian examples. At a meeting of the Colombo Buddhist Theosophical Society, Olcott cited the Christian practice of tithing in an attempt to shame his Buddhist listeners into increasing their offerings to ten percent. He incorporated into many of his other lectures the structure of the "widow's mite" story from Mark 12:41–44. In Olcott's version, however, the hero—a "poor, tired-looking woman, miserably clad"—contributed her pittance not to Christ but to Buddhist education. Apparently this woman, who earned a living grinding rice, had been "saving up coppers of the smallest denomination" for six months in hopes of buying some cloth for new garments, but in a demonstration of selflessness she gave the rupee instead to Olcott's Buddhist Educational Fund. Unlike the Biblical story, however, in which the widow was rewarded only spiritually, Olcott's story ended with a Horatio Alger twist. After the widow contributed all she had, a sympathetic onlooker tossed a rupee in her direction, and when others followed suit the widow walked away with a thirty rupee profit![18]

Given the phrenetic nature of his first Ceylon tour, Olcott welcomed what he described as a "wonderful falling off of crowds of visitors as compared with last year." But he remained disturbed by what he perceived as "the shocking ignorance of the Sinhalese about Buddhism."[19] This determination that the island's Buddhists did not know their Buddhism was an odd sort of judgment for a recent convert who had purportedly come to Asia not to teach but to learn. It was, however, a judgment that Olcott shared with many nineteenth-century academic Orientalists, whose books greatly influenced Olcott's Buddhist faith. Like Olcott, pioneering Buddhologists like Rhys Davids (whom Olcott eagerly read) tended to reduce the Buddhist tradition to what the Buddha did and what the Buddhist scriptures said. This tendency permitted them both to praise the ancient wisdom of the East and to condemn its modern manifestations—to view Asian religious traditions much like Calvin viewed the human race: as decadent creatures fallen from some Edenic past.[20] It was Olcott's uncritical and unconscious appropriation of this aspect of academic Orientalism that led him to the rather absurd conclusion that Ceylon's Buddhists knew little, if anything, about "real" Buddhism. Like his hated missionaries and his beloved Orientalists, Olcott assumed the right to define what Buddhism really was. Unlike them, however, he assumed the duty to stir the Sinhalese masses from their ignorance, to instill in them his own creole representation of their Buddhist faith.

Buddhist Catechism

In devising his strategy for this didactic mission, Olcott turned yet again to the missionary example. Apparently no longer convinced that Buddhist thinkers were "the only competent interpreters" of Buddhism, he decided to compile for use in his Buddhist schools a catechism of basic Buddhist principles, "on the lines of the similar elementary hand-books so effectively used among Western Christian sects," both Protestant and Catholic. Olcott's *A Buddhist Catechism*, which would eventually go through more than forty editions and be translated into over twenty languages, is in many ways the defining document of Olcott's creole Buddhism. It first appeared, in both English and Sinhalese, on July 24, 1881. Hugely influential, it is still used today in Sri Lankan schools.[21]

Not surprisingly, readers disagreed about the merits of *A Buddhist Catechism*. In a review entitled "Absurdities of 'A Buddhist Catechism,' " the *Ceylon Catholic Messenger* denounced the tract as "a fanciful agglomeration of fables worthy only to be classified with the Arabian Nights."[22] But a more trustworthy reviewer, Hikkaduve Sumangala, certified that the work was "in agreement with the Canon of the Southern Buddhist Church."[23]

One reason Olcott was able to earn the imprimatur of Sumangala was that he presented a draft to him before publishing it. But to Olcott's dismay, the high-ranking monk was initially less than enthusiastic. What troubled Sumangala was Olcott's discussion of nirvana. Aware of a longstanding disagreement between the Theravada and Mahayana schools about whether the human somehow survives nirvana, Olcott had noted that eminent Buddhist metaphysicians disagree "respecting the survival of a 'subjective entity' after the dispersion of the skandhas."[24] When Sumangala denied any such disagreement, Olcott cited various Mahayana texts. But Sumangala, who threatened to withdraw his sanction of the project, ultimately prevailed. "Nothing more to be said, as he has the whip hand now," Olcott concluded in his diary, "Our turn may come later." At least in the catechism, Olcott agreed that nirvana entailed "the total obliteration of everything that goes to make up the physical man."[25]

Olcott divided his catechism into five sections. The first three were clearly inspired by traditional Theravada Buddhism's "Three Refuges."

The White Buddhist

Olcott had promised, upon embracing Buddhism during his first tour, to rely on the Buddha, the Dhamma ("Teachings"), and the Sangha ("Monastic Community"). His organization of the first part of the book into three chapters on "The Life of the Buddha," "The Dharma or Doctrine," and "The Sangha" reflected this commitment. But if the first three chapters of the catechism reflected the Buddhist vows he took in Asia, the last two demonstrated his continued ties to the West. In chapter four, "The Rise and Spread of Buddhism," he outlined the history of Buddhism as he had learned it from academic Orientalists. And in chapter five, "Buddhism and Science," he allowed his theosophical accent free reign, conflating the Buddhist worldview with occult science and theosophical esotericism.

Drawing on the standard catechistic question-and-answer format initially popularized by Catholics, but later taken up with a vengeance by Protestants, Olcott's catechism commended itself from the start to beginning students of the Buddhist tradition. It began rather simply:

1. *Question. Of what religion are you?*
   Answer. The Buddhist.

2. *Q. What is Buddhism?*
   A. It is a body of teachings given out by a great personage known as the Buddha.[26]

But even this simple start was extraordinarily revealing. The Buddhist tradition was now one "religion" among many. And this reified "ism" was immediately reduced to the beliefs of the ancient Buddha. From the start, therefore, rituals were both marginalized (in typical Protestant style) as peripheral to the tradition and the beliefs of modern Buddhists and discounted through the introduction of a primitivist assumption (also widespread among Protestants) that the earliest manifestations of the tradition, namely the teachings of the historical Buddha, were also the most authoritative.

Interestingly, the major burden of the catechism that followed was not to define "Buddhism" more precisely on its own terms but to understand it in opposition to Christianity. Olcott himself characterized his catechism as an "antidote to Christianity."[27] And so it was. But if a desire to combat the Christian tradition drove the catechism's answers, a shocking reliance on that tradition was evident also in its explicitly Christian questions:

Q. Was the Buddha God?
A. No. Buddha Dharma teaches no "divine" incarnation.
Q. But some people imagine that Nirvana is some sort of heavenly place, a Paradise. Does Buddhism teach that?

A. No. When Kutadanta asked the Buddha "Where is Nirvana," he replied that it was "wherever the precepts are obeyed."

Q. Does Buddhism teach the immortality of the soul?
A. It considers "soul" to be a word used by the ignorant to express a false idea . . . there can be no immortal survival of a changeful thing.

Q. Do Buddhists accept the theory that everything has been formed out of nothing by a Creator?
A. . . . We do not believe in miracles; hence we deny creation, and cannot conceive of a creation of something out of nothing.[28]

Other question-and-answer pairings exhibited the reactionary nature of the text by responding quite explicitly to Christian missionary critiques of Buddhism:

Q. Do these precepts show that Buddhism is an active or a passive religion?
A. To "cease from sin" may be called passive, but to "get virtue" and "to cleanse one's own heart," or mind, are altogether *active* qualities. Buddha taught that we should not merely not be evil, but that we should be *positively* good.

Q. Did the Buddha hold with idol-worship?
A. He did not; he opposed it.

Q. Are charms, incantations, the observance of lucky hours and devil-dancing a part of Buddhism?
A. They are positively repugnant to its fundamental principles.[29]

Nowhere is this reactive yet imitative nature of the catechism more obvious than in its definition of Buddhism over against other "religions." In Olcott's telling, Buddhism taught "the highest goodness without a creating God; a continuity of life without adhering to the superstitious and selfish doctrine of an eternal, metaphysical soul-substance that goes out of the body; a happiness without an objective heaven; a method of salvation without a vicarious Savior; redemption by oneself as the Redeemer, and without rites, prayers, penances, priests or intercessory saints; and a *summum bonum*, i.e. Nirvana, attainable in this life and in this world by leading a pure, unselfish life of wisdom and of compassion to all beings."[30]

Olcott's tract thus mirrored, in form if not in content, standard Christian missionary pamphlets, which also defined and evaluated one religion in light of another. If the lexicon of this creole catechism was Buddhist, its grammar or deep structure was Christian, and its accent, clearly theosophical. In Olcott's version, of course, Buddhism rather than Christianity came out on top, but the Christian missionary practice of defining one tradition in opposition to another was perfectly preserved. Olcott's catechistic Buddhism was, more than anything, non-Christianity. Defined by a rhetoric of negation, his Buddhism did *not* preach miracles like the atonement, creation, or revelation; and it did *not* damn unbelievers to hell. Because it was a "scientific" rather than a "revealed" religion, it did not require its adherents to accept any dogmas on authority; every teaching was to be tested "by one's reason and experience." Finally, Buddhism distinguished itself from Christianity by its refusal to perpetuate itself through "cruelties and crimes." Buddhism was, according to Olcott, "a religion of noble tolerance, of universal brotherhood" with "no taint of selfishness, sectarianism or intolerance."[31]

Perhaps the strangest thing about Olcott's ostensibly non-Christian Buddhism was how much it sounded like liberal Protestantism. More than an antidote to Christianity, Olcott's catechism was a homeopathic cure, treating the scourge of Christianity with a dose of the same. His critique of Christianity shared many elements with liberal Protestants' critique of Christian orthodoxy, including: a distrust of miracles, an emphasis on reason and experience, a tendency toward self-reliance, and a disdain for hell. Like their Jesus, his Buddha was a quintessential Christian gentlemen. "Sweet and convincing," he was the personification according to Olcott of "self-culture and universal love."[32]

Olcott also echoed the liberal Protestant critique of Christian orthodoxy by defining his religion in moral rather than theological terms—as "a pure moral philosophy, a system of ethics." Emphasizing deeds over creeds, Olcott instructed his readers "not to waste time in intellectual speculations" and to concentrate instead on "leading the holy life and following the rules laid down." A Buddhist was not someone who simply believed in Buddhist things but one who practiced Buddhist precepts; and the path to nirvana was not so much right thought as right action. Among the ways to practice this right action was, according to Olcott, to become a social reformer. Thus Olcott joined liberal Protestants in championing in his catechism not only antislavery and temperance, but also gun control, chastity, and women's rights.[33]

Finally, Olcott's representation of Buddhism exhibited a typically Protestant disdain for clerics (and their ostensibly empty rites) and a concomitant celebration of the laity (and their supposedly simple faith). In language strikingly reminiscent of nativist diatribes directed by Protestant preachers against the ostensibly empty superstitions and rituals of Catholic priests, Olcott criticized the "intellectually and morally inferior" monks and blamed their "rich, lazy, and sensual" predecessors for Buddhism's flight from India. He undercut the authority of the Sangha (as Luther and other Protestant reformers had undercut the authority of Catholic priests) by redefining the monastic order as an ethical rather than a traditional elite. "Only those who diligently attend to the Precepts, discipline their minds, and strive to attain or have attained one of the eight stages of holiness and perfection, constitute [the Buddha's] 'Order,' " he argued. "The mere wearing of yellow robes, or even ordination, does not itself make a man pure or wise or entitle him to reverence."[34] By elevating the laity while undercutting the Sangha, Olcott championed a radically democratized and "Protestantized" Buddhism that embraced "people of all ranks, nations and castes; rajas and coolies, rich and poor, mighty and humble, illiterate and the most learned." Nirvana, which according to Olcott was reachable "while one is living on this earth," was now open not only to monks but to laypeople.[35] It too had become a "priesthood of all believers."

If Olcott's *Catechism* smuggled into Buddhism elements of liberal Protestantism, it also appropriated key features of academic Orientalism. Olcott followed pioneering Buddhologists in portraying Buddhism as a moral philosophy rather than a religion, and in condemning Buddhist monasticism.[36] But the Orientalist influence was most pronounced in Olcott's tendency to reduce the Buddhist tradition to the Buddhist scriptures. During the mid-nineteenth century the Orientalists' manifestly Protestant assumption that all religions were religions of the book resulted in a process that Philip C. Almond has described as "the textualization of Buddhism." By reducing Buddhism to a "textual object" delimited by its Sanskrit and Pali sources, the Orientalists were able to combine a positive evaluation of the Buddha and the sutras with a negative evaluation of modern Buddhism. This discourse thus served to legitimize not only Orientalist scholarship (which examined Buddhism's golden age) but also the Christian missionary enterprise (which aimed not at the venerable faith of the Buddha but at the superstitions of modern idolaters).[37]

Olcott—who claimed to have read over 10,000 pages of translations and commentaries while preparing the *Catechism*—relied almost entirely on the Orientalists for his understanding of Buddhism, so it is not surprising that he imbibed their textual bias. This bias surfaced, for example, in the catechism's disdain for popular Buddhism. Devotionalism he denounced as "pagan, mean and spurious"—a lamentable departure from the tradition's "pristine purity." And according to the catechism, Shakyamuni himself had condemned rituals such as "charms, incantations, the observance of lucky hours and devil-dancing" and had instructed his followers to be vigilant in opposing such "perversion[s] of the true doctrine." Olcott showed his fa-

miliarity with Orientalist discourse when he judged these practices "surviv-
ing relics of fetishism" and denounced the syncretism they represented as
"a sign of deterioration."[38]

In summarizing living Buddhism as "the decay of spirituality, the corruption of the Sangha, and the reaction of the populace from a higher
ideal of man to unintelligent idolatry," Olcott corroborated the negative
stereotypes of the Orientalists.[39] He would, of course, reject the missionary's efforts to translate these stereotypes into a justification for conversions
to Christianity. But by employing those same stereotypes to legitimize his
Buddhist revival, he would perpetuate them nonetheless.

Saraswati and the Arya Samaj

Following his second Ceylon tour and the successful publication of his
Buddhist Catechism Olcott returned to India, where he continued to portray
himself as a revitalizer not only of Buddhism but also of Hinduism, Zoroastrianism, and Islam. He remained focused, however, on Buddhism. This fact
prompted criticism not only from Blavatsky, who was becoming increasingly
certain that Olcott was neglecting his theosophical commitments, but also
from his most powerful Indian ally, Dayanand Saraswati of the Arya Samaj.
Olcott's utopian East-West union would be hard to find.

While Saraswati had embraced Olcott and Blavatsky in 1878 as partners
in his mission to restore to India the eternal Vedic religion in its pristine
purity, over time he grew to question their commitment to his cause. The
letters that Olcott and Saraswati had exchanged before the theosophists
came to India convinced both men that the merger of their two societies
was probably not a very good idea, so the amalgamation had been effectively annulled only months after it was effected.[40] But the leaders remained
on relatively good terms for over three years. In 1882, however, Saraswati
publicly denounced the theosophists, thus becoming the first of Olcott's
Asian allies to reject him as heterodox.

Saraswati's main contention was that Olcott had misrepresented himself
as a Hindu who believed in the eternal veracity of the Vedic scriptures. At
first, Saraswati had been concerned that Olcott's doctrine of God was impersonal rather than personal. But now he believed that Olcott was either
an atheist or a Buddhist or both. In any case, he was decidedly not, in
Saraswati's judgment, a proper Hindu. Olcott responded to Saraswati's
charges, not surprisingly, with denunciations of his own. Citing the Arya
Samaj's insistence on Vedic orthodoxy and its lack of tolerance for other
faiths, he denounced the organization as "a new sect of Hinduism" and

The Sinhalese Buddhist Revival

Saraswati as an authoritarian ruler roughly akin to a Catholic pope.[41] In Olcott's judgment, blame for the failure to sustain the merger of the Theosophical Society with the Arya Samaj fell entirely on the shoulders of Saraswati, and that failure consisted essentially in the Swami's refusal to see his religion (as Olcott demanded it be seen) as one among many and his scripture's truths as shared rather than unique. In this way, Olcott's first attempt at an East-West union ended in failure.

Mesmeric Healings and Messianic Expectations

Rather than dwelling on his difficulties with Saraswati and whatever future problems they might portend, Olcott dove into his Buddhist work. Returning to Colombo on July 18, 1882, for his third Ceylon tour, Olcott discovered that the Buddhist Theosophical Society was "lifeless" and the revival was "at a standstill." Of the 13,000 rupees that had been pledged to the National Education Fund, only 100 had been collected. More ominously, a contingent of Roman Catholic missionaries had converted a well near a Buddhist pilgrimage site in the town of Kelanie into a Lourdes-like healing shrine. There were reports of one miraculous cure, and Olcott feared "a rush of ignorant Buddhists into Catholicism." In an attempt to break the Catholic monopoly over this crucial segment of the religious marketplace, Olcott pleaded for a monk to step forward and perform healings "in the name of Lord Buddha." How diligently he searched for an indigenous Buddhist to respond to the Catholic offensive is not clear. But when no monk came forward, he decided to do the work himself.[42]

Olcott's first healing in Asia occurred on August 29, 1882. When a man said to be totally paralyzed in one arm and partially disabled in one leg approached him after a lecture, Olcott recalled his youthful experiments with mesmerism and made a few perfunctory passes over the man's arm. The next day the man returned with reports of improved health, and Olcott began to treat him systematically. Soon the man could, in Olcott's words, "whirl his bad arm around his head, open and shut his hand, . . . jump with both feet, hop on the paralyzed one, kick equally high against the wall with both, and run freely."[43] Equally importantly, he was also able to sign a public declaration testifying to his miraculous recovery. Thanks to a combination of Olcott's publicity and old-fashioned gossip, news of the Colonel's healing powers spread across the island "as a match to loose straw," and his fund-raising tour was immediately transformed into a roadshow featuring the miraculous healing hands of the instantly charismatic "White Buddhist."[44]

Olcott publicly attributed his healings to the Buddha, but privately he credited the Austrian physician Franz Mesmer. Dismissing the notion that his cures were miraculous, Olcott proffered a strictly physiological explanation for the healings. Neither his patients' faith nor his own powers of hypnotic suggestion caused the cures, he said, which resulted in his view from the passing of "nerve-aura" between himself and a patient whose "mesmeric fluid" was in "sympathy" with his.[45] Olcott arrived at this ostensibly scientific theory after hearing that a paralytic patient whose miserliness had angered him suffered a relapse. He explained his discovery like this:

> I postulated to myself the existence in each individual of a nerve-fluid which would be . . . conductible by another person's nervous system in which an identical state of vibratory thrills or pulsations of aura was occurring. . . . Therefore a healer like myself could not cause his nerve-aura to enter the nerve-system of any patient which was out of sympathetic vibration with his own system, any more than an electric current could be made to run through a non-conductor. *Per contra*, the certainty and rapidity of his cure of any given patient would be in proportion to the completeness of this sympathetic vibration. . . . To proceed upon [this] hypothesis would be to bring psychopathy within the domain of positive science.[46]

Although Olcott had conjured up his curative powers in response to what he perceived as a Catholic offensive, the awakening of his charismatic gift seems to have met more personal needs as well. Before the summer of 1882, the roles of Olcott and Blavatsky in the theosophical drama had been as distinct as they were separate: Blavatsky was the charismatic genius, a Bohemian parlor queen and materializer of cups and saucers; Olcott was, on the other hand, the organizational man, the competent Colonel, the administrative accompaniment to his chum's chicanery.[47] Previously, Olcott had questioned Blavatsky's authority only in his capacity as a bureaucrat: her book was too long to sell, her manner too crude to be accepted, her lifestyle too lavish for their society's resources. But Olcott now challenged, for the first time, Blavatsky's charisma itself.

When Olcott returned to India in November of 1882 to oversee the transfer of the headquarters of the Theosophical Society from Bombay to its current site in Adyar, a suburb of Madras, he received, through a conciliatory Blavatsky, "a most kind message" from the Masters congratulating him on his Ceylon success. He initially received the note as "blessed news," but soon the incongruous juxtaposition of its friendly tone with Blavatsky's earlier invectives prompted Olcott to reevaluate his partner's trustworthiness as a medium. "Thenceforward, I did not love or prize her less as a friend and a teacher," Olcott wrote, "but the idea of her infallibility, if I had ever entertained it even approximately, was gone for ever."[48]

The Sinhalese Buddhist Revival

Now that Olcott possessed a gift on a par with her conjuring abilities, equality with the mysterious Madame was becoming something to be grasped. Scores of patients lined up outside the new headquarters in Adyar, and on a 1882 tour of Bengal Olcott supposedly treated 2812 patients.[49] In an effort to keep up with the booming demand for his services, Olcott set aside a portion of each day for a saltwater swim. These daily baths gave Olcott a brief respite from the madding crowds and served, according to his mesmeric theory, to restore vital essences drained by his patients. Soon, however, the seemingly insatiable needs of his followers overwhelmed Olcott's recuperative capacities. His popularity became a burden and when, toward the end of 1883, the Masters handed down an order to stop the healings, Olcott happily complied.[50]

Before his healing tours of 1882 and 1883, Olcott had recruited most of his Sinhalese and Indian followers from among the English-speaking middle classes. But his celebrated cures popularized his message, especially in Ceylon, where he may have inspired messianic expectations among Sinhalese peasants. On Christmas in 1882, Governor of Ceylon James Longden forwarded a secret memo to London informing Colonial Secretary Lord Kimberley of rumors that a pamphlet prophesying the imminent overthrow of British rule was circulating among the island's Buddhists. Although Longden thought it was "tolerably well ascertained" that some sort of messianic prophesy was afoot, he discounted the rumor's significance. "The native population is generally in the enjoyment of perfect freedom and of great material prosperity," he boasted. "Food is cheap and plentiful, and the causes which usually goad men into insurrection are wanting." Convinced not only of the legitimacy but also of the beneficence of British rule, Longden attributed the prophesies to chance circumstances, including a "magnificent Comet . . . which certainly will be long remembered by generations in Ceylon as the most brilliant manifestation of light ever seen in Ceylon by night."[51]

Longden did not include Olcott's healings in his list of prophecy-inspiring circumstances, but he did come close to crediting the Colonel in later dispatches. At some point during the winter of 1882–1883, Longden came to believe that the dire predictions had issued from India. In a letter to Governor Duff of Madras he traced the prophecies to "that revivalism which is undoubtedly abroad among Buddhists." He then added that the hero of the revolutionary tales was a "King of Righteousness" who would "outturn the British Dominion and secure the reign of the Buddhistic saints."[52]

There is no specific reference, either in this letter or in Governor Duff's response, to Colonel Olcott. But numerous details of the prophecy—its Indian origin, the figure of the "King of Righteousness," the link with the Buddhist revival—seem at least to hint at Olcott. If the masses of Ceylon's Buddhists were awaiting a messiah to come from across the ocean to liberate them, then Olcott was more than willing to play the role.

Kotahena Riot and Buddhist Rights

Olcott solidified his role as a leader of the Sinhalese Buddhist Revival in the wake of a tragic Buddhist-Christian riot that occurred on March 25, 1883, in Kotahena, a Catholic stronghold of Colombo.[53] On that day a Buddhist procession marched through the streets on the way to Mohottivatte Gunananda's newly decorated monastery, the Deepaduttama Vihara, where a new Buddha image was to be dedicated. When the procession approached a Roman Catholic cathedral located a few hundred yards from the temple, the cathedral bell sounded, followed almost immediately by bells in other Catholic churches in the area. As if in response to this signal, about a thousand men descended on the procession and a bloody brawl ensued. Authorities summoned eighty policemen but their batons were no match for the clubs, swords and stones of the mob. During the three-hour melee, one man was killed and forty others were injured.

Governor Longden responded to this battle over the bounds of sacred space in Kotahena by appointing an investigatory Riots Commission. A correspondent for the Baptist *Ceylon Observer* accused the Buddhists of instigating the row and traced its roots to Olcott's arrival on the island.[54] But Colonial Office records show that Longden and his commission concluded that the Catholics were the aggressors.[55] Catholics worshippers had apparently been offended by images utilized in a previous Buddhist parade. They had interpreted an icon carried by Sinhalese worshippers on Palm Sunday as a caricature of the Virgin Mary, and another image was said to resemble a "monkey on the crucifix."[56] Incensed by such affronts to their faith and, according to Buddhist and government reports, inflamed by alcohol, they took up arms.

As the governor's Riots Commission investigated the affair, Catholics and Buddhists took each other to court. Numerous cases were filed, but authorities eventually dropped all charges because of a lack of "reliable evidence."[57] In a private communication to Lord Derby, who had recently replaced Lord Kimberley as colonial secretary, Governor Longden admitted that his inability to bring the offenders to trial constituted a "lamentable failure of justice." Longden was not, however, to lament this failure. After it had become clear that the Catholics would not be tried, a group of Sinhalese monks and laypeople cabled Olcott urging him to come to Ceylon.

The Sinhalese Buddhist Revival

Upon his arrival on January 27, 1884, Olcott organized a Buddhist Defence Committee, which elected him an honorary member and charged him to travel to London as its representative, "to ask for such redress and enter into such engagements as may appear to him judicious." Thus for the first time Olcott's role as an intermediary between East and West became apparent, not only to himself but to Buddhists and colonial administrators alike.[58]

Before leaving for London, Olcott traveled to Kandy to meet with Sir Arthur Gordon, who had succeeded Longden as governor of Ceylon. At a meeting on January 31, 1884, Olcott expressed the committee's displeasure at the colonial government's failure to bring the rioters to justice. He apparently convinced Gordon that his Buddhist clients had "real and just cause to feel aggrieved," but Gordon stood firm, insisting that, given the passage of time, nothing could be done to remedy the injustice. In a report on this meeting that he later sent to Lord Derby, Gordon included a telling estimation of Olcott's growing stature in Ceylon. "There can be no question," he wrote, "that Colonel Olcott really possesses considerable influence among the Buddhist Community; that he, to a great extent, enjoys their confidence; and that he may fairly claim to be a representative authorized by them on his present mission, of the nature of which they are fully aware." But Gordon's evaluation of Olcott's legitimacy as a culture broker was equivocal. "On the other hand," he added, "my own communications with leading Buddhists lead me to suspect that he somewhat overestimates both his own knowledge of their doctrines and affairs, and the amount of influence which he exercises over their Counsels."[59]

Olcott may well have overestimated both his knowledge of Buddhism and his influence among Buddhists, but before he left for London a group of high-ranking Buddhist monks gave him reason to believe that he possessed both. In a solemn farewell ceremony, they authorized him "to register as Buddhists persons of any nation who may make to him application, to administer to them the Three Refuges and Five Precepts and to organize societies for the promotion of Buddhism."[60] The first person of European descent to be given such an honor, Olcott became in the process the first Buddhist missionary to the West.

A London Mission

When Olcott arrived in London in April 1884, British colonial officials were already well acquainted with him. In a June 26, 1883, letter covering the Report of the Riots Commission, Governor Longden discussed Olcott while reviewing the root causes for the brawl. The most important such cause was, in Longden's view, the revival of Buddhism. There could be, he wrote, "no doubt" about the "genuineness" of the revival. Signs of it were everywhere:

> The outer evidence of it is to be seen in the rebuilding of old shrines, the repair of wihares, the building of new Dagobas, the larger offerings made to the Temples. Within the Buddhist Church the revival is signalized by a greater number of ordinations held with greater publicity, the care with which the Buddhist doctrines are being taught in the Pali language in the Vidyodaya College and in the monasteries, and the preparation of Buddhist Catechisms in the native and even in the English language.[61]

Longden appended to his report a copy of Olcott's catechism and remarked that the Colonel had "very warmly espoused the cause of Buddhism." The creole nature of Olcott's actions was not lost on Longden, who remarked that the Colonel "brought the energy of Western propagandism to [the revival's] aid."[62]

In a subsequent dispatch to Colonial Secretary Derby, Longden again mentioned Olcott, but now in more ominous terms. It was only a matter of time, he wrote, before one or two individuals would arise and take control of Buddhist affairs on the island. Given the "negligent character of the Sinhalese mind," he reasoned, it was likely that non-Asian Buddhists would fill these leadership roles. Longden then cited encouraging census figures which uncovered zero European Buddhists on the island in 1881, but added that "from time to time Europeans are attracted to Buddhism." Chief among these Europeans, he wrote, was "Colonel Olcott, the founder of a Theosophical Society and an eminent upholder of the Buddhists." "It is probable," he concluded, "that through some such channel as this European intelligence and energy would guide a Buddhist assembly either directly or more probably indirectly; and it is by no means certain that the actions of an assembly so guided could always meet with the approval of the government."[63] Longden closed his letter by calling for an indefinite postponement of legislation related to the thorny issue of "Buddhist Temporalities." In marginal notes appended to Longden's original dispatch, Lord Derby's assistant under secretary, R. H. Meade, recorded his agreement with Longden's position. "The result of the contemplated legislation," he wrote, "might be to throw [great] power into [Olcott's] hands."[64]

In May of 1884, almost a year after Longden had warned his superiors about the Colonel, Olcott arrived in London. Though officials were wary of augmenting his already significant influence, he was able to meet with Meade. Shortly thereafter he sent a memo to Lord Derby. The memo included six demands: (1) that Catholics accused of instigating the riot be brought to trial; (2) that Buddhists be guaranteed the right to exercise their religion freely; (3) that Wesak—the full moon day on which the Sinhalese commemorate the Buddha's birth, enlightenment, and death—be declared a public holiday; (4) that all restrictions against the use of tom-toms and other musical instruments in religious processions be removed; (5) that Buddhist registrars be appointed; and (6) that the question of the Buddhist temporalities (the supposedly negligent control of Buddhist properties by monks) be resolved.[65]

Olcott enclosed with his memo some accompanying documents that testified to the "discontent and despair" that had in his view gripped the island's Buddhists following the Kotahena riots. In this memo he hinted that, if ignored, their dissatisfaction might result in rebellion. An accompanying letter penned by a Buddhist named J. R. DeSilva called Olcott's mission "the great culminating point in the destiny of Buddhism in Ceylon." It warned that if his mission failed "the public would surely raise a tremendous outcry whose long-sounding echoes will help increase the prevailing feeling of distrust."[66] One final enclosure, a copy of a petition from Edward F. Perera to Governor Gordon, was even more apocalyptic. "We are as a community living over a social volcano," Perera wrote, "which at any moment may appall us with some bloody outburst."[67]

Olcott followed these not-so-veiled threats with two additional letters, and Meade responded on behalf of Lord Derby on June 17 and 27. The result was a qualified victory for Olcott and the Sinhalese Buddhist reformers. As he undoubtedly anticipated, Olcott was not able to negotiate a trial of the Catholic rioters. "In the absence of fresh evidence," Meade wrote, "it would be impossible to reopen the matter." But Meade did offer a few concessions regarding this first demand. He expressed Lord Derby's "great regret" about the impossibility of prosecuting the rioters, and he voiced the colonial secretary's conviction that the Buddhists had "real grounds for complaint."[68] After Olcott pressed him to clarify his position on the possibility of a new trial, Meade conceded that "if any fresh evidence had been forthcoming . . . a prosecution would have been instituted and pressed to its conclusions."[69] This response to Olcott's first demand was satisfactory to both parties. The British were able to close a troublesome case, and Olcott and his Buddhist clients received the crown's condolences, in addition to a promise that colonial authorities would not conspire in the future to block Buddhists from seeking justice through the legal system.

Meade also finessed Olcott's demand for some formal government proclamation of religious liberty. He refused to issue any declaration along the lines of the Kandyan Convention of 1815 but did promise "to put an end to any appearance of disregarding the Proclamations of Religious Neutrality which were made at the time when the English took possession of the island." Meade also sidestepped Olcott's demands for resolution of the Buddhist temporalities issue and for the appointment of Buddhist registrars. Governor Gordon, Meade promised, would "carefully consider" the former issue and would show "every consideration possible" in the latter.[70]

Only two of Olcott's requests were speedily granted. In the fall of 1884, colonial officials agreed to pursue "more of a hands off policy" regarding the use of tom-toms and other musical instruments in religious processions; and on April 28, 1885, Wesak became an official holiday in British Ceylon.[71]

Following his negotiations with Meade, Olcott wrote to the chairman of the Buddhist Defence Committee and informed him, over-optimistically, that his mission had been a complete success. British authorities, Olcott reported, had expressed not only "their abhorrence of the injustice inflicted upon the Buddhist community" but also "their readiness . . . to prosecute to the last possible extremity the ringleaders guilty of the outrages complained of, if the necessary proofs are forthcoming." "The chief point at issue has been settled," he announced, "and the principle of my mission accomplished."[72]

Colonial officials arrived, of course, at less sanguine interpretations of Olcott's accomplishments.[73] But the community that counted most—the Buddhist revivalists of Ceylon—deemed Olcott's mission a victory. Members of the Buddhist Defence Committee concluded that the British proclamation of Wesak as a public holiday was "primarily due to Colonel Olcott's appeal," and on April 28, 1885, during the first government-recognized celebration of Buddha's birthday, the now-venerable name of Olcott was invoked frequently and with great devotion.[74]

Thanks to the success of his London mission and his ongoing revivalistic activities in Ceylon, Olcott was beginning to resemble the "King of Righteousness" foretold by the island's prophets. While Buddhists praised his indefatigable efforts, missionaries once again attested to his successes by recording their mounting frustrations. One angry missionary, who characterized the opposition of Sinhalese Buddhists to the Christian Gospel as "very bitter," noted that this opposition was "being constantly stirred up by the influence of the American Agnostic, Colonel Olcott." Another, who also credited Olcott with "stirring up a good deal of Buddhist opposition to us in our work both in town and country" added that Olcott's far-reaching labors had made it "difficult in some places to get a hearing at all."[75]

And so the Sinhalese Buddhist Revival was undoubtedly under way.

But even as he was consolidating his status as a leader of the Sinhalese Buddhist Revival, Olcott was widening his sights. Satisfied that Ceylon's skirmishing Buddhist sects were beginning to work together to repel the Christian onslaught, he was retooling his objective of a nonsectarian Sinhalese Buddhist revival into an even more ambitious goal: the formation of a Buddhist ecumene—"An United Buddhist World."[76]

Five

A United
Buddhist World

<hr>

Among the ceremonies that marked the first official Buddhist holiday in British Ceylon was the unveiling of the Buddhist Flag. Designed, with some assistance from Olcott, by a committee of leading Sinhalese Buddhists, this new symbol first appeared in print on April 17, 1885, in the pages of the *Sarasavi Sandarasa*, a Buddhist biweekly. An article accompanying the illustration explained that the flag's six colors symbolized the six rays that according to ancient sutras emanated from the Buddha's body: blue from his hair; yellow from his robes; red from his lips; white from his teeth; orange from his skin; and a composite color emanating from his entire body. The flag represented, according to its designers, "a mark of respect to the All Knowing [Buddha]." Once unfurled on the first government-sanctioned Wesak Day, it would become "a symbol of the 'Day of Light' on which he was born." Like all potent symbols, however, the flag quickly outran the intentions of its designers, gathering a host of additional meanings.[1]

The fact that the flag was first unveiled at the Deepaduttama Vihara, the site of the 1883 Buddhist-Catholic riots in Colombo's Catholic stronghold of Kotahena, testifies to its first alternative meaning, as anti-Christian tapestry. The decision to tap Mohottivatte Gunananda, the island's most celebrated and vitriolic anti-Christian debater, as the flag raiser only underscored this interpretation of the flag as a weapon in the ongoing Buddhist battle against foreign missionaries for the souls (or skandhas) of the island's people. A second alternative meaning of the flag was provided by Olcott, who interpreted it as "an agent in that scheme of Buddhistic unity which I have clung to from the beginning of my connection with Buddhism." Olcott hoped that the flag, in addition to being adopted by Sinhalese Buddhists as a symbol of their national revival, could be embraced "by all Buddhist nations as the universal symbol of their faith." If so adopted, the ever-imitative Olcott hypothesized, the symbol of the Buddhist Flag could serve "the same purpose as that of the cross does for all Christians."[2]

These two alternative interpretations of the Buddhist Flag—as anti-Christian and ecumenical Buddhist symbol—were not, of course, incommensurable. In fact, it is reasonable to see the arguments against sectarian Christianity and for nonsectarian Buddhism as the warp and woof of the flag's fabric. Long before Olcott's arrival on the island, Buddhist reformers had held up Christian missionaries as a common enemy in an attempt to construct and maintain Buddhist coalitions. And the first two tracts Olcott contributed to the Buddhist-Christian debate in Ceylon were "Why I am not a Christian" and "Why I am a Buddhist."[3]

What was new about the anti-Christian and pro-Buddhist impulses that came together around the raising of the Buddhist Flag was that the Christian enemy was now conjured in an effort to bring together not simply Sinhalese Buddhists but Buddhists from all over the world. The unveiling of the Buddhist Flag thus initiated not only Wesak Day as a government holiday but also Olcott's program to weave all Buddhists everywhere into one unified Buddhist community and thus, in Olcott's words, to bring about "a complete unification in sympathy of the Northern and Southern 'Churches.' "[4]

Burma, Buddhism, and Blavatsky

Olcott's efforts to construct what he would soon describe as a "United Buddhist World" began in earnest in the Theravada Buddhist nation of Burma. Olcott first visited Rangoon in January 1885 at the invitation of Burma's King Theebaw, who had apparently learned of Olcott's contributions to the Sinhalese Buddhist Revival. As in Ceylon, where Olcott had labored to bridge the gaps between the island's three competing Theravada sects, he began in Burma to bring together South Asia's Theravada Buddhists.

Olcott had barely arrived in Rangoon, however, when he received "a thunder-clap out of a clear sky" informing him that Blavatsky was on her deathbed.[5] If it was clear by the mid-1880s that Olcott planned to juggle his roles as Theosophical Society president and Buddhist reformer, it was equally clear that Blavatsky was going to attempt to upstage his act with some jugglery of her own. Back in 1880, Blavatsky had pressed Olcott to emphasize theosophy over Buddhism by informing him that neither she nor the Mahatmas were pleased with his plan to return to Ceylon for a second tour. There was important theosophical work to attend to in Adyar, Blavatsky had contended, and he should not jeopardize that work by busying himself with less consequential matters. Now, consciously or unconsciously, Blavatsky interjected herself once again between Olcott and his Buddhist goals.

Olcott responded to the news of Blavatsky's malady by quitting Rangoon for Madras. His diary indicates that he spent his transit time preparing for the worst while reflecting on the intimacy he had once shared with his coworker in theosophy:

> My poor Chum, and is thy life of adventure, of anguish, of violent contrasts, and of unswerving devotion to Humanity ended? Alas! my loss will be a thousandfold greater than if thou hadst been wife, or sweetheart, or sister; for now must I carry alone the immense burden of this responsibility with which the Holy Ones have charged us.[6]

After leaving Burma, but before reaching India, Olcott received a second telegram. Learning that Blavatsky was apparently not so sick after all, Olcott quickly shifted gears. He now suspected that his chum had played "a scurvy trick" on him in order to shift his attention away from Buddhism and back to theosophy. "I half suspect," he wrote in his diary, "I am sold by the cry of 'Wolf.' "[7]

Whether Blavatsky was feigning her illness is unclear. But five days after Olcott's arrival she was up and about, attributing her miraculous recovery to a Master who, in Olcott's words, "came one night, laid his hand upon her, and suddenly snatched her back from death."[8] If Blavatsky had hoped that her illness would derail Olcott's nascent errand to the Buddhist world, his almost-immediate return to Burma must surely have disappointed her. Adyar remained Olcott's home and Blavatsky continued to be his friend, but she no longer resembled his guru, and his spiritual life no longer revolved entirely around Adyar.

On his second visit to Burma, Olcott accomplished much. He assisted in the translation of his *Buddhist Catechism* into Burmese and organized both a Buddhist branch of the Theosophical Society for Burmese Buddhists and a theosophical branch for Europeans interested in mesmerism. Olcott had only begun his Burmese work, however, when news of Blavatsky's poor health interrupted him again. Having suffered a relapse, she was requesting his company once more. This request placed Olcott's "Buddhism or Blavatsky?" dilemma in bold relief. Should he stay in Burma and play there the revivalistic role he had performed so brilliantly in Ceylon? Or should he return to Adyar and his entanglements with Blavatsky? Not yet indifferent either to Blavatsky's illness or to the danger her demise posed to the Theosophical Society, Olcott decided to return. Upon his arrival at Adyar, the atmosphere was, Olcott later wrote, "dark and heavy." Blavatsky "was struggling for life and as vehement as an enmeshed lioness."[9] What made her battle so poignant was the fact that she was fighting not only for her life but also for her good name.

Six months earlier, in September 1884, the Madras-based *Christian College*

A United Buddhist World

Magazine had begun publishing a series of exposés based on forty letters allegedly written by Blavatsky to Emma Coulomb, a staff member at Adyar and Blavatsky's longtime friend. The magazine's editor reported that Coulomb had admitted to conspiring with Blavatsky in exceedingly this-worldly ways to manufacture ostensibly other-worldly manifestations. She had, for example, supposedly dropped letters through ceilings and embroidered names on handkerchiefs. She had even reportedly constructed a dummy that paraded as a Mahatma by night![10]

In the winter of 1884–1885, Blavatsky's problems compounded when the London-based Society for Psychical Research (S.P.R.) published, in the midst of its investigation of Blavatsky's occult powers, a preliminary report which concluded that while there was evidence for the validity of some of her spiritual manifestations it was nonetheless certain "that fraud has been practised by persons connected with the [Theosophical] Society."[11] Shortly thereafter, the S.P.R. dispatched Dr. Richard Hodgson to Adyar to conduct interviews, to inspect the Coulomb letters, and to examine the shrine room where many of Blavatsky's alleged phenomena took place. Hodgson's prickly investigations kept the wound inflicted by the Coulomb affair open throughout the early months of 1885.

Blavatsky responded to the Coulomb charges and the Hodgson investigation with a mixture of denial and *ad hominem* argument. When Olcott saw her in March 1885 she was, in his words, "wild and violent." "It was awful to see her," he later recalled, "with her face empurpled by the blood that rushed to her head, her eyes almost standing out from their orbits and dead-looking, as she tramped up and down the floor, denouncing everybody and saying wild things." Among the wild things Blavatsky supposedly said (this time in a letter to Hodgson) was that Olcott was "an overgrown baby" whom she could hypnotize simply by looking into his eyes. Upon hearing of this boast, Olcott was devastated. "In my whole experience in the movement, nothing ever affected me so much as this," he later wrote. "It made me desperate, and for twenty-four hours almost ready to go down to the beach and drown myself in the sea."[12]

Instead of pushing him to suicide, however, this revelation quickened Olcott's resolve to distance himself from Blavatsky, if not from theosophy. Determined to bring the Coulomb affair and the Hodgson investigation to a speedy resolution, Olcott decided it was time for Blavatsky to go. Supported by a group of physicians (who argued that Blavatsky could not survive any additional stress) and theosophists (who contended that their society would not survive her testimony in a pending libel suit associated with the Coulomb case), Olcott finally confronted his friend, demanding that she resign as corresponding secretary and leave India immediately. Now more bitter toward Olcott than toward Coulomb and Hodgson combined, Blavatsky sailed for Europe on April 2, 1885. She would never see India again.

Over the next few months Olcott lived "in hourly dread of fresh revelations of [Blavatsky's] indiscretion."[13] But the only revelations that came, although disturbing, were rather stale. The S.P.R. concluded, in its final report of December 1885, that Blavatsky was "one of the most accomplished, ingenious, and interesting imposters in history."[14] Though harsh, this judgment was not unexpected, and Olcott was probably happy finally to have the charge out in the open.

In addition to precipitating a crisis within the Theosophical Society, Blavatsky's illness, the Coulomb affair, and the S.P.R. investigation combined to hasten a crisis in Olcott. When the charges against Blavatsky exploded, Olcott had been immersed in Buddhist activities. The Sinhalese Buddhist Revival was prospering and his "United Buddhist World" was beginning to take root in Burma. The temptation must have been great for Olcott to respond to the crisis by loosening, if not severing, his ties to theosophy and strengthening his bonds to Buddhism. A revealing letter Olcott wrote to Blavatsky in March 1886 indicates that he considered leaving Adyar to become a Buddhist monk:

> The robes and a pansala are ready for me whenever I am ready; and go I will unless I can have things go on decently henceforth. If ambition were my motive, I can be the biggest man among the Buddhists of either Burmah or Ceylon whenever I choose.[15]

But, significantly, Olcott did not take up the Buddhist robes and become a Theravada monk. He responded instead to his mid-life transition by quickening his commitment to theosophy. The Theosophical Society was sailing through its darkest storm, and Olcott saw it as his responsibility "to get the ship through the breakers."[16]

This decision to remain at the helm of the Theosophical Society is telling because it reveals that theosophy, rather than Buddhism, remained Olcott's first love. Given Olcott's self-identification as a Buddhist and the tremendous energy he poured into reforming Buddhism worldwide, this decision is curious. Exactly why Olcott remained throughout his life a theosophist first and a Buddhist second is not clear, but some attempt at an explanation may be in order here.

One possible reason for this preference is that the Theosophical Society was his organization and, as such, was under his control. Blavatsky, of course, contested his leadership, but nonetheless allowed him wide latitude in "exoteric" or administrative matters. The troubles that beset Blavatsky as a result of the Coulomb Affair, moreover, only strengthened Olcott's hold over the society. Olcott, of course, had much less control over Buddhism than he did over theosophy. While many Buddhists in Ceylon looked to him as a leader of their revival, they also looked to Hikkaduve Sumangala and Mohottivatte Gunananda. And while Olcott had wide latitude in defining (and redefining) the mission of the Theosophical Society, his freedom to interpret Buddhism was frustrated on a number of occasions by the alternative interpretations of other Buddhists, especially Buddhist monks, to say nothing of the weight of over two millennia of Buddhist tradition.

Another factor motivating Olcott's primary allegiance to theosophy was clearly the duty he felt both to Blavatsky and to the society that together they had brought into the world. Olcott was, it should be remembered, a middle-class American man, and he carried with him throughout his adult life a strong sense of responsibility. In addition, Olcott obviously felt an equally mighty attachment to Blavatsky, whose charismatic personality had drawn him first into theosophy and later into Buddhism. If with Olcott allegiance to these two worldviews was mixed, however, with Blavatsky Buddhism came in a distant second. This was probably because in Blavatsky's cosmos theosophy clearly functioned as a sacred canopy that stretched across all the world's faiths, Buddhism included. If in Blavatsky's view Buddhism and Hinduism were essentially one faith, that one faith was theosophy. In making theosophy a priority, therefore, Olcott was following the logic of Blavatsky's theosophy-centered worldview—a worldview that allowed him, not inconveniently, tremendous interpretive leverage in bending Buddhism in the direction of his own designs. Although Olcott embraced both Buddhism and theosophy, he construed Buddhism theosophically. He was a Buddhist rather than a Hindu or a Zoroastrian because Buddhism deviated least from the hoary truths of theosophy; and he chastised Christianity more than any other religious tradition because it deviated from theosophy most.

As Blavatsky set sail for Europe, Olcott was left alone at the society's helm. From that position, he steered the theosophical ship away from the dangers of Blavatsky's esotericism and toward the safety of his own exoteric agenda. Years earlier, Olcott and Blavatsky had together transformed their society from an American organ for the reform of spiritualism into an international body devoted to promoting Asian wisdom, constructing a pan-religious "Universal Brotherhood of Humanity," and investigating spiritual manifestations in the name of occult science. Now Olcott, acting largely on

The White Buddhist

his own, retooled the society once again. Less than a month after Blavatsky had left Adyar, Olcott circulated a statement aimed at undercutting her influence and downplaying the importance of her occult agenda. Attacking the "wrong impression that blind belief in Phenomena is a pre-requisite for membership and that Theosophy is based upon such belief," Olcott's "Special Orders of 1885" promulgated a list of Theosophical Society "ideals and duties" that omitted any reference to spiritual manifestations and the occult.[17] One month later, an article by Olcott on "Infallibility" found its way onto the front page of the *Theosophist*. Olcott began by recalling that the Brahmo Samaj had split into three warring camps after the death of its founder, Rammohun Roy, in 1833. Although he did not specifically mention Blavatsky, his message was clear. In an obvious reference to Blavatsky he stated, "One should accept nothing, whether written, spoken or taught by sage, revelator, priest of book, unless it reconciled itself with one's reason and common sense."[18] Finally, Olcott confronted Blavatsky directly in a private letter about the need for a "total abandonment of sensationalism":

There is . . . a firm determination to have no more to do (as the T.S.) with "phenomena." . . . If we keep things quiet, and go on steadily with useful work, we shall be stronger than ever. If there is a return to sensationalism, the defection will cripple us beyond expression. Now mark my words, my dear Chum. Adyar is your only home, the only refuge you have upon earth. . . . The proverb says: "It's an ill bird that fouls its own nest." Don't make yours uninhabitable.[19]

Blavatsky reacted to Olcott's offensive with a counteroffensive of her own. In September 1887 she established in London her own magazine, *Lucifer*, as an alternative to the Olcott-controlled *Theosophist*. One year later, in October 1888, she formed an "Esoteric Section of the Theosophical Society" and gathered around her a core group of followers similarly dedicated to pursuing the hermetic truths articulated in her second opus, *The Secret Doctrine* (1888).

Though Olcott agreed, albeit reluctantly, to allow Blavatsky to form and lead her own Esoteric Section, he remained disturbed about its emphasis on secrecy and its authoritarian structure. He filled his diary in the summer of 1890 with uncharitable references to his "insatiate" nemesis, who was in his view "bent upon grasping all power exoteric and esoteric." "This sort of thing drives me wild," he confided to a friend, "and so works my nerves that I am positively in such a state of nervous unrest as that of a person in a bombarded town."[20]

Despite Olcott's fears that Blavatsky was angling to break their longstanding agreement to tend to "separate spheres," their respective spheres of influence and control actually became more clearly delineated in the mid-1880s. Blavatsky labored to advance the occult aim of the Theosophical Society in Europe, while Olcott worked in Asia to define the organization exclusively in terms of the society's two exoteric objects. While reviewing the objects of the Theosophical Society in a speech in 1886, Olcott omitted any reference to its occult aim. The society's mission, he implied, was now twofold: "to form the nucleus of a Universal Brotherhood of Humanity, without distinction of race, creed or colour," and "to promote the study of Aryan and other Eastern literatures, religions and sciences."[21]

It is difficult to account for all the effects of this Olcott-Blavatsky rift, but one undeniable result was the slow but certain splintering of the Theosophical Society. Though the organization would not divide officially until 1895, Olcott's Adyar co-workers and Blavatsky's London followers were acting years earlier, as Blavatsky herself recognized, like "Methodists and Baptists tearing each other" apart. There was, she informed Olcott in a private letter in 1888, "an impassable chasm" between the society's founders.[22]

A second effect of the Blavatsky-Olcott impasse was the temporary derailment of Olcott's campaign for a "United Buddhist World." In fact, in the three years that followed Blavatsky's exile to Europe in 1885 Olcott took what amounted to an extended hiatus from his Buddhist work. Remaining for the most part in India, Olcott worked during those years to consolidate the gains his society had made in its first decade. In the midst of this recess, Olcott admitted that "the rapid increase of Indian work has compelled me to neglect that so successfully begun in Ceylon . . . and the effects have been bad."[23] The Sinhalese Buddhist reformer Mohottivatte Gunananda apparently agreed. In 1887 he became the first Buddhist reformer to publicly censure the "White Buddhist." On February 18 of that year, Olcott lectured at Mohottivatte's temple in Kotahena, and Mohottivatte responded, in Sinhalese, with what Olcott later described as "a venomous attack on the Colombo B.T.S. and myself." Olcott, he claimed, in a criticism that would gather force over the next decade, was woefully neglecting the Buddhist cause.[24]

Japan

Olcott responded to Mohottivatte's criticisms by returning to his campaign for a "United Buddhist World" in the winter of 1888. At that time a Japanese Buddhist reformer named Zenshiro Nogouchi arrived in Adyar and invited Olcott, whom he flattered as the "Bodhisat of the Nineteenth

The White Buddhist

Century," to come and lead a Buddhist revival in Japan. True to form, Blavatsky countered Nogouchi's effusiveness in a letter to Olcott by dismissing a Japan tour, as she had Olcott's earlier visits to Ceylon, as "tomfoolery." But Olcott soon came to view a trip to the Mahayana Buddhist country of Japan as an opportunity to expand his already considerable vision of Buddhist unity. Previously he had worked to bring together competing Theravada Buddhist sects in Ceylon and Burma. Now he aimed at a more spectacular ecumenism: a coming together of Theravada and Mahayana Buddhists from across the globe in "a rapprochement unknown since the great schism at the Vaisali Council two thousand one hundred years ago."[25]

Accompanied by Nogouchi, Olcott arrived in Kobe, Japan, on February 9, 1889. Also in tow was Don David Hevavitharana, the Sinhalese Buddhist reformer and theosophist who was rapidly becoming a leader of the Buddhist revival in Ceylon. Hevavitharana, who had by the time of the Japan tour taken the name Anagarika Dharmapala (meaning, roughly, "homeless defender of the Buddhist doctrine"), was the son of a leading Sinhalese businessman. As a boy he had attended English-language Christian missionary schools but also received private instruction in Buddhism and Sinhalese. He had met Olcott and Blavatsky in 1880, at the age of fourteen, and was initiated into the Theosophical Society during their first Ceylon tour. Eventually he would go on to represent Theravada Buddhism at the World's Parliament of Religions in Chicago in 1893 and to become a major figure in the Sinhalese Buddhist Revival.[26]

The day after his arrival in Japan, Olcott stood in a Buddhist temple in front of a statue of the Amida Buddha and recited Pansil, Sinhalese-style, in Pali. Years later, Olcott recalled the incident's incongruity:

> Was it not a unique experience for an American man to be standing there, as one of his race had never stood before, in the presence of those hundreds of priests and thousands of laymen, intoning the simple sentences which synthesise the obligations assumed by every professing Buddhist of the Southern Church? I could not help smiling to myself when thinking of the horror that would have been felt by any of my Puritan ancestors of the seventeenth century could they have looked forward to this calamitous day! I am sure that if I had been born among them at Boston or Hartford, I should have been hanged for heresy on the tallest tree within easy reach of their infant settlement. And very glad I am to believe it.[27]

Later, in Kyoto, Olcott organized a convention of monks from various Mahayana sects. Olcott began the convention by reading a letter of introduction in which Hikkaduve Sumangala described him as "a Buddhist, a

Pandit, [and] a courteous gentleman."[28] He then announced, with great rhetorical flourish, his grand plan to unite northern and southern Buddhists into a great Buddhist ecumene:

> Why should the two great halves of the Buddhist Church be any longer ignorant and indifferent about each other?
> Let us break the long silence; let us bridge the chasm of 2,300 years; let the Buddhists of [the] North and those of the South be one family again.[29]

As he had in Ceylon, Olcott based his call for Buddhist unity on the Christian threat. Buddhists, he argued, had two responsibilities: first, "to revive our religion [and] purify it of its corruptions" by challenging, in lectures, publications, and schools, the lies spread by Christian missionaries; and, second, to launch an anti-missionary counteroffensive by sending Buddhist "teachers and preachers to distant lands . . . to tell the millions now disbelieving Christianity . . . that they will find what will convince their reason and satisfy their heart in Buddhism."[30] Given the anti-missionary bent of his ecumenical appeal, the strategy Olcott proposed for carrying out these aims is striking. Once again, he urged Buddhist listeners to follow the example of the deceitful but administratively astute Christians. When asked about how Buddhists should organize for change, he responded, "I point you to our great enemy, Christianity, and bid you look at their large and wealthy Bible, Tract, Sunday School, and Missionary Societies—the tremendous agencies they support to keep alive and spread their religion. We must form similar Societies, and make our most practical and honest men of business their managers."[31]

At the conclusion of his speech, Olcott rejected the offer of a group from the militantly nationalistic and decidedly non-irenic Jodo Shinshu (True Pure Land) Buddhist sect to organize his tour. Intent on promoting "the pure religion taught by Shakya Muni . . . without distinction of sect" and worried that this arrangement might foster the misapprehension that he was partial to one Japanese Buddhist sect, Olcott insisted that a nonsectarian committee be formed to administer his campaign.[32] In the absence of such a united effort, he insisted, he would cancel his Japan tour.

Olcott's Japanese friends accepted his nonsectarian terms, and soon he departed on a four month crusade, which included short visits with pioneering American Buddhist sympathizers Ernest Fenollosa and William Sturgis Bigelow. Olcott attempted in his itinerant lectures to stir "the religious sentiment" that he believed was deeply rooted in the "national character" of the Japanese. "No country and no epoch," he claimed, "were ever

more ripe for religious reform than is Japan at this moment." Olcott's recipe for reform mingled Buddhist rhetoric with established liberal Protestant themes, including anticlericalism, temperance, and voluntaryism. The
main obstacle to this revival, Olcott argued, was a sectarian and slothful
Sangha:

> The restoration of your Buddhism to its full pristine health and vigor
> depends almost entirely upon the willingness of your priesthood to
> correct existing abuses in their monastic discipline. . . . Let me beg of
> you, one and all, to lay aside in this crisis all sectarian differences and
> personal bickering, and join with your co-religionists of other Buddhist
> countries to revive the noble aspirations of the times of Sakya Muni
> Budha [sic] and his disciples, and make all mankind see and appreciate
> the Noble Truths upon which Buddhism stands as a strong castle upon
> the living rock.[33]

In addition to attacking clerical abuses, Olcott preached temperance over
drunkenness ("Break thy Sake-bottle," he admonished one layman, "if thou
wouldst reach Nirvana") and assisted in the formation of a Buddhist
Women's Society and a Young Man's Buddhist Association ("after the
model of the Young Men's Christian Association," he noted).[34]

Predictably, missionaries in Japan cast Olcott's tour in a negative light,
claiming that public interest in Olcott's talks dropped precipitously after
his listeners discovered his ignorance of Buddhism. "The Buddhists of
Japan do not think highly of Colonel Olcott," the *Missionary Herald* editori-
alized, "They do not recognize his teachings as good Buddhism." Emphasizing the creole nature of Olcott's newfound faith, another critic wrote that
"the Buddhists were much disappointed [because] he taught a system
utterly at variance with theirs" while another complained, "We are not to
be treated to a revival of Buddhism but to the old worn out 'dodge,' called
'spiritualism.' "[35]

Nonetheless, according to the *Dandokai*, a Japanese Buddhist periodical,
Olcott's presence caused "great excitement" among Christians and "remarkable enthusiasm" among Buddhists. "His success was far beyond our
most sanguine expectations," a Japanese Buddhist wrote. "Buddhism took
life again, and Buddhists began everywhere to undertake the revival of
their ancient faith."[36] The ever-optimistic Olcott deemed his Japan junket
a success. "The mission is accomplished," he proclaimed, "the work is
done." Given an average attendance of 2500 at each of his 76 lectures,
Olcott calculated that he had addressed nearly 200,000 people. The result
of this prodigious effort was, in his view, "a great revival of our glorious
religion among Buddhist nations."[37]

A United Buddhist World

Olcott's crusade was no doubt less triumphant than he believed yet more successful than his opponents claimed. The missionaries were surely correct in discerning Olcott's obvious departures from certain venerable Buddhist beliefs and behaviors, but they clearly overestimated the importance of adhering to some ostensible orthodoxy in Buddhism. Even if some Japanese Buddhists were disappointed with Olcott's mission, others soon requested Olcott to return to their island to continue his work. Like earlier Burmese backers, these Japanese supporters prompted Olcott to think about retiring from the presidency of the Theosophical Society in order to devote himself full-time to Buddhist labors. "If I could be spared from the Theosophical movement proper, and were free to occupy myself exclusively with Buddhistic interests," Olcott conjectured, "I could very soon build up an International Buddhistic League that might send the Dharma like a tidal wave around the world."[38]

Buddhist Platform

Still, Olcott remained forever tied first and foremost to theosophy, so he was never able to commit himself to the goal of setting this great Buddhist tsunami in motion. He did, however, continue to work to transform his dream of a "United Buddhist World" into reality. Shortly after the annual meeting of the Theosophical Society in December of 1890, Olcott convened at Adyar an unprecedented ecumenical convention of Theravada and Mahayana Buddhists from Ceylon, Burma, Japan, and Chittagong (now in Bangladesh). His aim was nothing less lofty than "a religious pact of the Buddhist nations, and the unification of the two schools of Buddhistic Philosophy."[39]

The transnational Buddhist coalition Olcott hoped to construct was not unlike the contemporaneous Evangelical Alliance of American Protestantism. Founded in 1846 as a domestic anti-Catholic association, the Evangelical Alliance had come under the direction of Josiah Strong in 1886 and had taken up the mantle of "Anglo-Saxonizing" the world for Christ. Like Strong's association, Olcott's Buddhist union would combine parochial, even racist, rhetoric with benevolent sentiments and global aspirations. Olcott's two-fold plan involved theological and missionary aims: first, to arrive at a common doctrinal statement on which all Buddhists could agree; and second, to launch from this common platform a united mission to reform along Buddhist lines both Occident and Orient. For Olcott, as for Strong, the kingdom was coming. And, in that coming kingdom, Buddhists too had a sacred duty to be their brother's keeper.

Following an extensive dialogue among Mahayana and Theravada delegates regarding their respective worldviews, Olcott drafted a fourteen-point "Buddhist Platform" encompassing key points of agreement. These points encompassed an intriguing concatenation of traditional Buddhist and modern western values. In addition to a restatement of the Four Noble Truths and the Five Precepts for lay Buddhists, the fourteen propositions included: an affirmation of religious tolerance and of the evolution of the universe, a rejection of supernaturalism, heaven and hell, and superstition, and an emphasis on education and the use of reason. The essence of Buddhism, the platform concluded, was summed up in these pious and moralistic words of the Buddha:

> To cease from all sin,
> To get virtue,
> To purify the heart.[40]

When the assembly adopted this set of propositions, Olcott became more hopeful than ever about the prospects for his "United Buddhist World." He canceled plans to travel to theosophical branches in Australia and accepted instead an invitation to return to Burma to discuss a united Buddhist mission to Europe and to gather signatures for his Buddhist creed.

Within a week of his arrival in Rangoon on January 21, 1891, Olcott had devised a "skeleton plan" that would give institutional form to his dream of a "United Buddhist World."[41] Following the organization of American politics into national, state, and local governments, Olcott's plan included an "International Buddhist League" subdivided into national "Buddhist Leagues" and local "Buddhist Brotherhoods." The local societies would promote local interests, including "Grants-in-aid of Buddhist schools, publication and circulation of religious literature, assistance to poor pagodas for support of Priests, repair of temples and other religious structures, and other objects promotive of the revival and spread of Buddhism." The national societies would work for "the promotion of Buddhism throughout the world, and the drawing of all Buddhists together into close brotherly relations." Olcott, of course, would manage the international organization and would control its revenues, which would be raised locally.[42]

With this plan in mind, Olcott traveled to Mandalay and met with a monastic council on February 3. He recapitulated in his address to the council his triumphs in Ceylon. Then he read the fourteen points of his Buddhist Platform. One by one, the assembled monks assented to their orthodoxy. They then certified Olcott's "Fundamental Buddhistic Beliefs" as "accepted on behalf of the Buddhists of Burma."[43]

Signatures in hand, Olcott worked quickly to translate this hard-won doc-

A United Buddhist World

trinal consensus into cooperative action for religious reform. Citing the *Dhammapada*'s injunction that "the merit of spreading the Dharma is greater than that to be acquired by the building of 84,000 Viharas," Olcott tried to convince his listeners to devote less time and money to building monasteries and more of both to launching a Buddhist mission to the West.[44] He also insisted that any Burmese efforts should avoid the specter of sectarianism by including leaders from all the country's major Buddhist sects. "In so important a work the merit should in equity be shared by all Buddhist nations," he argued diplomatically, and the assembly was apparently swayed. It pledged its support for an "international committee of propaganda" to be represented and supported by all Buddhist nations.[45] Emboldened by his success in Burma, Olcott returned to Ceylon in February of 1891, hoping to add the signatures of the island's monks to his Buddhist Platform and to enlist their participation in his "International Buddhist League." He accomplished the first objective when Hikkaduve Sumangala and five other monks approved his fourteen theses on behalf of the Buddhists of Ceylon. But he was unable to sell the second plank of his plan. He formed no Sinhalese Buddhist League, and his appeals to institute a "Wesak Fund" to support a Buddhist mission to the West fell on deaf ears.[46]

Following his successes among the Buddhists of Burma and Ceylon, Olcott set sail once again for Japan. His Buddhist Platform still awaited the imprimatur of the Mahayana Buddhists, and Olcott was determined to gather at least a handful of Japanese signatures. Upon his arrival in Yokohama on October 28, 1891, Olcott was confronted with two problems: his co-religionists in Ceylon had failed to notify the Japanese of his arrival and a great earthquake had just struck the island, prompting a number of leading monks to leave Kyoto to assist elsewhere in disaster relief.

Olcott did manage nonetheless to gather a representative body of monks to discuss his fourteen points. During the discussion, one Buddhist objected that Olcott's propositions were so general and vague that they failed to do justice to his beliefs. There was, of course, considerable merit to this objection; Olcott's platform was an exceedingly simplified statement of Buddhist beliefs. But Olcott was able to respond to this criticism with a winning reply:

> I said: "If I should bring you a basketful of earth dug out of a slope of Fuji San, would that be part of your sacred mountain or not?" "Of course it would," he answered. "Well, then," I rejoined, "all I ask is that you will accept these Propositions as included *within* the body of Northern Buddhism; that they are a basketful of the mountain, but not the whole mountain itself."[47]

This koanic quip apparently sufficed. By the time Olcott left the island on November 10, all but the Jodo Shinshu sect, the most stridently sectarian of Japan's major Buddhist groups, had sanctioned his Buddhist Platform.[48]

The acceptance of his Buddhist Platform by representatives of the Mahayanists of Japan and the Theravadins of Ceylon and Burma fell short of Olcott's hope for what he termed (in an obvious reference to the Christian Trinity) "a vast international tripartite Sangha, *tria juncta in uno.*"[49] But it did transform Olcott from an important contributor to the Sinhalese Buddhist Revival into a key figure in the emerging movement for international Buddhism. No longer merely the "Father of the Sinhalese Buddhists," he was now revered as "The Apostle of Asia."[50]

Helena Blavatsky's Death

While Olcott was busy fashioning himself into someone resembling Buddhism's Paul, he was interrupted again by news of Blavatsky's poor health. This time the bulletin was no ruse: Blavatsky had died after a battle with influenza on May 8, 1891. Olcott responded to news of Blavatsky's death by tabling his Buddhist work and sailing immediately for England and a final encounter with his long-time friend and sometime adversary.

Arriving in London on July 4, 1891, he met Annie Wood Besant and William Quan Judge, theosophists who, with Blavatsky deceased and Olcott ever-teetering on the edge of retirement, represented the future of the Theosophical Society. Judge, a lawyer and the Theosophical Society's vice-president, would soon lead a group of American dissenters out of the old organization and into the "Theosophical Society in America."[51] "Annie Militant," as Olcott dubbed Besant, was, before she joined in common cause with the theosophists, a prominent freethinker and socialist in her English homeland. She would eventually ascend to the presidency of both the Theosophical Society and the Indian National Congress.

Given the presence of these leaders, Olcott might have used his friend's death as an occasion to emancipate himself from many of his theosophical responsibilities. But he did not. Rather than bidding farewell to Blavatsky and ceding his theosophical authority to Judge and/or Besant, he entered Blavatsky's bedroom and swore a solemn oath "to be true to the Cause and to each other." On his first night in London, Olcott half-expected that Blavatsky would appear to him in a dream. She did not, but her absence only strengthened Olcott's resolve "to carry the heavy burden that had fallen upon my shoulders, and do my best to keep the vital power unweakened within the body of the Society which we two had built up together."[52]

A United Buddhist World

In a eulogy published in the *Theosophist*, Olcott omitted for the first time in years the now-customary references to his partner's manifold foibles. And in an effort to purify her admittedly blemished reputation, he defended her against charges of fraud ("I do not consider the charges proven"), of sexual impropriety ("If there were ever a sexless being, it was she") and of immorality ("She was neither thief, harlot, drunkard, [nor] gambling-house keeper").[53] Olcott also attempted in the article to decode the cryptic spirit of the deceased. Blavatsky, he noted, possessed "a double-selfed [*sic*] personality." She was, on the one hand, a glutton whose love for a well-spoken curse was exceeded only by her seemingly insatiable need for cigarettes. At her worst—and, because of her poor health, she was frequently at her worst—she was "very antipathetic . . . irritable, unquiet and often . . . unjust." There was, however, another side to her personality, and Olcott's encounters with this finer face had convinced him that he shared with her "a psychical consanguinity" that began in previous incarnations and would surely continue into future lives. "I loved her," Olcott explained, "for the other, the higher self."[54]

Blavatsky's passing provided an important turning point in Olcott's life. Rather than causing him to despair over the future of the Theosophical Society, her death convinced Olcott that the Theosophical Society could survive his own demise. "This movement has acquired an individuality of its own," he affirmed, "and . . . nothing in the world can drag it down."[55] Blavatsky's passing also inspired Olcott to pledge once again his primary allegiance to theosophy over Buddhism. "My family was now the members of the Society," he came to recognize, "my friends, my working colleagues; my home, the Adyar Headquarters; my ambitions, aspirations, hopes, loves and very life had passed into the Society."[56]

The widespread acceptance of his Buddhist Platform and the survival of the Theosophical Society beyond Helena Blavatsky's death provided the dual climaxes of Olcott's Asian life. By the time of Blavatsky's passing in 1891, the Theosophical Society had grown from a bold idea at a New York gathering of spiritualists into an international organization with 258 branches on six continents. And Olcott was responsible, if not for the society's germination, then at least for its sustained growth. He was also responsible for the transformation of the Sinhalese Buddhist Revival into a broader movement to conjoin competing Theravada and Mahayana sects into one "United Buddhist World." These twin triumphs—in theosophy and in Buddhism—allowed Olcott to look back at his life at the end of 1891 and pronounce it good. While at Blavatsky's deathbed in London, Olcott felt for the first time "ready and willing to die." "Though I should not live to see another year," he affirmed later that year, "my life will not have been quite useless to mankind."[57]

Convinced that it was time for summing up the past rather than moving forward into the future, Olcott sat at his desk on January 16, 1892, and penned the first words of a series of reminiscences that would eventually comprise his six-volume history of the Theosophical Society, *Old Diary Leaves*. Less than a week later, he wrote to Judge and Besant, informing them of his decision to step down as Theosophical Society president. "In the ordinary course of nature the young replace the old," Olcott noted. "I feel I have a full right to my freedom and I take it." Soon friends were collecting an "Olcott Pension Fund," and the "old wheel-horse," as Olcott now called himself, began constructing a retirement cottage at Ootaca- mund, a summer resort community popular among British elites snuggled in south India's Nilgiri Hills.[58]

As Olcott prepared to go into retirement, the Masters dusted themselves off and ended their self-imposed exile from the Theosophical Society head- quarters. In the years that followed Blavatsky's adieu to Adyar in 1885, Olcott had received precious little advice from the Masters. Blavatsky's ex- planation for this silence was that they had withdrawn with her in anger. And withdrawn they apparently had. From 1885 until Blavatsky's death in 1891 the Mahatmas were conspicuously absent from the pages of Olcott's diary.[59]

Some time before daybreak, however, on the morning of February 10, 1892, the Mahatmas returned. Olcott recorded the visitation in his diary:

> This morning before dawn I received clairaudiently a very important
> message from M about H.P.B., a messenger coming from Tibet, the
> unbreakable relation between HPB and myself, . . . and declaring his
> constant watch over me. . . . Rebuked me for trying to resign
> prematurely and spoke discouragingly about the Buddhist scheme.[60]

On the night of March 13, 1892, Olcott heard a voice intoning cryptically the word "Banan." The next morning another voice informed him that there was "no use to bother about H.P.B. She was safe now and her bad and good record was made up and could not be changed." On April 8 Olcott noted that he "heard distinctly last night two calls of a voice pronouncing one word. . . . The word sounded like 'Wy!' or 'Wife!.' "[61] Finally, in the spring of that same year tarot card divinations informed Olcott that Blavat- sky would soon be reborn in Tibet. There are many ways to interpret these messages, including on the one hand that they were hallucinatory nonsense and on the other that they were genuine revelations.[62] But at the very least these experiences indicate that Olcott remained haunted by Blavatsky's spirit; he could not yet let her (or her disapproval of his Buddhist ventures) go.

In his adieu to Blavatsky, published in the *Theosophist*, Olcott had invoked the virtues of Yankee self-reliance. "Nothing is so pernicious, nothing is so weakening, as the encouragement of the spirit of dependence upon another, upon another's wisdom, upon another's righteousness," he had argued.[63] And at the Theosophical Society convention of 1891 he had resumed his denunciations of Blavatsky-worship by protesting against "the temptation to elevate either [the Masters], their agents, or any other living or dead personage, to the divine status, or their teachings to that of infallible doctrine." "I have been taught to lean upon myself alone," he added, "to look to my Higher Self as my best teacher, best guide, best example and only saviour"[64] But these admonitions seem to have been aimed as much at Olcott himself as they were at his listeners. Perhaps more than any other single theosophist, it was Olcott—the same man who, for the bulk of his life with Blavatsky, had struggled to keep her at arm's length—who remained tied to his chum and her Masters.

Whether he was prompted by Mahatmic messages, by memories of Blavatsky, or by a fear of death is not known. But in the spring of 1892 Olcott postponed indefinitely his retirement. The events of the early 1890s—his attempt at retirement, his writing of his memoirs, his return to Mahatmic guidance—suggest that Olcott was aware that his grandest achievements were behind him. Soon Annie Besant would emerge as theosophy's new leader, and Anagarika Dharmapala would rise to lead the nascent international Buddhist movement. The main acts in Olcott's drama had been played out. All that remained was the denouement.

Six

The Indian Renaissance

Colonel Olcott is now best known as the president-founder of the Theosophical Society and a major figure in the Sinhalese Buddhist Revival, but he resided during his last three decades in India rather than Ceylon, and he worked to revitalize not only Buddhism but also Hinduism and, on occasion, even Zoroastrianism and Islam. In India, he operated very much as he did in Ceylon, promoting the publication of Hindu catechisms, agitating for various social reforms, and working to found a Hindu Tract Society, a Young Men's Hindu Association, and a Hindu Sunday School Union. He was, as a result, a contributor not only to the Sinhalese Buddhist Revival but also to the Indian Renaissance.

The Indian Renaissance was a cultural and religious movement of English-speaking intellectuals and reformers in nineteenth-century British India.[1] These intellectuals and reformers sought to modernize and westernize Indian religious beliefs and practice even as they edged the Indian people toward political independence. Just as leaders of the earlier European Renaissance looked back to Roman and Grecian antiquity while laboring to bring their continent into a new age, these Indian revitalizers conjured up the grandeur and glory that was India while struggling to accommodate the subcontinent to the modern West. In this way they too produced creole cultural and religious forms.[2]

Among the individuals frequently cited as major contributors to this revitalization are Rammohun Roy (1772?–1833) of the Brahmo Samaj, Ramakrishna (1836–1886) and Swami Vivekananda (1863–1902) of the Ramakrishna Mission, Keshub Chunder Sen (1838–1884) of the "New Dispensation," and Dayanand Saraswati (1824–1883) of the Arya Samaj. Each of these men shared with Olcott the tendency to split the world into two separate spheres and then to ascribe to the "masculine" West superiority in technology and material life and to the "feminine" East superiority in spiritual disciplines and religious thought. Also like Olcott, each hoped for a marriage of East and West and worked to reform India by improving the positions of untouchables and women in Indian society.

Olcott's contributions to the Indian Renaissance were greatest in the late

1880s and the 1890s but his participation in the movement can be traced to New York and his first correspondence, in 1877, with prominent members of the Arya Samaj. After his arrival in India in 1879, Olcott was able to effect a short-lived union between the Theosophical Society and that organization. He also succeeded in aligning the Theosophical Society, at least for a time, with two pundit's societies: the Benares-based Sanskrit Sabha and the Hindu Sabha of Southern India. These successes fueled Olcott's more ambitious hopes for a pan-Indian "Pandit's League" and an even broader "National Samaj of Aryavarta" that would create out of many Indian Samajes one grand union. In fashioning these hopes, which mirrored his unitive dreams of a Buddhist Ecclesiastical Council and a broader "United Buddhist World," Olcott relied once again on the model of his inherited rather than his adopted homeland. "My own country, the Great Republic of the West, has this motto: E Pluribus Unum—one out of many," he wrote. "Just so it might be *one* National Samaj of Aryavarta, out of a shoal of local societies."[3]

Some of Olcott's admirers have contended that Olcott contributed to the Indian Renaissance not only culturally and religiously but also politically. These backers argue that Olcott should be credited with inspiring the Swadeshi Movement, later popularized by Mahatma Gandhi, by organizing during his stint in Bombay an exhibition of all-Indian products. An even more popular argument among Olcott's admirers is that the Theosophical Society's annual meeting provided the first example of a yearly pan-Indian gathering and thus paved the way for the founding of the Indian National Congress in 1885. It is no coincidence, they argue, that many of the founding members of the Indian National Congress were theosophists and that Annie Besant, who would succeed Olcott as Theosophical Society president and theosophy's main stump speaker, also served for a time as president of the congress.[4] One friend of Olcott has taken this line of reasoning so far as to describe Olcott as the "Father of the Indian National Congress" and the driving force behind Indian independence.[5]

There is some basis in fact for this assessment. Attendance at annual meetings of the Theosophical Society rose when the Indian National Congress met on the same dates in the same city and declined when the congress met at the same time in different cities. This fact suggests that the two organizations enjoyed overlapping constituencies. Still Olcott and his fellow theosophists worked hard to maintain at least the appearance of an apolitical stance. And when Olcott did opine or act politically, neither his words not his deeds supported independence. Olcott clearly believed that Indians were better off under what he saw as the benign if not benevolent rule of the British, who were in Olcott's view as fit to rule as the Indians were to be ruled.[6] And on more than one occasion he bragged that he and his society had made India's natives "more tractable as subjects."[7] Given these statements, to say nothing of the fact that he saw to it that "the American National hymn" was played at his celebrated all-native goods exhibition, Olcott should not be seen as a progenitor of either the congress or Indian independence.[8] Olcott made his most important contributions to the Indian Renaissance not in the political arena but in the realms of religion and culture.

Caste and the Education of Untouchables

Like virtually all other contributors to the Indian Renaissance, Olcott made no secret of his disdain for the system of caste and of his concern for those at the bottom rung of Hinduism's social ladder: the untouchables whom Olcott called "Panchamas" and Gandhi would later christen "Harijans" ("children of God"). While living and traveling in India Olcott was frequently confronted with what he described as the "hopeless misery" of Hindu untouchables. He compared the treatment of those outcasts with "the treatment of the American Indians by those rapacious, intolerant human animals, the Conquistadores."[9] Recalling his roots in the American antislavery movement, he likened their degradation to the enslavement of African Americans:

> Their social status is wretched beyond expression, infinitely worse physically than that of our former slaves in the South; they are not allowed even to drink water from the village well, nor to pass a high caste man on the public road—they must step aside into the field, till he has passed by. In fact, one may truly say of them that their condition warrants the phrase used by the late Chief Justice Taney in his famous decision on the Dred Scott Fugitive Slave case; these Pariahs have no rights which a high caste man is bound to respect.[10]

But despite his view that the caste system was an immoral infringement of individual liberty, Olcott refrained until very late in his life from speaking out publicly on the issue. The Theosophical Society had a stringent policy of noninterference in political matters, so Olcott was careful to note whenever he did speak out on caste that he was only expressing a personal opinion.

Not until after his flirtation with retirement from the Theosophical Society in the early 1890s did he begin to transform his relatively private disdain for the caste system into public action. He did so in two ways. First, he worked to improve the lot of untouchables *within* Hinduism by providing them with technical education that would enable them to perform their allotted duties more effectively. Second, in an attempt that presaged similar efforts in the twentieth century by the untouchable reformer Dr. Bhimrao Ramji Ambedkar (1892–1956), Olcott attempted to lift untouchables out of the caste system by converting them to a casteless Buddhism.[11]

Like other members of New York City's metropolitan gentry, Olcott was convinced that education was the key to "uplifting" the masses to a level of "culture" worthy of the best men and women of his age. But he veered away from at least some of those reformers and in the direction of Booker T. Washington by advocating technical rather than liberal education in India. In "The Theosophical Society and Its Aims," the first speech he delivered in India, he had made this preference plain. And that preference was reflected in the curricula in his Sinhalese schools.

Olcott's first effort at educating untouchables, the "Olcott Free School," opened in Madras on June 18, 1894. Modeled after Ceylon's B.T.S. schools, which were themselves patterned after Christian missionary examples, this modest schoolhouse measured forty feet by twenty feet and was constructed, at Olcott's personal expense, out of mud and palm thatch. In addition to the students who flocked eagerly to the school, two governors of Madras visited the site and encouraging government grants followed in their wake.

Eventually Olcott opened a number of additional "pariah schools." These institutions were administered by two female reformers from the United States: Miss Sarah E. Palmer and Mrs. N. Almee Courtwright. Courtwright, who had worked previously as an educational reformer in the slums of Chicago, introduced the latest western educational methods (including kindergarten-style reforms) into the curriculum. She also effected a pedagogical shift, then being popularized in America, from the "abstract, mental cram method" to the "objective or 'personal experience' method."[12]

These schools were clearly reform-minded, but they were in no way revolutionary. Not unlike Washington's Tuskegee Academy, they aimed not to provide future doctors, lawyers, and government employees with a liberal education but to provide a technical education to working people. Their goal was almost shockingly modest: in Olcott's words, "to fit [pupils] for their most lucrative employment, that of house servants to Europeans and Eurasians."[13] Students learned how to adjust to their stations in life, not how to overcome them; they studied not economics and political theory but cooking and cleaning and a bit of the grammar of their vernacular language of Tamil. Eventually the list of model occupations for graduates of Olcott's school expanded to include "tally-keepers in small bazaars, time-keepers under contractors, teachers in [untouchable] schools, petty shopkeeping, local guides to travellers." As a result of this shift, teachers began to instruct students in languages such as English and Hindi and skills such as money, weights, and measures.[14] Still the goals of these schools remained far more modest than those of the Buddhist schools of Ceylon. While the B.T.S. schools sought to produce English-speaking aspirants to the new middle class, Olcott's schools for untouchables aimed merely to turn out competent domestic servants.

In formulating these circumscribed aims for his "pariah schools," Olcott was clearly motivated by an American penchant for practicality. In fact, what he described as "technical education" mirrored in many details what Horace Greeley, his former boss at the *New York Tribune*, had described (and advocated) years earlier as "practical education." Painfully aware that he could not eradicate the stigma of caste, Olcott aimed not to encourage his students to strive for equality but to equip them to advance as far as possible in an unequal world.

Olcott was also motivated, however, by some rather unattractive biases. Unlike a friend who maintained in the *Theosophist* that "under the Law of Karma the pariahs are but suffering for their misdeeds in a former birth," Olcott apparently never publicly utilized the doctrine of karma as an apology for the untouchables' situation.[15] But on at least one occasion, he did use the idea to justify economic inequality. "If a Christian boy were asked why one man is poor and another is a millionaire, he would say it is God's will," Olcott reasoned. "Hindu Books, on the contrary, would point out that what man is, is what he made himself by his past Karma."[16] Thus the doctrine of karma led Olcott to a conclusion shared by Social Darwinists and laissez-faire economic theorists in the West: that individuals somehow deserved the hand that life had dealt them. Another bias that informed the educational aims of Olcott's "pariah schools" was his racialism. Though a tireless defender of the "heathen," Olcott shared with many of his hated missionaries and his beloved Orientalists a belief that Indians and Sinhalese were a lesser breed not naturally equipped for higher tasks. Like missionary James Tennent, who described the Sinhalese people as torpid and indolent, Olcott viewed them as "lazily recalcitrant."[17] Burmese he characterized as an "awfully lazy people," and African races as "backward" and "intellectually so inferior."[18] Finally, Olcott lamented the childlike slothfulness of Indians even as he praised the manly industriousness of Europeans and Americans. "The Hindus are almost like children as regards the management of public affairs," he had noted in 1891. "Look at the workers in England and America. They are always forward in action."[19]

Olcott's racial condescension and his socially reactionary reading of karma clearly found a place in his pariah schools. Superintendent Court-wright assented to the standpoint, which she labeled "biological" and "scientific," that "the limitations and possibilities for mental training of the child are almost entirely a matter of the child's ancestry." Because untouch-ables were "mostly destined to be servants," she concluded, their teachers should not attempt to pull them up to "too high a mark of culture."[20]

Olcott's antidotes to the social sickness of caste thus incorporated both the insights and biases of American Protestantism and metropolitan gen-tility. Like many American Protestants, Olcott believed that lasting social reform resulted from the transformation of individuals and, therefore, that the ablest agents of such change were not governments but voluntary asso-ciations (especially private schools). Like his liberal Protestant con-temporary Horace Bushnell, Olcott believed that individuals were better transformed through the gradual process of character-building than the once-and-for-all event of conversion.[21] Finally, Olcott shared with genteel educational reformers like Horace Mann the certainty that the proper place for this nurture was the schoolhouse. "No Government in the world," Olcott asserted, "can lift a great body of five millions of people from the degradation of brutish ignorance to the dignified condition of a self-re-specting, self-sufficient community, save by passing their children through the schoolmaster's hands." Ignorance, according to Olcott, was the source of India's problems. The remedy, he argued in terms that were simultane-ously genteel and Buddhist, was " 'Get wisdom.' "[22]

Dravidian Buddhist Society

In addition to offering up the remedy of "getting wisdom" for India's untouchables, Olcott commended, at least for a time, the remedy of "getting Buddhism." Here Olcott's reasoning, which would be utilized in the twen-tieth century by Dr. B. R. Ambedkar, was simple. Gautama Buddha opposed caste; Buddhism did not recognize caste; therefore, untouchables should convert to casteless Buddhism rather than suffering under Hinduism's caste system.

Olcott's agency for converting untouchables into Buddhists was the Dravidian Buddhist Society (or Southern India Sakya Buddhist Society). Formally inaugurated at a meeting in Madras on June 8, 1898, the D.B.S. issued on that day a petition ostensibly addressed to Olcott but clearly influenced and probably written by him.[23] Anticipating the dangers of the participation of the president of the India-based Theosophical Society, which was officially committed to a policy of religious neutrality, in a project to convert Hindus to Buddhism, the petitioners advanced a historical argument that Madras' untouchables were originally (and therefore, by Protestant, Orientalist, *and* theosophical logic, essentially) Buddhists. As Olcott later explained, "They were convinced, from a study of Tamil literature, that their ancestors were of the Dravidian race and Buddhists; that they had been conquered in war and reduced to slavery; that they had never been able to recover their former social condition; and that the conquerors had destroyed their temples, slaughtered their priests and extirpated their religion from Southern India. Their earnest wish," he added, "now was to revert to it."[24] The petitioners supplemented this historical argument with an appeal to liberal notions such as liberty, equality, self-reliance, and social reform that sounded strikingly like the American Declaration of Independence. "We hope to restore our self-respect," they announced, "to win by our own exertions, domestic comfort and untrammeled personal liberty of action, which are denied us in the Hindu Social system of caste."[25]

Following a public reading of this petition, Olcott and Anagarika Dharmapala addressed the inaugural assembly. Olcott reserved judgment regarding the historical claim, but he pledged nonetheless his aid (in his private and unofficial capacity as an individual Buddhist, of course). Olcott appealed in his speech more to modern western notions of rights and liberties, however, than to ancient Buddhist principles. In addition to anticlericalism, social mobility, and opposition to caste, Olcott's Buddhism also inculcated "honesty, moral living, truthfulness and temperance."[26] His clearly creolized text, which contained clear echoes of liberal Protestant antislavery tracts, included no references to Buddhist enlightenment. Individual freedom was instead the goal:

> [Buddhism] will make every man, woman and child among you *free*
> of all the oppression of caste; *free* to work; *free* to look your fellowmen
> bravely in the face; *free* to rise to any position within the reach of your
> talents, your intelligence and your perseverance; *free* to meet men,
> whether Asiatics, Europeans or Americans on terms of friendly equality
> and competition, according to your individual refinement, courtesy and
> self-respect; *free* to follow out the religious path traced to the Lord
> Buddha without any priest having the right to block your way; *free to
> become teachers and models of character to mankind.* [Emphasis in original][27]

At the conclusion of this inaugural meeting, the leaders of the Dravidian Buddhist Society assented to Olcott's suggestion to forward a petition to monk Hikkaduve Sumangala and the Buddhist Sangha of Ceylon. In this petition the society begged for help in organizing its "Mission for the conversion of the people to the religion of their Buddhistic forefathers." It asked, more specifically, for Tamil-speaking missionaries to come to Madras and for money to construct and maintain a building to house them. "Our friend Col. Olcott will aid us so far as lies within his power," the petition read, "but it lies with you and our brethren of the Sangha to start this moment."[28] A few weeks after inaugurating their society, two untouchables from Madras—Dr. C. Iyothee Doss and a teacher named P. Krishnaswami—accompanied Olcott to Ceylon to convey their petition personally to Sumangala. Then, at a "monster meeting" in Colombo on July 3, they followed the examples of Olcott and Blavatsky by taking Pansil and dramatically becoming Buddhists.[29]

Given the commitment of the Theosophical Society to nonsectarianism, to say nothing of its frequently articulated anti-missionary bent, the fact that Olcott fretted about his involvement with the Dravidian Buddhist Society should not be surprising. What is surprising is that these concerns did not prevent Olcott from manipulating the movement from both ends. When it came time for Sumangala to reply to the pariah's petition, Olcott prepared the draft, as he had probably prepared the petition.[30] But because he feared that the Dravidian Buddhist Society might lead to confrontations between Buddhists and Hindus, he continued to maintain the ruse that the organization was an indigenous initiative unaided by external influence.

The D.B.S. was apparently destined to become nothing more than a short (and largely forgotten) preface to Dr. Ambedkar's modern movement for converting India's untouchables to Buddhism, because Olcott abandoned the organization shortly after establishing it. One reason Olcott withdrew from the cause was his abiding theosophical commitment to a liberal theory of religious unity. During his speech at the D.B.S. inauguration, Dharmapala, who was moving in the direction of militant Sinhalese Buddhist chauvinism, had distinguished himself from the more liberal Olcott by celebrating rather than sidestepping the issue of Buddhism's Indian origins. Buddhism is "a pure Aryan religion founded upon the Aryan Dharma, promulgated by an Aryan, preached by the Aryans to the Aryans," he proclaimed. And he stressed Buddhism's central place in India's sacred geography and mythology:

Although to-day there is no Buddha Dharma in India, yet one finds scattered all over the Indian continent traces of this great religion. On the coast of Orissa, the romantic spot at Udayagiri shows that at one period Buddhist Arhats had lived there. In the temple of Jagannath, at Puri, the characteristic feature of brotherliness peculiar to Buddha

Dharma is manifested. . . . The coming Buddha Maitreyya will be born, ages hence, in Benares.[31]

The militant conclusion to Dharmapala's speech could not have contrasted more with Olcott's decidedly conciliatory call for Buddhism to return to India not as conqueror but as one religion among many. "India belongs," Dharmapala insisted in a sentence Olcott would never have considered uttering, "to the Buddhas."

In the face of statements such as this, Olcott gradually distanced himself from the Dravidian Buddhist Society. He explained that growing distance in an 1899 address in which he noted that the untouchables of Madras had not been able to produce the promised historical documents that would prove their Buddhist lineage and thereby justify their Buddhist mission as a revival. But, more tellingly, he lamented Dharmapala's "injudicious and quite unnecessary . . . attacks upon [Hindu] religious beliefs and customs."[32] Dharmapala's indiscretions, coupled with the unavailability of the crucial historical evidence, again forced Olcott to make a choice between Buddhist work and his theosophical vision. And once more Olcott chose theosophy over Buddhism. The decision to jettison his efforts to convert India's untouchables to his beloved Buddhist tradition must have been a difficult one for Olcott. But the success of his "pariah" schools undoubtedly made that decision a bit more palatable.

Aryavarta and Academic Orientalism

In addition to working in the 1890s to "uplift" the untouchables of India either through education in a trade or through conversion to Buddhism, Olcott labored throughout his time in India to "uplift" the Indian bourgeoisie. His strategy here mirrored the strategy he employed with Ceylon's middle classes. And once again, the watchword was education. Olcott's educational efforts in India were directed at two fronts. First, he aimed to awaken in India's middle classes a reverence for ancient India by rekindling in them an understanding of and appreciation for the Sanskrit language and the Hindu scriptures. Second, he hoped to reduce their supposed moral and intellectual deficits by encouraging them, as he had encouraged American spiritualists decades earlier, to cultivate "culture" and "character."

Olcott's love of ancient India, its language and scriptures was clearly rooted in the work of pioneering academic Orientalists—work which clearly influenced his creolized Buddhism. Before moving to India, Olcott had read widely in the work of men like Rhys Davids, Emil Burnouf and Max Müller. And after he arrived on the subcontinent, he corresponded with a number of leading Orientalists and actually met Müller, as well as Burnouf, Sir Edwin Arnold, and E. B. Tylor. Olcott was, therefore, very much a part of the broader community of discourse of academic Orientalists.

Earlier in his life, Olcott had demonstrated his ties to academic Orientalism through repeated efforts to publish translations of Asian scriptures and to promote the study of ancient Asian languages. Interestingly, these efforts had begun not in India but in New York, where in 1878 Olcott had devised a plan to publish a series of translations of Oriental scriptures. Though that initial plan fell through, Olcott did eventually produce numerous Sanskrit editions of ancient Indian texts and his *Theosophist* regularly published scriptural translations. Those editions and translations were funded through the Theosophical Society's Publication Fund, which Olcott had modeled, once again, after "the example of the Christians, who long ago founded their publication societies and organized excellent systems of distribution throughout the world."[33] Not surprisingly, Olcott's work in this arena earned him the disdain of the Christian missionaries he was imitating. Accompanying that disdain, however, were the plaudits not only of Max Müller, who subscribed to the society's Oriental series and applauded its translations, but also of Rhys Davids, who read the *Theosophist* for its translations of Oriental classics.

Along with a penchant for Sanskrit studies, libraries, and professional societies, Olcott imbibed two important biases from those Orientalists who together transformed "the Orient" into an academic field: a primitivist bias that equated the original form of a religious tradition with that religion's essence, and a textual bias that saw a religion's scriptures as its authoritative manifestation.

Richard T. Hughes has argued that the quest for the primitive church has been a predominant feature of American religion. "Primitivism," according to Hughes, demands that " 'first times' are in some sense normative or jurisdictional."[34] But if this primitivism characterizes American religion, it practically constituted nineteenth-century academic Orientalism, which legitimized through its professional societies and journals the colonial dichotomy between the "civilized" self and the "primitive" other. Thus Olcott's *Heilsgeschichte* moved, like the Puritan preachers' Jeremiad and the academic Orientalists' historical and philological reconstructions, from ancient greatness to modern apostasy—from the grandeur of "ancient Aryavarta" to the "idolatrous lethargy and fatalism" of modern times:

> The union of the olden days is replaced by disunion, province is
> arrayed against province, race against race, sect against sect, brother
> against brother. . . . The brow of a once proud nation is laid in the dust,

and shame causes those who revere her memory to avert their gaze from the sickening spectacle of her fallen greatness. Mighty cities, once the homes of hives of population, the centres of luxury, the hallowed repositories of religion and science, have crumbled into dust; and . . . the filthy beast and carrion bird inhabit their desolate ruins.[35]

Closely aligned with this primitivist bias was Olcott's textualist bias. Given the assumption of most academic Orientalists—an assumption they shared, significantly, with many Protestants—that the original form of a religious tradition was also its essential form, it was natural to view a religion's ancient sutras as its definitive expression and then to criticize on the basis of ancient scriptural authority that religion's modern beliefs and practices. And this Orientalists did with a vengeance. Following the lead of these Orientalists and the example of Blavatsky's theosophical hermeneutic, Olcott identified the essence of a religion with the inner meaning of its scriptures. From this textualist perspective, he criticized Hinduism and Buddhism as "but brutalizations of their primal types."[36]

When put together, the Orientalists' textualist and primitivist biases allowed Olcott, as they had allowed a generation of academics, simultaneously to damn and to praise Asian religions. But Olcott took one important step beyond the Orientalists, by endeavoring to reform Asian religious traditions—to root out their damnable modern traits and plant in their stead the praiseworthy beliefs and behaviors of ancient times. Though Asia was once great, Olcott argued, she was now in ruins. And it was his job to rebuild her. Part archeologist and part architect, he would resurrect her ancient truths from under a pile of modern rubbish. Then he would reconstruct out of ancient scriptural materials her venerable magnificence. By combining ancient truths with modern organizational and communications techniques, Olcott would force "the sap of a new spring-time to rise in the ancient trunks of Indian Brahmanism and Buddhism, causing their hoary crowns to be once more covered with luxuriant leafage." Thus Olcott set himself up not only as Asia's savior but also as her reformer. "These religions, when fully resuscitated," he prophesied, "will be as different from their immediate 'forbears,' as the adult is from the youth."[37]

Instilling Character: The Hindu Boys' Association

Making adults that are superior to the youths they had once been was Olcott's main strategy in his campaign to "uplift" the India's middle classes. As in Ceylon, Olcott directed his reforming work in India in the last decade of the nineteenth century largely at Indian youth aspiring to middle-class status. Olcott initiated among this group a juvenile magazine called the

The Indian Renaissance

Arya Bala Bodhini (est. 1895) and formed juvenile organizations such as the short-lived Aryan League of Honor (est. 1884) and the more enduring Hindu Boys' Association (est. 1894).

Not unlike the YMCA that preceded it and the Boy Scouts of America that it antedated, the Olcott's Hindu Boys' Association aimed to promote "moral and spiritual education" among youth.[38] Its objects, as expressed in its constitution, were threefold:

> First.—To form the nucleus of a brotherhood among the Hindu boys of India. Second.—To induce the Hindu boys to put into practice their religious rites and ceremonies, study and understand their significance, and make them true to their own faith. Third.—To spread among them a substantial knowledge of their literature, religion, philosophy and morals.[39]

But despite this emphasis on Hindu rituals and beliefs, the organization revealed its creole nature by promoting modern western values as much if not more than ancient Hindu norms. The *Arya Bala Bodhini*, the official organ of the Hindu Boys' Association, was published in English. Later renamed the *Central Hindu College Magazine*, its children's stories had more in common with the popular morality tales of Jacob Abbott and Horatio Alger than with the Vedas. In addition to a regular column on "Western Wisdom," the *Bodhini* included a recurring feature on "How an English Boy is Brought Up." One article in the series discussed the etiquette of knives, forks, and spoons and the niceties of using cups and saucers at tiffin. Another article described cricket, fox hunting, lawn tennis, and rowing—activities open only to the most leisurely of Indian elites. Even Indian contributors to the magazine satisfied the editor's seemingly insatiable taste for articles about "character" and they quoted Matthew Arnold (whom one dubbed the "Western Sadhu") as much as Hindu sages.[40] Thus the *Bodhini* exhibited a form of cultural schizophrenia characteristic not only of Olcott but also of most nineteenth-century Hindu reformers; at the same time it was denouncing English dress among Indian schoolboys it was commending the cultivation of cricket.

In addition to these youth clubs and periodicals, Olcott promoted (as he had done among Buddhists in Ceylon) a series of popular catechisms and instruction manuals for the moral and spiritual edification of youth. Here Olcott was, not surprisingly, self-consciously imitating the strategies of Protestant and Catholic publication and tract societies. And once again he did a credible job of imitation. In 1886, Olcott edited and published, after the model of his *Buddhist Catechism*, a Hindu *Dwaita Catechism*. He also promoted an *Epitome of Aryan Morals* (1887), another creole text, which like his own *Golden Rules of Buddhism* (1887) and similar etiquette manuals in the West, distilled centuries of moral wisdom from various scriptures into one easy-to-read pamphlet. The *Epitome* contained, as Olcott himself remarked in his introduction to the volume, "free" rather than "literal" translations from Sanskrit scriptures. Its injunctions against gambling and for hard work would no doubt have pleased Puritans as well as Hindus. And this rendering of a section from the *Laws of Manu*—"It is certain that man commits some sin or other by the attachment of his organs to sensual pleasure. He ought therefore to subdue them rigorously and he will then attain a lasting bliss."[41]—could easily have been drafted by a Victorian rather than a Hindu ethicist.

By promoting, publishing, and distributing publications such as these, and by organizing Hindu youth clubs, Olcott was able to reach with his genteel gospel of character-building through education a number of young Indians aspiring to bourgeois status and Raj-related jobs.

Adyar Library Opening

Although Olcott's interactions with Hinduism and with Hindus was probably most evident in his early years (when he was working with Saraswati and the Arya Samaj) and in his later years in India (when he was addressing the problem of caste and "uplifting" bourgeois Indian youth), there was really no time during his Indian career that his Buddhist and theosophical concerns entirely overwhelmed his Hindu interests. One reason Olcott did not feel compelled to choose between his work on behalf of Buddhism and his work on behalf of Hinduism was his abiding commitment to a liberal theory of religious unity. In order to understand the contributions Olcott made to the Indian Renaissance in the 1890s, it may be helpful to edge back a bit in time to consider both his related work in previous decades and his religious universalism.

Although Olcott clearly contributed to the Indian Renaissance through his speeches and writings, his affinities with other Indian reformers may be most visible in an event that he orchestrated at the headquarters of the Theosophical Society in December of 1886. At the Theosophical Society's Convention of 1885, held almost exactly one year earlier, Olcott had spoken about the necessity of a revival of Sanskrit learning and ancient Aryan morality. This revival, Olcott proclaimed in typically grandiloquent terms, would serve as "the *aes perenne* or everlasting bronze that in India will compose our Society's monument." To this end, Olcott had proposed youth organizations for Indian children, Sanskrit schools, translations of Sanskrit scriptures into English and Indian vernaculars, and, finally, a library at

The Indian Renaissance

Adyar that, by attracting "the cleverest Brahman pandits and the most learned Western orientalists," would transform the headquarters of the Theosophical Society into "a second Alexandria."[42]

The Adyar Library opening, held on December 29, 1886, represented a rite of passage for theosophy in India and a baptism of sorts for Olcott's religious universalism. The ceremonies began with congratulatory poems intoned in Sanskrit, Pali, and Avestan. Ritual specialists from the Zoroastrian, Islamic, Buddhist, and Hindu traditions then paraded before a common platform, invoking blessings upon the library in their own languages and according to their respective traditions. Reviewing the objects of the Theosophical Society in his welcoming address, Olcott continued the now-established tradition of modifying those objects to suit current circumstances. He omitted any reference to the society's third, occult, aim, implying that the society's mission was now twofold: to construct a pan-religious "Universal Brotherhood of Humanity" and to foster the study of Asian religious traditions. The purpose of the Adyar Library, according to Olcott, was to advance these two objects by gathering in one place the best thoughts of the best sages and thus "to reestablish the dignity of the true pandit, mobed, bhikshu and maulvi."[43] Toward the end of his speech Olcott announced his intention to publish catechisms for Islam, Zoroastrianism, and various schools of Hinduism.[44]

After Olcott's welcoming address, the pluralistic parade continued, appropriately enough in an array of ancient tongues. A Hindu pundit called upon Saraswati, the Goddess of Wisdom and Learning. Some schoolboys from local Sanskrit schools chanted benedictions from the Vedas in the original Sanskrit. Zoroastrians lit a fire and along with that sacred flame offered a prayer to Ahura Mazda. A Theravada Buddhist intoned some Buddhist sutras in Pali. And a Muslim followed the injunction of Allah to "Recite!" by reciting some suras from the Koran. While some may have found this panoply confusing, Olcott enjoyed immeasurably its dizzying diversity. "It was," he later recalled, "one of the happiest days of my life."[45]

As the Adyar Library opening makes plain, Olcott's participation in the Indian Renaissance was not limited to Hindu activities and his theory of the unity of religions embraced not only Hinduism and Buddhism but also Islam, Zoroastrianism, and other great faiths. Just as he had worked in Ceylon, Burma, and Japan to purge Buddhism of its modern execrations and to educate modern Buddhists about their tradition's ancient glories, he labored in India to awaken Indians of all faiths to their common roots in the core teachings of all ancient scriptures.

If we view the events that constituted the Adyar Library opening as a social drama, we might conclude, in fact, that the main purpose of the opening was to promote just that sort of religious awakening by articulating and, indeed, enacting Olcott's theory that the unity of all of today's religions lay in a shared, ancient past. As a social drama, the events attempted to address the problem of the spiritual fragmentation of the world by bringing all the world's religions together under the theosophical banner of religious unity.

The Unity of All Religions

Olcott was, of course, neither the first nor the last to hoist this banner, but he did much to popularize it, both in India and, through the activities of the Theosophical Society, in the United States. Virtually every leader of the Indian Renaissance shared Olcott's conviction that the differences between religious traditions were more apparent than real. Rammohun Roy, Swami Vivekananda, and a host of other Indian reformers attempted during the nineteenth century to create a sentiment of unity among all the people of India and a sense of participation in a common endeavor between people in India and people in the West, but standing in the way of such lofty goals was the astonishing linguistic, cultural, and religious diversity of the inhabitants of the Indian subcontinent. Contributors to the Indian Renaissance worked to resolve these diversities into unity by speaking in a common tongue (the colonial language of English), by infusing their diverse cultural actions with common British norms, and by practicing their various religious traditions under the canopy of a liberal theory of the unity of religions. If British colonial administrators had worked to transform, for example, Telugu-speaking Hindus and Arabic-speaking Muslims into English-speaking and religiously tolerant British subjects, then leaders of the Indian Renaissance struggled to infuse in those same people a pan-Indian consciousness that would enable them to stand together one day as free citizens of a post-colonial India.

Of all these forms of unity, leaders of the Indian Renaissance stressed a goal they shared with other religious liberals around the globe: religious unity. This unity they hoped to fashion not by converting all Indians to one religion but by instilling in Indians of different religious traditions a common faith in the fundamental spiritual unity underlying religious differences. Hence Ramakrishna's contention that each religion was a different path to the same goal, Rammohun Roy's argument for one universal monotheistic religion, and the later claim of Gandhi that "All Religions Are True."

Back in America, Olcott's contemporaries were making similar claims.

In an oft-delivered address on "The Sympathy of Religions," Thomas Wentworth Higginson, America's universal reformer *par excellence* and a popularizer of liberal religion himself, had collapsed the world's religions into one "Natural Religion." All religions shared the "same aim, the same symbols, the same forms, the same weaknesses, the same aspirations," he argued. "All seek after God and give their lives for the service of man."[46] Olcott too argued for the unity of religions, but he located their point of sympathy in history rather than psychology. All religions, according to Olcott, were rooted in the ancient wisdom of ancient scriptures. Because all religions shared this common foundation, all were equally true. But because each had deviated from the now-lost *Urreligion*, each was also partially false and in need of reform. "What we do is to preach the majesty and glory of all the ancient religions," Olcott wrote, "and to warn the Hindu, the Sinhalese, and the Parsi, to beware how they depart from the teachings of the *Veda*, the *Tripitakas*, and the *Avesta*."[47]

Olcott's interest here not only in the Hindu and Buddhist scriptures but also in the Avesta, a sacred text of Zoroastrianism, is telling. It points to the fact that his reformer's zeal and creolizing tendencies extended beyond Buddhism to Hinduism and other faiths. Given Olcott's express concern with reforming all of India, to say nothing of the fact that India has been the home of multiple religious traditions for millennia, this extension is eminently reasonable. If India was to be reshaped in the image of ancient India or "Aryavarta," not only Hinduism but also Zoroastrianism and even Islam would have to be revitalized. And not only the Vedas but also the Qur'an and the Avesta would have to be invoked.

Revitalizing Zoroastrianism and Islam

Olcott first expressed an interest in Zoroastrianism while still in New York. During the time of his correspondence with various reformers from India and Ceylon, Olcott had recruited at least one Parsee to join the Theosophical Society. After arriving in Bombay, a Parsee stronghold in India, in 1879, Olcott attempted (unsuccessfully, apparently) to interest influential Zoroastrian adherents in what he was calling the "Parsi Research Society"— an organization that by conducting scholarly explorations of the roots of Zoroastrianism might accomplish, in Olcott's words, "for their faith, by archaeological research and exploration, what the Christians have done for theirs in Egypt and Palestine."[48]

Although Olcott's Zoroastrian interests can be traced back to New York and the 1870s, he first brought these interests to public view in a speech he delivered in February 1882 in Bombay. He began "The Spirit of Zoroas-trianism" by praising the religious tradition of Bombay's predominantly Parsee population as "noble" and "rich" and its founder, Zoroaster, as "a great man who discovered secret truths." In keeping with his tendency to see unity rather than diversity among the world's religions, however, Olcott praised Zoroastrianism not for its individual genius but for its congruence with other religious traditions. Olcott cited the preface to one of Max Müller's *The Sacred Books of the East* in arguing that "The Avesta and the Veda are two echoes of one and the same voice, the reflex of one and the same thought." He then contended for the harmony of that one voice with the voices of the Hindus' Yoga Sutras, the Jews' Kabbala, and even the Bud-dhists' Tripitakas. He compared Zoroastrian priests with Hindu yogis and Theravada Buddhist arhats; and the Parsee spiritual goal he likened to the Hindu's moksha and the Buddhist's nirvana. Finally, Olcott commended Zoroastrianism for its remarkable correspondence with and, in some cases, superiority to modern science. "Zoroaster," Olcott contended, "knew more about nature than Tyndall does, more about the laws of force than Balfour Stewart, more about the origin of species than Darwin or Haeckel."[49]

What Olcott was praising, however, was not the Zoroastrianism practiced by modern Parsees but an ostensibly ancient yet clearly creole Zoroastrian-ism of his own imagining. In Ceylon, he had praised the pristine wisdom of "pure, primitive Buddhism" even as he had damned its modern decline into hackneyed ritual and superstitions. Now Olcott contended with equal rhetorical flourish that modern Zoroastrianism had fallen precipitously from an Edenic past:

> . . . the old life has gone out of Zoroastrianism. Originally a highly spiritual faith . . . it has shrunk into a purely exoteric creed full of ritual-istic practices not understood, taught by a numerous body of priests as a rule ignorant of the first elements of spiritual philosophy, and repre-sented in prayers of which not one has a meaning to those who recite them daily—the shrivelled shell that once held a radiant soul.[50]

Nowhere was this declension more evident, Olcott argued, than in the moral failures of Parsee youth. "Gathering in clubs to drink pegs and play cards . . . defiling themselves by evil associations, smoking in secret . . . and prating glibly the most sceptical sophistries they have read in European books," they portended a dark future for the tradition of fiery light. If the Parsee community did not repent and return to the ancient wisdom of Zoroaster, Olcott concluded, "the time will come when it will be only the occasional brave heart that will dare call himself a Mazdean."[51]

The Indian Renaissance

As students of Puritanism will immediately recognize, Olcott's speech was a Jeremiad, a prophetic lament of a community's spiritual diminution.[52] And just as Olcott borrowed his sermon's form from his Puritan ancestors, he borrowed his praise of the Parsees from the Puritans, too. Previously Olcott had lauded his Puritan forebears (and, implicitly, himself) for leaving behind the land of their birth in order to practice their religion freely in a foreign land. Now he commended the Parsees' "forefathers [who gave] up everything they prized rather than repudiate their faith . . . who, for the sake of conscience, fled from [their] native land."[53]

Olcott's Parsee readers could redeem themselves, Olcott continued, only by committing themselves, as New England's Puritans had centuries earlier, to a Great Awakening. This revival should incorporate four practical reforms. Each of these reforms was strikingly Protestant, and each mirrored the anticlerical criticisms that had been advanced for centuries by Protestant reformers against Catholic priests.

First, Olcott argued, Parsees should uplift their priests by educating them in oratory, as well as European and Asian languages and literatures. Second, they should uplift popular Zoroastrianism by purging common folk of ignorant superstitions and empty rituals. Third, they should bring Zoroastrianism to the laypeople by translating prayer books into English and vernacular languages, by explaining those texts in simple language in footnotes, and by publishing commentaries that reconcile hoary Zoroastrian truths with the laws of modern science. Finally, they should found, on the model of the Christians' Palestine Exploration Society, an organization that could sift the sands of ancient civilizations for historical proofs of the veracity of the Zoroastrian scriptures. In order to support these stunningly Protestant reforms, which he summarized in the activist injunction, "be up and doing," the ever-practical Olcott proposed the establishment a "Fund for the Promotion of the Mazdean Religion."

Olcott returned to this theme of a Zoroastrian revival in an open letter to a Parsee published fourteen years later. In this 1896 letter, Olcott praised Zoroastrianism as "one of the noblest, simplest, most sublime religions in the world" even as he damned the "criminal indifference" of many Parsees to the rampant "apostasies of ignorant, untaught, or feeble-minded [Zoroastrian] children." Once again, Olcott invoked in his remedy the Puritan and Orientalist model of ancient apostasy and modern redemption. Parsees needed to follow more closely, he argued, the examples of their Zoroastrian forebears whose sturdy faith, according to Olcott, "made them— like my own Pilgrim forefathers—quit country, wealth, friends, comfort and all, and smilingly face every unknown danger for the dear sake of their religion." And once again he suggested that Parsees follow the example of the Christians' Palestine Exploration Fund and enlist scholars in recovering their lost scriptures.[54]

Such was the strikingly Protestant substance of Olcott's plea for a Parsee revival. Like Luther and Calvin centuries earlier and a continent away, Olcott criticized puffed-up priests who made a living by foisting empty rituals on an ignorant and superstitious public. Olcott too called for clergy and laypeople alike to commit themselves to reading scripture in the vernacular and to understanding it in their hearts. And his strategy once again was, in his words, "to emulate the successful attempts of the Christians."[55]

Even more noteworthy than Olcott's attempted creolizations of Zoroastrianism, however, was his ostensibly Zoroastrian voice. In both his 1882 speech and his 1896 letter, Olcott addressed would-be Parsee revivalists as an insider. At the center of his earlier sermon he intoned these two remarkable sentences:

> I have, you must remember, been speaking from the standpoint of a
> Parsi. I have tried to sink my personality and my personal religious
> preferences for the moment and put myself in your place.[56]

Thus Olcott represented himself once again not as a particular man but as an *homme universel* who could leave behind both the American Protestantism of his youth and the Buddhism of his adulthood and miraculously become, if only for an afternoon, a native Parsee. This representation apparently convinced at least one Parsee, who concluded that "though [Olcott] was an American by birth and a Buddhist by religion, the fire of Zoroastrianism was ever burning within his bosom . . . he was at heart a true Zoroastrian."[57]

Olcott's claim to speak from a Parsee standpoint is all the more remarkable given the fact that he made similar claims during his Asian sojourn to speak authoritatively as a Muslim insider. In Lucknow, India, in August 1885, Olcott was asked to deliver a lecture on Islam. The challenge daunted him at first, since by his own admission, "I had then no more than the slight knowledge of the subject which one gets in the course of his general reading." But as he sat down, in anticipation of his speech, to read the Qur'an he was able, in his words, miraculously "to grasp all that lay between the lines." And when he delivered the speech he was able to speak, once again, authoritatively as an insider of a religion that was not explicitly his own. "As I proceeded, I seemed to be able to put myself in Mohammed's place, to translate his thoughts and depict his ideal, as though I were 'a native here, and to the manner born,' " Olcott wrote. And at least in his version of the tale, his listeners eagerly embraced him as one of their own. The audience was "aroused to a pitch of enthusiasm . . . and the next day a Committee waited on me with an address of thanks, in which every blessing of Allah was invoked for me, and the wish was expressed that their children knew 'one-tenth as much about their religion' as I did."[58]

At least to the reader employing a hermeneutics of suspicion, Olcott's claim that his three years of residence among Parsees in Bombay qualified him to speak as a "White Parsee" rings as hollow as his claim that one night of Qur'anic study enabled him to speak as "a native here" among Muslims. These claims are at least understandable, however, when it is understood that Olcott made them neither as an orthodox Parsee nor an orthodox Muslim but as a theosophist. When Olcott read the Avesta or the Qur'an he employed neither a Parsee nor a Muslim but a theosophical hermeneutic. When he spoke in the language of the creole faiths that he spun out of these great traditions, he spoke with a Protestant grammar and a theosophical accent. And thus his "insider" representations differed by his own admission from how non-theosophical Parsees or Muslims might represent their own traditions. Olcott accounted for these interpretive differences, however, not by questioning his own views but by damning non-theosophical interpretations. Most Parsees and Muslims, he reasoned, knew only about the externals of their traditions. But he was able to penetrate to the more real, more true internals. Thus Olcott's claims to speak as a Muslim or a Parsee are even more extraordinary than they might appear at first blush. Olcott was not simply denying his earlier affirmation that members of a given religious tradition were its only legitimate interpreters. Neither was he claiming merely to stand *alongside* Muslims and Parsees as a coequal interpreter of their traditions. Rather he was claiming, much more audaciously, to stand *above* "other" Muslims and Parsees as a more authoritative interpreter of the Islamic and Zoroastrian faiths. Both the creole Zoroastrianism and the creole Islam of his own making were in his view superior to traditional understandings of those faiths.

Evaluations

Given Olcott's engagement, not only in the 1890s but also in the preceding two decades, with Hindu, Zoroastrian, and even Islam reform, Olcott ought to be seen as at least a peripheral contributor to the Indian Renaissance. He contributed to that movement in at least four ways: first, by promulgating a theory of pan-Indian religious unity; second, by encouraging the revitalization of Zoroastrianism and Islam; third, by promoting the revival of Hinduism and Sanskrit; and fourth, by working to reform Hinduism, especially regarding the rights and liberties of untouchables. In each of these efforts, Olcott remained true to his roots in American Protestantism, academic Orientalism, and metropolitan gentility. Just as he had worked in quintessentially genteel fashion to "uplift" both spiritualists in America and Buddhists in Asia, so did he labor to instill what he saw as the "best thoughts" in the soon-to-be "best men" of India. Although a number of Olcott's efforts in this regard came in the 1890s (around the time he was considering retiring from his presidency of the Theosophical Society) there was really never a time in India when he was not in some way involved with one of these four activities.

While in the midst of his Indian labors in 1890, Olcott summed up his contributions to the Indian Renaissance in typically grandiloquent fashion. "India's spiritual renaissance [began] through our efforts," he concluded. A decade later, he remained convinced that theosophists were "the chief agents for bringing about [the] revival of Hinduism in India."[59] Missionary critics in India evaluated Olcott's efforts differently but noted their effectiveness nonetheless. One reported that Olcott "attracted many educated Hindus" in India and that theosophy was a "great and formidable" enemy of Christianity.[60]

Still, Olcott clearly overstated his case. The Theosophical Society was not, as he claimed, "doing the very same thing for Hinduism that it [was] doing for Buddhism in Buddhist countries."[61] But it did contribute significantly, among both middle-class Indians and South India's working poor, to the Indian Renaissance, helping to foster what one missionary termed "the quickening of the religious zeal in the defense of Hinduism."[62] At the popular level, Olcott worked, ultimately unsuccessfully, to "save" Hindu untouchables by converting them, through the agency of the Dravidian Buddhist Society, to Buddhism and, more successfully, to "uplift" them by preparing them in his "pariah schools" for useful work within their allotted station in life. At the elite level, Olcott worked to instill in English-speaking Hindus, Parsees, and Muslims an understanding and a love for their ancient languages and scriptures and a commitment to hoary moral principles. All this work Olcott conducted under the assumption that not only Buddhism but also Hinduism, Zoroastrianism, and Islam (or at least his own imaginative constructions of them) were true, that not only the Buddhist sutras but also the Hindus' Vedas, the Parsees' Avesta, and the Muslim's Qur'an were inspired books of ancient wisdom.

In the last analysis what is striking about all of Olcott's Indian campaigns is how much they resembled Protestant missionary attempts to "civilize" the "primitive" natives. Like those missionaries who found it difficult to separate their duty to evangelize from their instinct to civilize, Olcott seemed unaware that in his attempt to "build up the Aryan ideal" he was using many of the cultural materials and construction techniques of modern western civilization.[63] Olcott's work to resuscitate ancient Aryavarta in India thus shared a crucial characteristic with his labor to revive primitive Buddhism in Ceylon: while both were billed as purifications, they were instead creolizations. In both cases, deep structures from Olcott's American Protestant past lurked beneath beliefs and actions that seemed, at least on the surface, to be ancient and Asian. In both cases, Olcott fused elements of the culture of his birth and the South Asian cultures of his adoption. In the process he unwittingly promoted among Hindus, Parsees, and Muslims of South Asia the ideologies and morphologies of American Protestantism, frequently reinterpreted in accordance with his decidedly theosophical voice.

Though Olcott was himself unaware of his attempted transformations of Hinduism, Zoroastrianism, and Islam on the subcontinent, his Hindu, Parsee, and Muslim coworkers were not. Almost invariably they noticed Olcott's theosophical accent and eventually discerned the American Protestant grammar lurking beneath Olcott's pro-Asian lexicon. And equally invariably at least some of them eventually resisted his attempted grammatical shifts.

Seven

Things Fall Apart

From his early years as a Union colonel in the American Civil War, to his later years as an advocate for a global Buddhist union, Olcott dreamed optimistic dreams of boundless unities and worked hard to transform those hopes into realities. Some of the unities Olcott sought to construct were clearly complementary, but others were at least potentially conflictual. At first glance, there would seem to be no apparent dissonance between, for example, Olcott's desires for an "International Buddhist League" that would gather all Buddhists into one "United Buddhist World," for a "Universal Brotherhood of Humanity" that would unite all people of faith into one harmonious family, and for a "National Samaj of Aryavarta" that would unite all of India's Hindus. But such conflicts did arise, and Olcott was reminded of them frequently and from many quarters.

Christian theosophists, for example, complained that Olcott violated theosophy's core maxim of religious neutrality whenever he denounced the Christian missionary enterprise. Buddhist sympathizer Lafcadio Hearn advanced a similar complaint, arguing that the theosophists belied their laudable "dream of a universal religion" whenever they spewed anti-Christian vitriol.[1] One missionary put the critique succinctly: "Any religion but the true one . . . is apparently their motto."[2] This complaint was not without grounds. Especially in Ceylon, Olcott repeatedly and bitterly conjured up the Christian missionary onslaught in an attempt to unite the island's Buddhists against a common enemy. According to the official *History of the Church Missionary Society* (1899), Olcott vowed during his first trip to Ceylon to "entirely uproot Christianity in the Island" and had taken pleasure in witnessing the Bible being publicly kicked about on the streets.[3] While this testimony may be hyperbolic, Olcott's own statements, which were clearly influenced by Blavatsky's more strident, European-style anticlericalism, seem to bear out the substance of the missionary complaint.

It should be noted, however, that Olcott was not entirely unfriendly to Christians and Christianity. In fact, a number of Christian missionaries working in Asia became his friends[4] and he learned greatly to admire not only the revivalistic techniques but also the "unselfish earnestness" of the

Salvation Army.[5] Moreover, Olcott clearly tempered his anti-Christian back-biting over time, and though he never considered returning to the Christian fold he did attend church services on occasion in the last years of his life. There seem to have been two reasons for this shift. The first was Blavatsky's death in 1891, which clearly served as a turning point in theosophical-Christian relations. The second is the fact that as the Theosophical Society matured it attracted more and more Christians. For both of these reasons, Olcott's anti-Christian statements after 1891 were both more nuanced and less frequent. In fact, at the end of 1891 Olcott began his President's Address to the Theosophical Society Convention with what can only be described as a confession. After noting that theosophical ideas "are flowing into the heart of the Christian church" and that "some most spiritually-minded Christian men and women . . . have taken office or simple membership in our Branches," Olcott sounded a note of contrition:

> if less intolerance towards Christianity had been shown hitherto by the Founders of our Society and their colleagues, we should have suffered and made to suffer less, and would to-day have had a thousand Christian well-wishers where we have one. . . . I deplore our intolerance, counting myself a chief offender.[6]

This confession must have satisfied those Christians who remained members of the Theosophical Society, but other church members remained troubled by Olcott's longstanding tendency to fail to apply his society's non-sectarian policy to the Christian Church.

The second reminder that Olcott's various attempts at unity might not be entirely harmonious came from Blavatsky herself, who vigorously opposed nearly every one of Olcott's Buddhist initiatives. Two concerns informed Blavatsky's opposition: first, that such Buddhist work drained his energies away from theosophical matters; and second, that his eager advocacy of Buddhism (unlike her own, less vociferous preference for the tradition), might compromise the Theosophical Society's neutrality by fostering the misconception that its goal was Buddhist unanimity, rather than pan-religious unity. According to Blavatsky Olcott was, in short, too Buddhist too often.

Olcott countered Blavatsky's criticism of his ostensibly excessive advocacy of Buddhism by appealing to the popular Gilded Age distinction between the "public" and the "private" self. While healing people in the name of the Buddha or delivering fundraising speeches to support Buddhist education, Olcott contended, he was acting in his "private" capacity as an individual Buddhist. But while presiding over Theosophical Society conventions or lecturing on the fundamental unity of all religions he was acting in his "public" role as Theosophical Society president.

This defense justified, at least in Olcott's mind, the simultaneous pursuit of both a "United Buddhist World" and a "Universal Brotherhood of Humanity." And at least for a time these goals did not collide. A Buddhist to the Buddhists, a Parsee to the Parsees, a Muslim to the Muslims, a Hindu to the Hindus, and a theosophist to the theosophists, Olcott was able for most of his Asian sojourn to market himself as an *homme universel* who belonged to no nation or religion precisely because he belonged to all. But being all things to all people is no simple task. The persistence and intensity of the complaints leveled against him by Christian theosophists, by Blavatsky, and by others, point to the fact that Olcott's quests for unity continued to produce upon contact with one another considerable friction. While Olcott was able in theory to harmonize his theosophical and Buddhist work, in practice he was not always so successful.

As early as 1885, Buddhists whom Olcott dismissed as sectarians had argued that the *Buddhist Catechism* should be burned.[7] And before that, Hikkaduve Sumangala had threatened to oppose that same document because of Olcott's ostensibly unorthodox characterization of nirvana. As the nineteenth century drew to a close, however, such tensions between Olcott's various quests for unity grew greater and greater. As Anagarika Dharmapala began to press him to work to reintroduce Buddhism to India, Olcott was forced to choose, once and for all, between his theosophical and his Buddhist commitments.

The Maha Bodhi Society

On May 31, 1891, around the time that Olcott abandoned as unmanageable his skeletal scheme for an "International Buddhist League," Anagarika Dharmapala established the Buddha-Gaya Maha Bodhi Society and drafted Colonel Olcott as its director and chief advisor. This organization, which was dubbed the "Heathen Missionary Society" by a Christian critic, was soon renamed the Maha Bodhi Society and still exists under that designation today.[8] Its aim was to establish Bodhgaya, the town in the modern Indian state of Bihar, where Gautama Buddha is said to have experienced enlightenment under a Bo tree, as a sacred center and pilgrimage site for all the world's Buddhists. By establishing a Buddhist college and an interdenominational monastic center near that Bo tree, the Maha Bodhi Society hoped to attract pilgrims from "the Buddhist countries of China, Japan,

Siam, Cambodia, Burma, Ceylon, Chittagong, Nepaul, Tibet and Arakan."[9] Olcott shared with Sumangala the titular leadership of the Maha Bodhi Society but Dharmapala was the driving force behind it. Thus the ascent of Dharmapala and the M.B.S. on the heels of the demise of Olcott's "International Buddhist League" signaled both a shift in leadership and a change in strategy for the international Buddhist movement.

Dharmapala, moved by Edwin Arnold's quintessentially Orientalist lamentation of the degradation of the site of Gautama Buddha's enlightenment, traveled to Bodhgaya in January of 1891 to witness the desecration firsthand. What he found were ancient statues buried under garbage heaps and Ashokan pillars propped up as posts in the kitchen of the Hindu priest who maintained the property. Returning to Ceylon, Dharmapala devised, in consultation with Sumangala and Olcott, a plan to organize a society to purchase the land surrounding the Bo tree temple at Bodhgaya, to restore the site as an interdenominational Buddhist shrine and pilgrimage site, and then to draw Buddhist representatives from around the world to nearby rest houses.[10] Bodhgaya would thus become to Buddhists "what the holy sepulchre is to the Christians, [what] Zion [is] to the Jews and Mecca [is] to the Mohammedans"—a bona fide sacred space.[11]

This plan to reclaim, restore, and reconsecrate Bodhgaya as a sacred center for all Buddhists was not unlike a dramatic enactment of Olcott's more abstract and propositional errand to the Buddhist world. If Olcott's aim was to recapture the Buddhist tradition from hostile missionary forces, to reunite warring Buddhist sects into a harmonious whole, and thus to restore the Buddhist tradition to its primitive purity, Dharmapala's proposal translated that goal into social drama and political action. He would wrest the temple at Bodhgaya from a hostile Hindu cleric, restore the building to its primitive purity and, in so doing, provide a sacred center for world Buddhism. Dharmapala, in short, would build from the ruins of Bodhgaya the Buddhist unity that Olcott had attempted to construct from propositions. The rise of Dharmapala and the Maha Bodhi Society thus shifted the focus of the international Buddhist movement away from text toward space, away from Olcott's Protestant emphasis on scripture and doctrinal consensus to a more traditional Theravada emphasis on pilgrimage and sacred place. This shift in emphasis was accompanied by an equally significant shift in the movement's constituency. Whereas Olcott's Buddhist Platform reached almost exclusively English-speaking elites, Dharmapala's Maha Bodhi scheme commended itself, at least theoretically, to all the world's Buddhists.

Dharmapala claimed that he received the idea of restoring Bodhgaya in a flash of inspiration during his initial visit there, but at least two more mundane influences were at work. First, there was the precedent in Ceylon of using the restoration of sacred sites as a rallying point for Buddhist revival and reform. In the 1840s, for example, leading Sinhalese Buddhists had responded to efforts by the British government to distance itself from its 1815 pledge to "maintain and protect" Buddhism by mounting a campaign to restore temples and schools overrun or overlooked during the Portuguese and Dutch occupations.[12] Second, there was the more recent precedent of a British program, begun in 1888 with archeological excavations at the Abhayagiriya Dagoba in Anuradhapura, to restore, presumably for scholarly and cultural purposes, Buddhist sites judged to be of "historical and archeological interest."[13] Dharmapala's strategy thus represented not only a return to the earlier site-oriented strategy of the Sinhalese Buddhist revival but also an attempt to wrest the restoration initiative from British archaeologists.

Before the foundation of the Maha Bodhi Society, Olcott's path to a "United Buddhist World" had skirted India, and although his cosmopolitan brand of Buddhism had offended Hindus, such as Saraswati and the members of his Arya Samaj, he had maintained a largely amiable coexistence with India's largest religion. But Dharmapala's Maha Bodhi Society threatened, like the Dravidian Buddhist Society discussed earlier, to upset this balance. The main goal of Dharmapala's strategy, after all, was to seize from a hostile Hindu a piece, however small, of India's religious pie. Dharmapala's route to a global Buddhist union cut through the geographical and spiritual center of India, and his more caustic revivalistic rhetoric chided not only Christian missionaries but also orthodox Hindus.

In the fall of 1892, Olcott and Dharmapala traveled to Calcutta, Darjeeling, Chittagong, Arakan, and Burma in order to raise money and enlist support for the Bodhgaya restoration project. In Calcutta, a group of Bengalis voiced concerns about the direction the Theosophical Society and the Maha Bodhi Society were taking. The theosophists were pursuing a secret policy of Buddhist propaganda, they feared, and the Maha Bodhi Society was in their view temperamentally anti-Hindu.

Hindus had voiced similar fears seven years earlier, and Olcott had attempted to mollify them by delivering a lecture entitled, "Theosophy Not Antagonistic to Hinduism."[14] Olcott's speech this time argued for "The Kinship Between Hinduism and Buddhism." He began this "Kinship" lecture by reaffirming the theosophical principle of religious impartiality, and by insisting that the Maha Bodhi Society entertained "no thought of sectarian hatred." He also pledged that precisely because of his Buddhist beliefs he did not believe, except in exceptional circumstances, in proselytization for the purpose of conversion. This was especially true, he added, in the case of the "sister cults" of Hinduism and Buddhism. Olcott then presented both a historical and a philosophical argument for Hindu-Buddhist consanguinity. In ancient times, he maintained, Hindus and Buddhists respected and revered one another. Moreover, the two traditions have for centuries shared important "points of resemblance," including their doctrines of karma, reincarnation, and "the *summum bonum* of Nirvana-Moksha."[15]

Finally, Olcott appealed in his lecture to nascent Indian nationalism. Referring to the apocryphal declaration of Mary I of England that should her chest be opened upon her death, inscribed upon her heart would be the name "Calais," Olcott averred that the sacred name etched upon his heart was neither "Buddha" nor "Buddhist" but "India."[16] This was a strange statement for a man who believed the boundaries of nation-states to be ephemeral. But Olcott was a practical man. If, as Indians, Buddhists and Hindus could learn to live together peacefully, then Indians they should be.

Maha Bodhi Society Resignation

As "The Kinship Between Hinduism and Buddhism" indicates, Olcott was acutely aware that the Maha Bodhi Society might flame a Buddhist-Hindu conflagration and thus threaten yet another of his quests for unity. He had attempted to mollify Hindu fears of Buddhist antagonism by conflating the Hindu and Buddhist traditions, but he refused to give up the Bodhgaya scheme. At least initially, Olcott supported Dharmapala's initiatives. He seemed willing to cede the reins of the international Buddhist movement to Dharmapala—to turn that portion of his life's work over to younger, indigenous reformers. As the 1890s wore on, however, Olcott gradually distanced himself from Dharmapala and his new society.

Olcott's troubles began in Bodhgaya, the planned center of the new Buddhist cosmos. Olcott and Dharmapala had originally planned to purchase the site surrounding the Bo tree temple. But they experienced problems raising the capital, and the resident Hindu expressed no interest in the funds they did collect, so the matter soon wound up in court.[17] Though a lawyer himself, Olcott was not comfortable with the adversarial nature of these proceedings, which plainly pitted Buddhists against Hindus. As the legal battle wore on and fundraising languished, it became clear that the Maha Bodhi Society could not, at least in the near future, either buy the site or win it in court. So Olcott improvised. Instead of purchasing the Bo tree temple, the Maha Bodhi Society would purchase a nearby home and convert it to a rest house for Buddhist pilgrims. Following Olcott's lead, Dharmapala negotiated successfully in the winter of 1895–96 for a home in the nearby town of Gaya. Olcott traveled there in February to close the deal, but when he saw the property he vetoed its purchase, and suggested that the M.B.S. buy a plot of land and build instead. Olcott's caprice irked Dharmapala, and the two men were locked in a power struggle that eventually issued in Olcott's resignation from the Maha Bodhi Society in May of 1896.[18]

Olcott and Dharmapala subsequently viewed each other with ambivalence, but they continued to cooperate. In December 1897, while he was working with Olcott and the Dravidian Buddhist Society to bring Buddhism to the untouchables of Madras, Dharmapala recommended that Olcott resign the Theosophical Society presidency, move to Sri Lanka, and concentrate on Buddhist work.[19] Although Olcott had seriously weighed this option previously himself, he was irritated by Dharmapala's suggestion. Dharmapala exhibited in Olcott's view "a marked tendency to fly kites, the strings of which persist in getting broken." He was, in short, a dreamer who possessed none of the administrative acumen necessary to transform an inspired idea into practical reality. Thus Olcott interpreted Dharmapala's hint as a selfish attempt to seize Olcott's organizational skills, to reverse the ill effects of his own managerial ineptitude. "Stript of all covering of fine talk," Olcott later remarked, "the idea was simply that I should pull his chestnuts out of the fire."[20]

Tensions between Olcott and Dharmapala increased in July of 1898 when Dharmapala moved to change the name of the "Colombo Buddhist Theosophical Society" to the "Colombo Buddhist Society." What prompted this move was the rise to prominence within the Theosophical Society of Annie Besant. Unlike Olcott, Besant described herself as a Hindu rather than a Buddhist. Moreover, she had been working overtly to revive Hinduism in India and had made some indiscreet remarks concerning the superiority of the Hindus' Vedas over the Buddhists' Tripitaka. To Dharmapala, Besant's indiscretions supported the conclusion that, despite Olcott's best intentions, the Theosophical Society was now partial to Hinduism and hostile to the Buddhist faith.[21] Olcott, of course, disagreed. Recalling, no doubt, his experience in America's Civil War, he denounced Dharmapala's motion to distance the Colombo B.T.S. from theosophy as an attempt at "secession," and informed the members of that organization that "while they were perfectly at liberty to expunge the word 'Theosophical' from the title of their Branch, if they did it I should immediately break my relation with them and never answer another appeal for help."[22] In the end, Olcott won the battle. Dharmapala's proposal was defeated, but the bitterness it engendered between the two men remained.

Religious Unity Rebuffed

If Dharmapala's falling away was all Olcott had to endure in the 1890s, he probably could have maintained, at least for a while, the plausibility of his self-representation as an *homme universel* existing above and beyond the fray of nationalistic and sectarian loyalties. But Dharmapala was not Olcott's only former friend who finally insisted that Olcott was a particular rather than a universal man. And he was not the only one to decide that Olcott's particular religion was ultimately irreconcilable with his own.

One of the first to make such a determination was William Q. Judge, one of the Theosophical Society's founding members and, for a time, one of Olcott's closest friends. There is no need to dwell on the Judge-Olcott battle here, since it has been scrutinized exhaustively in the theosophical literature.[23] What is significant for our purposes is that tensions between Olcott and Judge arose shortly after Blavatsky's death in 1891 and peaked three years later, after Olcott reneged on a promise to yield his executive authority to his friend. When Judge threatened Olcott's authority by announcing in 1894 that he was receiving Mahatma messages, Olcott attempted unsuccessfully to rein Judge in. Judge responded in April of 1895 by declaring the "complete and absolute autonomy" of the American section of the Theosophical Society and by reconstituting it under his own leadership as "the Theosophical Society in America"[24]

Both Olcott and Judge interpreted this split in light of American history. But while Judge likened his cause to that of the colonists in the American Revolution—and his group *was* both underrepresented and overtaxed by the Theosophical Society hierarchy—Olcott viewed Judge's dissent (as he had the criticisms of Dharmapala) as an "Act of Secession" aimed at destroying the theosophical "Union."[25] Olcott continued to hope that Judge's schismatics, like General Lee's Confederate rebels, would eventually return to the theosophical nation, but they never did. Much to Olcott's chagrin, the Theosophical Society in America survived Judge's death in 1896. Now centered in Pasadena, California, and known as the Theosophical Society International, it is the second-largest theosophical organization in the world. Although it produced its own splinter group, the United Lodge of Theosophists, in 1909, it survives today as one of three major theosophical organizations.

While Judge and his American followers were denouncing Olcott for not being theosophical enough, some Hindu reformers were excoriating Olcott for speaking with too strong of a theosophical accent—for attempting to introduce unwanted and unwarranted foreign elements (Buddhism included) into Hinduism. Among these Hindu critics, the most outspoken was Swami Vivekananda, the dashing Hindu reformer and Advaita Vedanta philosopher who dazzled American audiences at the World's Parliament of Religions in Chicago in 1893.[26] Shortly before departing for the United States and the World's Parliament, Vivekananda had solicited Olcott's support for his mission to the West on behalf of his nondualistic form of Hinduism. But Olcott had, for unknown reasons, rebuffed him. Vivekananda responded to the slight by pillorying Olcott and theosophy in, among other places, the *Hindu*. He began one of his critical articles by professing "regard and estimation and love" for many theosophists and by admitting that "it goes without saying that a certain amount of good work has been done to India by the [Theosophical] Society." But he went on to dismiss theosophy as an unwanted "Indian grafting of American Spiritualism—with only a few Sanskrit words taking the place of spiritualistic jargon—Mahatma missiles taking the place of ghostly raps and taps. . . . " Hindus, he added angrily, "do not stand in need of dead ghosts of Russians and Americans." They have "no need nor desire to import religion from the West."[27]

Advancing a similar argument was Orientalist Max Müller, who wrote a long letter to Olcott on June 10, 1893, criticizing the theosophists' imaginative constructions of both Hinduism and Buddhism. While Olcott was committed to "uplifting" those religious traditions, Müller accused Blavatsky and him of "lowering" both. Though he applauded Olcott for promoting the translation and publication of Oriental scriptures, he took aim at Blavatsky's esotericism. "There is nothing esoteric in Buddhism . . . Buddha protests against the very idea of keeping anything secret. There was much more of that esoteric teaching in Brahmanism. . . . But I do say that even in Brahmanism there is no such thing as an esoteric interpretation."[28]

In this way Müller, Vivekananda, and Judge chipped away at Olcott's self-representation as an *homme universel* by pointing out the particularities and peculiarities of Olcott's religious views and administrative actions. But it was left to Dharmapala to blast away any vestiges of Olcott's grand schemes of union. As the nineteenth century yielded to the twentieth,

Olcott and Dharmapala engaged in a struggle that continued even beyond the Colonel's grave.

A Declaration of Independence

While Vivekananda had denounced spiritualist elements in Olcott's Hinduism and Judge had decried nontheosophical elements in Olcott's theosophy, Dharmapala objected to Hindu elements in Olcott's creole Buddhism. In the spring of 1899, Dharmapala publicly proclaimed the failure of the Sinhalese Buddhist Revival and denounced the Theosophical Society for abandoning the Buddha's cause. Buddhism was declining in Ceylon, he complained, and he faulted the theosophists for emphasizing Hindu reform over Buddhist revivalism. "[In] the time of Mdme. Blavatsky, most of the theosophists embraced Buddhism and took *pansil*," Dharmapala argued, but "now the Theosophical Society upholds Hinduism as the supreme cult."[29]

Predictably, Olcott dismissed as "rubbish" Dharmapala's allegations that Buddhism was on the wane in Ceylon. Any setbacks that the Buddhist revival was experiencing he blamed on the administrative incompetence of Dharmapala, who was in his view "a reforming idealist" pursuing "impracticable, if not utopian" schemes. "A poor man of business," he exhibited a striking "ignorance of the business methods by which only can one carry on social reforms to practical results." How else to explain, Olcott asked, the failure of Dharmapala's Ethico-Psychological College and the simultaneous success of the Buddhist Theosophical Society colleges at Kandy and Galle? Or the failure of Dharmapala's *Journal of the Maha Bodhi Society* and the success of the theosophists' *Saravasi Sandarasa*?[30]

One might think that such rancor would have prompted each man to cut off relations with the other, but Dharmapala's ties to Olcott and Blavatsky ran deep. The co-founders of the Theosophical Society had, after all, brought him from Ceylon to Adyar while he was still a boy, and Olcott had introduced him to the wider world by taking him to, among other places, Japan. After his tremendous reception at the World's Parliament of Religions—a reception that lagged behind only the fawning over Vivekananda—Dharmapala no longer needed the support of his former mentor, but he wanted his blessing nonetheless.

In 1905 Dharmapala attempted for one last time to reconcile with Olcott. In a cordial letter punctuated by an affectionate salutation, Dharmapala asked Olcott for a number of favors. Could he find work in the Adyar

Library for a friend? Could he write an article on "The Future of Buddhism in India"? Could he provide a small bungalow for a monastery for Buddhists at Adyar? Could he assist in establishing a small Buddhist temple in Madras? Finally, and most importantly, might he honor an 1886 promise to make a home for Dharmapala at Adyar?[31]

Olcott responded to these entreaties angrily. After rebuffing the less important requests, he addressed the issue of Dharmapala's relocation to Adyar:

> Whatever I may have offered in 1886, you are now a totally different man. . . . In the old time you were entirely friendly to the Society and to myself, whereas of late years you have been very hostile to both. . . . As the society members all know this, and as you have no intention whatever of coming back again to the old standard of reverence for the Masters and desire to share in Their work, you may imagine what they would say about me if I took so bold an enemy into our family circle.[32]

Olcott concluded his rejoinder to his "enemy" by stating that while he continued to have "paternal" feelings for Dharmapala, he regarded him more as a "spoiled child" than a favorite son.[33]

This description of Dharmapala as "a spoiled child impatient of the advice of his elders" is intriguing, since the crux of Olcott's complaint seems to have been that his former protégé now exhibited all the unlikable traits of a child. But what irked Olcott most was neither Dharmapala's impracticality nor his inexperience—traits one normally associates with children—but his independence, his reluctance to follow advice. Thus, while Olcott's argument posited a developmental scheme from "docile boy pupil" to "vainglorious boy," his rhetoric pointed to a more typical transition from adolescence to adulthood.[34] The problem, in short, was not that Dharmapala remained a child but that he was becoming an adult, and as such was beginning to grow weary of Olcott's paternalism. This transformation might not have threatened Olcott if he had taken to heart his own admonition (uttered years earlier when he had first considered retirement) that "in the ordinary course of nature the young replace the old."[35] If he had been prepared to hand over the movements he had fostered to a new generation of leaders, Olcott might have interpreted the indisputable self-confidence not only of Dharmapala but also of Judge as evidence of adult competence rather than child-like vanity. But Olcott had no intention of stepping aside from either his theosophical or his Buddhist responsibilities.

A few weeks after sending his angry rejoinder, Olcott carried his battle with Dharmapala onto the pages of the *Theosophist*. There he attacked not only Dharmapala but the relic at the revered Temple of the Tooth in Kandy and, by implication, many if not most Sinhalese Buddhists. He described as "bigoted and ignorant" those Buddhists who judged the tooth genuine, and derided their thinking as ahistorical "nonsense." In a clear effort to demythologize the legends surrounding the Temple, Olcott argued that the original Buddha tooth was destroyed by the Portuguese in the sixteenth century, and the current relic had been fabricated from a deer's horn.[36]

Dharmapala responded to Olcott's call to arms with a trumpet blast of his own. In a letter to Olcott he complained that, while Blavatsky's Theosophical Society had pursued a friendly policy toward Buddhism, the society of Olcott and Besant (who, unlike Blavatsky, preferred Hinduism to Buddhism) was "only consolidating Krishna worship." Theosophy, in short, was unfit for Buddhism. "The planks of the Theosophical platform are not for the Buddhist," Dharmapala argued, "for Theosophy enunciates the existence of the Great Lifegiver, the fundamental identity of all souls with the Universal Soul, emanation of souls from the Central Logos, etc." Dharmapala then lamented that these heresies, which were in his view "absolutely opposed to Buddha's Doctrine," had rubbed off on Olcott, who in the fortieth edition of his *Buddhist Catechism* had answered several key questions "in the spirit of pantheism." Finally, citing Olcott's "most diabolical attack" on the Tooth Relic, Dharmapala broke with Olcott and the Theosophical Society. "As a Buddhist I value truth more than my life and life is worth more than limbs and limbs more than wealth," he wrote, "and as a Buddhist I sever my connection with the Pantheistic Theosophical Society."[37]

A day after mailing this declaration of independence, Dharmapala persuaded Sumangala to send a similar protest letter. Sidestepping Dharmapala's feud with Olcott, Sumangala's complaint concentrated on two issues: the heterodoxy of the fortieth edition of Olcott's *Catechism* and the impropriety of Olcott's statements regarding the Temple of the Tooth. Sumangala isolated seventeen answers in the catechism revision that were in his view "opposed to orthodox views of the Southern Church of Buddhism," and he demanded that Olcott either withdraw the edition from circulation or publicly admit its heterodoxy. Finally, he castigated Olcott for insulting the island's Buddhists—"Such an uncalled for attack we could expect only from an enemy of our religion"—and announced his own break with the Theosophical Society.[38]

Olcott dismissed Dharmapala's defection as "child's play," but he was deeply troubled about Sumangala's resignation. "If Sumangala turns against me," Olcott worried in a letter to a friend, "Dharmapala may stir up an angry feeling against me among the masses, so that I might think it time to sever my connection with the Island."[39] Hoping to avoid this outcome, Olcott worked to regain Sumangala's imprimatur for the *Catechism*. In 1906 and 1907 Olcott negotiated with him on a new edition that excised or edited the offensive questions and answers. Although Olcott did not capitulate entirely (he challenged as contrary to "science" and "common sense" the contention that Gautama Buddha was eighteen feet tall), he did manage to regain Sumangala's sanction for the catechism and to bring him back into friendly relations with his fellow theosophists.[40]

Olcott was unable to negotiate, however, a similar truce with Dharmapala. When push came to shove—and it did increasingly with these two men—Dharmapala was as intent on grasping power as Olcott was determined to retain it. Like the Christian missionaries of India who belied their indigenization theory by refusing to turn over their churches to native ministers, Olcott failed to fulfill earlier promises to yield the reins of the Buddhist movement to Asian reformers. And like the Indian Christians who faulted their American and British co-religionists for failing to keep their promises, Dharmapala insisted on taking charge. In the end neither side was satisfied. Olcott denounced Dharmapala's increasingly militant Sinhalese Buddhist nationalism as anti-Hindu and anti-theosophical, and Dharmapala criticized Olcott and his followers as "theosophical degenerates."[41]

It is difficult to account for all the sources of conflict between these two men, but at least one source of the mutual distrust is clear. Olcott and Dharmapala held two competing visions of the nature of religious commitment in a religiously pluralistic world. In Olcott's more liberal cosmos, his public theosophical vow to embrace all religions existed in a creative tension with his private Buddhist commitment to the Buddha, the Dharma, and the Sangha. For him, it was possible to be a Buddhist and a Hindu simultaneously. In Dharmapala's less irenic world, a "yes" to Buddhism implied a "no" to all other religious traditions. "Buddhism is absolutely opposed to the teachings of other existing religions," Dharmapala ultimately concluded, and "Theosophy is irreconcilable with Buddhism."[42]

As Olcott's life neared an end, his discussions with Judge, Vivekananda, and Dharmapala degenerated into shouting matches, and his visions of a "Universal Brotherhood of Humanity" and a "United Buddhist World" collapsed under the weight of mutual recriminations. The Theosophical Society was rent in two and, unlike his hero Lincoln, Olcott was unable to coax his "secessionists" back into his union. Finally, even the Sinhalese Buddhist Revival was itself on the verge of collapse, and the Maha Bodhi Society and the Dravidian Buddhist Society had proved more adept at raising the hackles of the Hindu community than at unifying the world's Buddhists. If

Olcott had been allotted more time, he might have been able to create out of this chaos some sort of order. But his time was running short.

The Fall

Throughout his adult life, Colonel Olcott had described theosophy as "the quintessence of common sense, and of scientific probability," and he considered himself both a reasonable and a practical man, a thinker swayed more by common sense than by superstition.[43] In this sense, he resembled during most of his Buddhist life what Thomas Tweed has described as the "rationalistic" American Buddhist sympathizer at least as much as he resembled its "esoteric" type.[44] When crises struck Olcott late in his life, however, he returned to esoteric comforts. As he struggled to make sense of the schism in his "Universal Brotherhood" and the splintering of his "United Buddhist World," he sought solace in occult speculations. He reported meetings with Helena Blavatsky in his dreams, and encounters with friends "on the Astral Plane."[45] With the help of a specialist in past-life regressions, he learned that in his previous incarnations he had lived in Atlantis and in Cuzco, and had inhabited the body of an Egyptian king and the form of the great Buddhist emperor Ashoka.[46] Finally, on a number of occasions Olcott turned to the prophesies of seers and seeresses. In an article on "The Coming Calamities," Olcott reported, on the basis of his reading of the Puranas, Nostradamus, and a number of contemporary prophets, that the calamitous end of the five-thousand year cycle of Kali Yoga was rapidly approaching. Europe, Olcott predicted, would fall first.[47] Olcott was, at least by most accounts, wrong about Europe, but he was prescient about a "coming calamity."

Olcott made his last trip to the West in the spring of 1906. In London he adjudicated yet another theosophical crisis, which resulted in the resignation of the Anglican cleric turned theosophical Buddhist, Charles W. Leadbeater.[48] And in New York he visited with family members before sailing one final time for his adopted homeland of India. While on board the *Cretic* bound for Genoa in October 1906, Olcott suffered at the age of seventy-four a serious accident. Catching his shoe on the top of a set of stairs, he fell fourteen steps to the bottom of the flight. Olcott considered it a miracle that he did not break his neck, but the accident shattered his health nonetheless. He convalesced in his stateroom for six days, then spent twenty-eight days in a hospital in Genoa before continuing his trek to Adyar.

While crossing the Arabian Sea, Olcott added to his injuries a bronchial cold. Upon his arrival in Ceylon in November, he was diagnosed as "dangerously ill with heart disease" and spent the next two weeks slipping in and out of delirium in a Colombo nursing home. His physicians judged him unfit for travel but he insisted on returning to his Indian home. Finally he arrived at Adyar on December 11, but his health only worsened. From January 14 to February 11, he was unable to sleep for more than one hour at a time. His mind wandered, and he began to hallucinate. According to his friends, however, he remained both patient and courageous and maintained his "gentle gaiety."[49]

One reason for Olcott's good cheer was his assurance that his beloved Mahatmas were once again at his bedside. As he lay in a state between delirium and death in January and February of 1907, he reported numerous visitations of the Masters. In fact, these visits were so frequent that Olcott was reminded of the "old days in N.Y. when they came so often through H.P.B."[50] These sages comforted Olcott, counseled him about theosophical controversies, instructed him not to resign, and informed him that they had tapped Annie Besant as his successor. The Masters also used the now charismatic Olcott—for the first and only time in his life—as a vehicle for transmitting a message to the Theosophical Society. One last call for unity, this entreaty reads like an encapsulation of Olcott's life-effort to construct unity out of diversity. It was, as such, his last and final wish:

> Cease from such turmoil and strife, and from causing such disturbance in the Unity of Brotherhood, and thus weakening its strength; but instead work together in harmony, to fit yourselves to be useful instruments to aid us, instead of impeding our work. . . . Cease rushing headlong into strife, or taking part in dissensions! Hold together in brotherly love, since you are part of the Great Universal Self. Are you not striving against yourselves? Are not your Brother's sins your own? Peace! Trust in us.[51]

In accordance with his Masters' wishes—wishes which he admitted were also his own—Olcott addressed an open letter to the Theosophical Society naming Annie Besant his successor.[52] He also addressed a private farewell to his closest friends:

> Good-bye, dear good old friends. The Blessed ones have come to take me home. They have all been here—we all saw them, and They say my life is done. They are waiting for me, H.P.B. is with them and I have seen and spoken with her. . . . What a glorious thing it is to die among the blessed on earth and the Thrice Blessed above.[53]

On February 5, Olcott affirmed his allegiances to Buddhism and theosophy as well as his roots in American Protestant notions of eternal peace in heaven when he called on the Buddha and his Masters "to take him to the Higher Planes to rest." But rest did not come until he slipped into unconsciousness one week later. On February 17, 1907, Colonel Olcott finally passed, as he might have said, into the universal Akasha. According to Annie Besant, Blavatsky officiated "in astral presence" at Olcott's death. "The cord is broken," H.P.B. reportedly declared, and Olcott was free.[54]

Last Rites

Friends and admirers carried Olcott's body on a bier on the afternoon of February 17 to the main hall at Theosophical Society headquarters in Adyar. On the south side of the hall a statue of Helena Blavatsky lorded over the proceedings, and to the east tables displaying the scriptures of Zoroastrians, Hindus, Buddhists, Christians, Muslims, Sikhs, and Jains defined the room as a sacred space to all the world's believers. In the center of this theosophical space lay Olcott's body, encircled by a ring of flowers and draped with twin symbols of his personal allegiances: the Buddhist flag and America's "Old Glory."[55]

Admirers filed past the body and offered flowers until only Olcott's white head and beard remained visible. A memorial liturgy then began with Buddhists chanting Pali sutras on life's transiency. A Buddhist praised Olcott's contributions to Buddhism. He must have been Olcott's sort of creole Buddhist, however, because he added to his praise a prayer that Olcott he would "attain to heaven without any evil obstacles." After two Brahmins chanted verses in Sanskrit from a sacred book, one recognized Olcott's contributions to the Indian Renaissance, praising him for initiating a Sanskrit and Hindu revival in India. "May the Rishis of Aryavarta," he prayed, "continue to grant Their protection to the cause to which he was so deeply attached and which he so nobly served." Next, a Parsee read from the Avesta and a Christian from the Book of Wisdom, and each praised Olcott in turn. Finally, Annie Besant delivered a eulogy and the service ended with a reading of another sacred text, a final message from the disembodied spirit of the dead, one last poignant plea from Olcott for progress toward interreligious unity:

> To my beloved brothers in the physical body: I bid you all farewell. In memory of me, carry on the grand work of proclaiming and living the Brotherhood of Religions.
>
> To my beloved Brothers on the higher planes: I greet and come to you, and implore you to help me to impress all men on earth that "There is no Religion higher than Truth," and that in the Brotherhood of Religions lie the peace and progress of humanity.[56]

The White Buddhist

Six Hindus and four Buddhists then lifted the bier and carried it to a cremation site near the banks of the Adyar River. Clothed with relics of the land of his birth and the faith of his adoption, Olcott's body was placed on a sandalwood pyre. The pyre was lit, and Olcott's body met the same end that Baron de Palm's famous corpse had met decades earlier.

Following Blavatsky's death, Olcott had seen to it that a portion of her ashes made their way to the United States. But none of Olcott's remains found a resting place in America. On the morning after his cremation, friends gathered the ashes and deposited them in two urns. One they placed in a locked wooden box, destined for a pilgrimage to Benares where its contents would be scattered (as had some of Blavatsky's remains) across the sacred Ganges. The other they paraded down to the sea and cast upon the waves of the Indian Ocean. In death, at least, Olcott's fidelity to Aryavarta was complete.

Shortly after his funeral, a statue of Colonel Olcott was placed next to that of Helena Blavatsky in the main hall of the theosophical headquarters in Adyar. Across the ocean in Ceylon, a bust of the "White Buddhist" was commissioned for the monastery in Galle, where Olcott and Blavatsky had first taken Pansil and publicly professed themselves Buddhists. With such acts of theosophical and Buddhist commemoration, the life of Colonel Henry Steel Olcott began its transmigration into legend.

As news of Olcott's passing made its way across Adam's Bridge to Ceylon and across the oceans to the United States, Olcott's acquaintances attempted to sum up his life. Friends praised him, and most of his enemies found something good to say. But such niceties escaped Dharmapala, who continued to denounce his former mentor as a wolf in sheep's clothing and his creole faith as bastardized Buddhism. "Although he became a Buddhist he does not seem to have grasped the fundamentals of Buddhism," Dharmapala complained. "To say that all religions have a common foundation only shows the ignorance of the speaker . . . Dharma alone is supreme to the Buddhist."[57]

Conclusion

Since Olcott's death in 1907, supporters and opponents alike have attempted to sum up his life. Typically those summations have hinged on the contentious question of the authenticity of the spiritual phenomena attributed to Helena Blavatsky. Those who judge those phenomena genuine have tended to praise Olcott as the organizational genius who adroitly built on the foundation of her charisma a towering international society devoted to unlocking the secrets of occult science, while those who see her phenomena as crafty parlor-room shenanigans have typically denounced him as a sinister accomplice or credulous dupe. Although this book has in no way sidestepped the conflicts that marked Olcott's association with Blavatsky, it has not weighed in on the question of her occult powers and has, as a result, deliberately left open the issue of Olcott's complicity in any alleged trickery. But the book has not avoided judgments entirely. Some synthesis of those judgments may be in order here.

The first such judgment is that Olcott's Asian odyssey was by many standards a striking success. Although the Theosophical Society languished in Bombay as it had in New York, it thrived after its 1882 move to Adyar, especially among English-speaking British and Indian elites. And Olcott was the person who guided the organization through a myriad of embarrassing controversies, financial problems, and changes of direction with the finesse of a master administrator. In the year of Olcott's death, the organization claimed 655 branches scattered across the globe.[1] Perhaps the strongest evidence of Olcott's theosophical successes came from his missionary critics. According to one such critic, the Theosophical Society gathered "a tremendous following" in the last two decades of the nineteenth century. "Even Englishmen of the highest social standing subscribed to their society, and Hindus with a British education were soon in a state bordering intoxication with regard to the new doctrines." That same missionary admitted reluctantly that at the time of Olcott's death the Theosophical Society had "a certain importance in Indian affairs."[2]

Olcott's educational efforts in Ceylon were also remarkably successful. Upon his arrival on the island in 1880 there were four Buddhist schools. But in 1907 an administrative report from the Director of Public Instruction in Ceylon counted over 20,000 students attending 183 grant-in-aid Buddhist schools.[3] Not surprisingly, Olcott's brand of Buddhism spread as these schools multiplied. According to one observer, Olcott's creole Buddhism was taught so effectively in Ceylon's Buddhist schools that it "diffused into the society and became the basic religious ideology of the educated Buddhist bourgeoisie."[4] Around the turn of the century, a missionary working on the island of Ceylon expressed amazement at how strong Buddhist opposition to Christianity remained in some quarters. The marks of Olcott's imitative method were everywhere:

> You commonly now find Buddhist lay preachers standing at street-corners ... plainly an adoption of our methods; Buddhist schools, on the model of our grant-in-aid schools, springing up everywhere ... Buddhist Sunday-schools, taught from modern Buddhist catechisms ... and Buddhist carols chime in our ears.[5]

Despite claims that Olcott initiated the Sinhalese Buddhist Revival, his connection with the movement was, as he himself recognized, neither as originator (credit Mohottivatte Gunananda) nor as culminator (credit Anagarika Dharmapala) but as organizer and articulator. It was Olcott who agitated for Buddhist civil rights before British colonial administrators, and who gave the revival its organizational shape by founding voluntary associations, publishing and distributing tracts, and, perhaps most important, establishing schools. It was he who articulated most eloquently the "Protestant Buddhism" synthesis. The most Protestant of all early "Protestant Buddhists," Olcott was a culture broker with one foot planted in traditional Sinhalese Buddhism and the other in liberal American Protestantism. He was the man who took these two sources, along with other key influences such as theosophy, academic Orientalism, and metropolitan gentility, and transformed them into a creole language that native speakers of both Buddhism and Protestantism could understand.

Finally, Olcott succeeded in influencing Asian religious traditions other than Buddhism. Not simply a reformer of Buddhism, he was, as one of his contemporaries noted, a "Reformer of Religions."[6] Among Hindus, he founded schools for untouchables, promoted a Sanskrit revival, established Hindu Boys' Associations, published Hindu tracts and magazines, and thus contributed to what scholars have described as the Indian Renaissance. And along the way he somehow found time to attempt to reform Zoroastrianism and even Islam as well.

Given this résumé, it is undoubtedly true, as Olcott once speculated, that his Puritan ancestors "would have made short work of their descendant, his colleagues, and their Theosophical Society, if we had come within reach."[7] But if Olcott was no orthodox Puritan, he was no orthodox Buddhist either.

And so Olcott has been portrayed here not as an outsider in the story of nineteenth-century American religion but as someone who stood near, if not in, the liberal Protestant mainstream. Among the influences that Olcott carried with him on his trek from America to Asia were an unflagging commitment to reform and a fervent desire to resolve diversity into unity. Olcott's commitment to reform would become evident as he worked through various means to "uplift" Hindu and Buddhist schoolchildren. But that commitment was also evident in his earlier struggle to "uplift" spiritualism into a higher, theosophical synthesis. Olcott's quest for unity also played itself out not only in Asia, in attempts to construct a "United Buddhist World," a "National Samaj of Aryavarta," and a "Universal Brotherhood of Humanity," but also in America in efforts to end slavery and to reconcile northerners and southerners after the Civil War. In fact, it may be the case that the crucible in which Olcott's lifelong commitment to constructing unity through reform was forged was the Civil War. That struggle's carnage convinced many in Olcott's generation to commit their lives to overcoming antagonisms of region, gender, race, and religion, and it no doubt played a part in Olcott's decision to invoke the motto of the United States (*E Pluribus Unum*—out of many, one) as a mantra of sorts for all his Asian work.

Some will view this argument that the continuities between Olcott's American and Asian lives outweigh the discontinuities as an attempt to demean the man and thus to make light of his considerable accomplishments. But that is not the intention here, since it is my conviction that Olcott was not at all unusual in acting as a culture broker standing between two very different cultural and religious systems. Specialists in African American religion have been aware for some time that West African slaves who converted to Protestantism in the American South imported elements of their inherited religions into the faith they adopted, and some have recognized the subsequent religious ideas and actions of African American Protestants as religious creations as novel, for example, as the Gullah language spoken by blacks in the South Carolina lowcountry.[8] The intent of these scholars is, of course, not to chastise African Americans for bastardizing Protestantism or for failing to become "real" Protestants but, on the contrary, to note their creativity and thus their contributions to American religious history. With Olcott my intent has been similar.

Still, Olcott's life does present itself to contemporary readers as a cautionary tale. One of the most intriguing aspects of Olcott's adult life in Asia was his ambitious attempt to construct himself as a cultural and religious everyman or *homme universel.* Nearly 2000 years before Olcott was born, the Christian apostle Paul had boasted of his ability to tailor his message to his audiences—to speak as a Jew to the Jews and as a Greek to the Greeks. But Olcott went much further. Two decades before his death, at the Theosophical Society's 1885 convention, Olcott noted that while other convention speakers had represented one country, one religion, one nationality, he alone represented all. Though born in the United States and baptized a Presbyterian, he was only superficially American and Protestant. Inside he was Indian—"a Hindu with white skin."[9] Olcott made similar representations while in Ceylon regarding his essentially Buddhist nature. And before Zoroastrian and Islamic audiences he presented himself again as a cultural and religious chameleon who could become a Parsee or a Muslim, depending on his surroundings. On at least one extraordinary occasion, Olcott also represented himself as a Jew. After dressing up in what he described as "a Jewish costume," he paraded past a neighboring Jewish family. "All thought me a Jerusalem rabbi," his diary proudly notes, "and an octogenarian Jew present saluted me as such!"[10] Thus Olcott contended in the presence of Hindus, Buddhists, Parsees, Muslims, and even Jews that his Asian adulthood had utterly erased both the familiarity of his American Protestant youth and the foreignness of his Asian adulthood—that he had, in effect, become one of them.[11]

Skeptics, of course, questioned Olcott's alchemy. Discerning what I have referred to as the creole nature of his adult faith, they saw both his Asianization and his dechristianization as less than complete. Regarding his conversion to Buddhism, Governor of Ceylon Arthur Gordon noted Olcott's tendency to overestimate his understanding of Buddhist doctrines and affairs. Other colonial administrators viewed Olcott as an odd hybrid of eastern and western influences—a "neo Buddhist" and an "oriental Calvinist."[12] One Christian missionary decried Olcott's faith as "mongrel Buddhism" and Mark Twain called it "Blavatsky-Buddhism."[13] But in the end it was a Sinhalese Buddhist (Anagarika Dharmapala) who questioned most stridently Olcott's Buddhist credentials just as it fell upon Hindus (Dayanand Saraswati and Swami Vivekananda) to denounce most vociferously Olcott's claim to be "a Hindu with white skin."

One way of understanding this perhaps inevitable resistance is to recall that both the Buddhism and the Hinduism that Olcott imaginatively constructed were creole faiths. When Buddhist and Hindu reformers first heard Olcott speaking about their religious traditions, they recognized that he was, in a word, "speaking their language." His lexicon sounded both familiar and friendly. Here, after all, was a white man denouncing missionary claims of Christian superiority and championing the wisdom of the Hindu and Buddhist scriptures. But after extended interaction, Dharmapala, Saraswati, Vivekananda, and others began to attend to the Protestant grammar of Olcott's creolizations and the theosophical accent with which he articulated them. Gradually they began to discern in Olcott's faith unwanted American, Protestant, and theosophical retentions. The Colonel had promised to come to Asia as a humble student, to listen to and learn from Buddhist monks and Hindu gurus. But shortly after his arrival in Asia he set himself up as a teacher, and began chastising monks and gurus alike for being ignorant of their own traditions. Perhaps because of his stated belief that Indians were not fit to rule India, he reneged on promises to yield the reins of many of his initiatives to indigenous reformers. In the end, many of Olcott's former friends recognized that he was not really "speaking their language" (at least not with the fluency of a native) and rejected his influence as both foreign and unwanted.

In an attempt to make sense both of the initial attraction of Hindu and Buddhist reformers to Olcott and their eventual resistance, it may be helpful to discern that the nineteenth-century encounter of Americans with the religions of the East involved not one but two overlapping contests. The first of these contests was the well-known battle between Christianity and the religions of Asia. In this contest Olcott and American sympathizers who preceded and followed him—Ralph Waldo Emerson, Henry Thoreau, William Sturgis Bigelow, Ernest Fenollosa, Lafcadio Hearn, e.g.—were clearly on the side of Asian religions, while Christian missionaries and the vast majority of British colonial administrators weighed in for Christianity and against the Orient's "heathen" traditions. It was the side Olcott took in this first battle that commended him, at least initially, to Asian reformers and that transformed his speeches in Ceylon, India, Burma, and Japan into mass spectacles.

Overlapping this well-documented contest, however, was a more subtle and perhaps more significant contest for the right to define Asian religions and the right to determine what Ceylon and India were to become. And here Olcott stood alongside rather than against most Christian missionaries, a living example of the odd persistence of both the Puritan errand to the New World and the nineteenth-century American missionary errand to the world. Long before Olcott first went to India or Ceylon, Christian missionaries had sent back to their boards reports describing the strange customs and defining the curious beliefs of the "heathen." Now Olcott mimicked the missionaries by publishing reports in the pages of the *Theosophist* that blasted both popular rites and pundits' precepts. When it came to constructing his understanding of Buddhism, for example, Olcott relied not on the living example of Asian Buddhists but on the scholarly works of academic Orientalists, most of whom were committed Christians. This key decision to attend to the bookish Buddhism of Orientalists rather than the lived Buddhism of Buddhists tilted Olcott's imaginative construction of Buddhism in a decidedly Protestant direction.

Drawing on a primitivist bias that defined a religion in terms of the ideas and practices of its earliest adherents and a textualist bias that defined a religion in terms of its scriptures, Olcott came to the striking conclusion that there was nary a "real" Buddhist to be found in Ceylon. Rather than interpreting the cognitive dissonance between his Buddhism and the Buddhism of the Sinhalese as evidence of his own theoretical shortcomings, Olcott chastised his Buddhist contemporaries for bastardizing the pure dharma of ancient Buddhism and deviating from what was clearly a Buddhist "tradition" of his own invention. Convinced that virtually everyone on the island was ignorant of Buddhism, he set about to "uplift" its Buddhists from a polluted to a purified faith. In this way Olcott joined his despised missionaries in assuming not only the right to define the religious traditions he encountered but also the responsibility to "uplift" his interlocutors from false to true religion. Therefore, despite his conversion to Buddhism and his love of India, Olcott participated along with many Christian missionaries in what Ashis Nandy has referred to as "the colonialization of consciousness."[14] His aim was to "civilize" his Asian acquaintances and the "civilization" he aimed to impart was his own. It was not without reason, therefore, that Olcott claimed that he and his society exerted a "wholesome and conservative influence upon the natives."[15] In fact, because of his adoption of Buddhism and his friendliness toward Hinduism and other Asian faiths, Olcott may have been a more effective "civilizer" of South Asia than his missionary contemporaries. Certainly it is the case that some missionaries were far more wary than Olcott about the dangers of cultural imposition.[16]

Friends of Olcott will undoubtedly detect some harshness in this final lesson—this judgment of a man who devoted his adult life to fostering religious tolerance and to attempting to create out of the dizzying diversity of human cultures a "Universal Brotherhood of Humanity." But Olcott's undoubtedly laudable intentions are not at issue here. What is under scrutiny are his actions. In a provocative book entitled *The Conquest of America* (1984), Tzvetan Todorov has argued persuasively that liberal theories of the equality of human beings can function as efficiently for colonial and imperialistic purposes as hierarchical theories of inequality. It is not controversial, he argues, that theories that begin by underscoring the differences between people of two cultures almost inevitably lapse into theories of superiority and inferiority that legitimate the enslavement or control of the inferior "other" by the superior "self." What is less widely recognized, however, is that liberal theories that begin by postulating the equality of two cultures can lapse equally readily into equally dangerous theories of identity in which the colonizer projects his or her values on the ostensibly equal "other" and thus legitimates a hostile assimilationism. Todorov's analysis is eerily relevant to Olcott's case.[17]

Olcott plainly eschewed religiously intolerant theories that would label Asians as inferior to westerners and Asian religions as inferior to Christianity. He refused, in short, to damn non-Christians to hell or to a perpetually lower level of "civilization." But his theory postulated not only the fundamental equality of religions but also their identity. Although this theory led Olcott away from the facile sorts of denunciations of Asians uttered by some Christian missionaries, it made it difficult for him to account for the significant cultural and religious differences he inevitably encountered between himself and his Asian friends. So when Olcott encountered differences between, for example, his creole Buddhism and the Buddhisms of Ceylon, his liberal theory of the equality of religions allowed him only two rather primitive responses: either to deny the differences themselves, or to eradicate those differences by forcing the Buddhists of the island to conform with the Buddhism of his invention. More often than not, Olcott took the latter course, insisting, in Todorov's terms, on a forced assimilationism. Rather than modifying his representations of Buddhism to match the Buddhism of the Sinhalese, he tackled the much more difficult task of modifying their beliefs and behaviors to match his own creole faith. Thus Olcott too engaged in what missionaries described as "fine spiritual imperialism."[18] The tragedy of this response is that it prevented Olcott from engaging in genuine dialogue with Asian religious reformers.[19]

To say that Olcott failed to engage in genuine dialogue does not mean that he did not talk with his Asian friends. In fact, one of the singular achievements of Olcott's adult life is that he was in all likelihood the first American personally to engage in friendly discussions with Zoroastrians, Muslims, Hindus, Buddhists, and Christians about their respective faiths. He succeeded, moreover, not simply in talking but in effecting historic East-West alliances with individuals such as Dayanand Saraswati and Anagarika Dharmapala and with voluntary associations such as the Arya Samaj. But the most notable of Olcott's interreligious and intercultural discussions ended in enmity, and his most notable affiliations in schisms. Both Saraswati and Dharmapala justified their splits with Olcott intellectually, reasoning that in the last analysis he didn't truly understand their traditions. But the splits were undoubtedly also politically motivated. Saraswati, Dharmapala, Vivekananda, and others recognized, in short, that Olcott was using his power and privilege as a westerner in Asia to make his imaginative constructions of Buddhism and Hinduism seem, to borrow a term from anthropologist Clifford Geertz, "uniquely realistic."[20] Though these Asian reformers initially believed that Olcott would wield his considerable power to help their causes, they decided in the end that his work was doing little to either extend the authority of their religions and cultures or to undermine the religious and cultural authority of the colonists. So eventually they resisted.

Although Olcott should be criticized for failing to enter into genuine dialogue with his Asian friends, it should be noted that some of his Asian friends were also poor dialogue partners. Dharmapala, who was initially attracted to the Theosophical Society because of the contention of many of its members that "All Religions Are True," drifted, especially after his break with Olcott, in the direction of a militant Sinhalese chauvinism, denouncing not only Olcott's liberalism but also virtually all Hindus as polluted enemies of the Buddha's pure dharma. So if Olcott can be chastened for providing subtle legitimation for British rule, Dharmapala should be criticized for stoking the fires of ethnic and religious hatred that erupted so violently between the Hindu Tamils and the Buddhist Sinhalese in Sri Lanka in the 1980s. At least on this score, Olcott's hands are clean.

Olcott must also be admired for his sheer audacity. Especially from the perspective of postmodernism, Olcott's grand reinterpretation of the American imperative to fashion "out of many, one" appears first ludicrous and then admirably audacious. One cannot help applauding Olcott, even as he applauded his Puritan forebears, for his evident sincerity, for remaining true, come what may, to his convictions. If one of the hallmarks of moderns was their willingness to dream bold dreams and to work fiercely to turn them into realities, then Olcott was one of the modern age's boldest dreamers and fiercest workers. Engaged in a lifelong quest for unities of many stripes, Olcott not only imagined a "United Buddhist World," a "National Samaj of Aryavarta," and a "Universal Brotherhood of Humanity," he struggled mightily to establish each of them in history. In fact, it is the depth of Olcott's commitment to unities of many kinds and the extent to which he labored to construct them that make his failures so poignant. To men of lesser imagination the splintering of the Theosophical Society or the defection of Dharmapala might have been shrugged off as understandable if not inevitable. But Olcott must have received these events as headlong assaults on his dreams.

Conclusion

There are, I trust, numerous scholarly implications to draw from this interpretation of Olcott's life. Specialists in American religious history may justifiably conclude after considering Olcott's Asian work that it is possible to affirm *both* the thesis that American religion was becoming more pluralistic in the last quarter of the nineteenth century *and* the argument that Protestant influence remained strong in that period. This concatenation of two seemingly antithetical theses is possible, of course, only if Olcott's experience is to some extent generalizable. But Olcott's case suggests at least the possibility that Protestant authority extended beyond the lives of individual Protestants and Protestant denominations into non-Protestant individuals and institutions. The power that Protestantism continued to wield in Olcott's case was the power to define on its own terms both "religion" in general and particular instances of "religion" (including Buddhism and Hinduism). This power worked not so much by making Asians Protestants as by Protestantizing Asian religions. And it was this power that gave rise, for example, to Olcott's assumption that the truth of Buddhism and Hinduism lay in their ancient sutras and to his attempts to create Buddhist and Hindu Sunday Schools. It surfaced, moreover, in America around the turn of the century with the appearance of institutions such as the Young Men's Buddhist Association and publications such as the *Imitation of Buddha*, and it continues to wield influence today.

If Olcott's life muddies the waters regarding the rise of religious pluralism and the supposedly concomitant decline of Protestant influence, it also problematizes the now-popular enterprise of interreligious dialogue. In the last analysis what is remarkable about Olcott's Asian sojourn is not how much he understood Asians and their religions but how much he misunderstood them (and they, him). Again one is tempted to criticize Olcott for his failure to live up to his initial promise to sit humbly at the feet of Asian teachers and to learn what their religious traditions had to teach, but it may make more sense to conclude that the sort of misunderstanding that Olcott exhibited in Asia may be the expected rather than the unexpected outcome of interreligious encounters. To put it another way, it may be inevitable that individuals are going to capitalize on the ambiguity that lies at the core of all world religions by bending the texts and rituals of those traditions in their own peculiar direction—by conforming the lexicon of those religions to their own grammar and by speaking the resulting creole language in their own particular accent.

Finally, Olcott's life calls into question simplistic models of religious conversion, especially in situations of crosscultural contact. Although it is no doubt possible for Protestants to convert to Buddhism and for Buddhists to convert to Protestantism, it would seem to be the case (if Olcott is at all representative) that such conversions are rarely, if ever, utterly complete. Olcott's inability to separate his adopted religion from his inherited culture suggests, in short, that the notion that individuals can convert *from* some hypostatic religious tradition *to* another equally hypostatic one may be ill-conceived. Not unlike physicists observing quantum mechanical experiments, converts clearly alter the religious traditions they embrace even as they are embracing them. To put it another way, religious converts are not exempt from the "Christ and culture" dilemma so well known to historians of American Protestant missions. If missionaries tend to persist, frequently unwittingly, in the grammars of their home culture even as they preach the Christian gospel, converts also tend to persist in their inherited grammars even as they adopt a new religious lexicon. Crosscultural religious conversions may, in the parlance of creolization theory, typically involve lexical rather than grammatical shifts. Just as it is easier to learn the words of a foreign language, so is it simpler to adopt the rhetoric and the forms of the rituals of a foreign religious tradition. What is difficult is to change one's deep-structure assumptions—the grammar of one's faith.

Conversion may be the engine, therefore, not only of individual religious transformation but of religious change in society. If converts typically retain the grammar of their previous faith even as they adopt the lexicon of a new tradition, the result of their synthesis is bound either to be creative, resulting, in all cases, in religious and cultural transformations and, in some cases, in wholly new creole religious and cultural forms. Hindu conversions to Protestantism may result, therefore, not only in the Protestantization of India but also in the Indianization and Hinduization of Protestantism. And American Protestant conversions to Buddhism may result in both the Buddhistization of America and the Americanization and Protestantism of Buddhism. Olcott's life points, therefore, not only to the complexity of Protestant Buddhism in colonial Ceylon and modern Sri Lanka but also to the inevitability and multiplicity of creolizations in American religious history.

Abbreviations

ABB	Arya Bala Bodhini
BL	*Banner of Light*
CO	Colonial Office Records, Public Records Office, London
Graphic	*New York Daily Graphic*
HSOC	Henry Steel Olcott Correspondence, Theosophical Society Archives, Adyar, Madras, India
HSOD	Henry Steel Olcott Diary, Theosophical Society Archives, Adyar, Madras, India
JMBS	*Journal of the Maha Bodhi Society*
MCBL	The Manuscript Collections, British Library, London
ODL	Henry Steel Olcott, *Old Diary Leaves: The History of the Theosophical Society,* 6 vols., 1895–1935 (reprinted Adyar, India: Theosophical Publishing House, 1974–75)
PRO	Public Records Office, London
SS	*Spiritual Scientist*
ST	*Spiritual Telegraph*
Sun	*New York Sun*
Tribune	*New York Tribune*
TSA	Theosophical Society Archives, Adyar, Madras, India

Notes

Introduction

1. "Buddhist Homage for an American," *New York Herald Tribune* (February 18, 1962) 2.

2. Olcott was, as far as I have been able to determine, the first American of European ancestry to undergo a Buddhist initiation rite. Nineteenth-century Chinese and Japanese immigrants to the U.S. brought their religious traditions with them, and as early as 1856 there were reports from San Francisco that "Buddhism has been formally inaugurated on American soil" ("Buddhism," *ST* 5.13 [July 26, 1856] 103). Spiritualist periodicals, moreover, published in the 1870s a number of articles on Buddhist topics, signed pseudonymously "Buddha" or "A Buddhist." As Thomas Tweed notes in *The American Encounter with Buddhism, 1844–1912: Victorian Culture and the Limits of Descent* (Bloomington: Indiana University Press, 1991), Dyer Daniel Lum was probably the first non-Asian American to proclaim himself a Buddhist, but he did not participate in any formal rite affirming that affiliation (23, 39). Ernest Fenollosa and William Sturgis Bigelow both formally embraced the precepts of Tendai Buddhism in Japan in 1885, but that was five years after Olcott first recited the Theravada Buddhist precepts in Ceylon in 1880.

3. Dudley Senanayaka, quoted in Saddhamangala Karunaratne, ed., *Olcott Commemoration Volume* (1967) 7. Olcott is described as a bodhisattva in Buddhadasa P. Kirthisinghe, "Henry Steel Olcott Is a Bodhisattva," *Modern Review* 140.3 (October 1976) 201–206; and "Tribute to Olcott," *Davasa* (February 20, 1962). For Olcott as Ashoka, see HSOD, September 17, 1895; and for Olcott as the Buddha, see HSOD, October 17, 1904.

4. "Olcott and Miller," *New York Times* (October 18, 1871) 4:5; "Harmless but Incurable Col. Olcott," *New York Times* (December 29, 1895) 27:4.

5. Dumas Malone, ed., *Dictionary of American Biography* (New York: Scribner's, 1934) 14.10.

6. The hint regarding Olcott's importance comes in a discussion of Paul Carus, a German-American Buddhist popularizer, in Thomas Tweed, *The American Encounter with Buddhism*, 65 (Tweed describes Carus as similarly influential). Those who have called for scholarly attention to Olcott include Buddhologist Michael M. Ames who has lamented that "an objective assessment of Olcott's contributions towards, and the extent to which he influenced the directions of the Buddhist resurgence [in Sri Lanka], has yet to be made" ("Westernization or Modernization: The Case of Sinhalese Buddhism," *Social Compass* 20.2 [1973] 139–70), and Americanist Carl T. Jackson, who has twice specifically requested a critical biography of Olcott ("The Influence of Asia upon American Thought: A Bibliographic Essay," *American Studies International* 22.1 [1984] 3–31; and *The Oriental Religions and American Thought: Nineteenth Century Explorations* [Westport: Greenwood, 1981] 174).

7. Despite the recent interest in "outsiders" in American religion, neither Olcott nor theosophy have received much scholarly scrutiny. The only extant biog-

raphy of Olcott—Howard Murphet, *Hammer on the Mountain: Life of Henry Steel Olcott (1832–1907)* (Wheaton, IL: Theosophical Publishing House, 1972), revised as *Yankee Beacon of Buddhist Light: The Life of Colonel Henry S. Olcott* (Wheaton, IL: Quest, 1988)—is a hagiographic, insider's account. The Theosophical Society does receive careful, if divided, attention in Mary Farrell Bednarowski, *New Religions and the Theological Imagination in America* (Bloomington: Indiana University Press, 1989); Robert Ellwood, *Alternative Altars: Unconventional and Eastern Spiritualism in America* (Chicago: University of Chicago Press, 1979); Rick Fields, *How the Swans Came to the Lake: A Narrative History of Buddhism in America* (Boulder: Shambala, 1981); and Carl T. Jackson, *The Oriental Religions and American Thought.* The only critical, scholarly history of the Theosophical Society is Bruce F. Campbell, *Ancient Wisdom Revived: A History of the Theosophical Movement* (Berkeley: University of California Press, 1980), but Michael Gomes' *The Dawning of the Theosophical Movement* (Wheaton, IL: Quest, 1987) is also helpful.

8. HSOD, July 20, 1891.

9. Happily, Olcott's theosophical labors have been narrated exhaustively in a string of works by theosophical researchers. Of these, the most helpful is Olcott's own *Old Diary Leaves: The History of the Theosophical Society* (6 vols.; New York: Putnam's: 1895–1935).

10. I am borrowing here from the postmodernist theorist Jean-François Lyotard, who in *The Postmodern Condition: Report on Knowledge,* trans. Geoff Bennington and Brian Massumi (Minneapolis: University of Minnesota Press, 1984) differentiates between modernism's penchant for grand schemes and postmodernism's "incredulity toward metanarrative" (xxiv).

11. Olcott, "The Genesis of Theosophy," *National Review* 14.80 (October 1887) 213.

12. Olcott, *The Descendants of Thomas Olcott* (Albany: J. Munsell, 1874) xxx–xxxi.

13. Perry Miller, *Errand into the Wilderness* (Cambridge: Harvard University Press, 1956) 1–15.

14. *ODL*, 4.101.

15. I am influenced here by William R. Hutchison's argument in *Errand to the World: American Protestant Thought and Foreign Missions* (Chicago: University of Chicago Press, 1987) that the foreign missionary enterprise of American Protestants ought to be seen as a "new version" of the Puritans' "errand into the wilderness" (7).

16. Olcott, "A Great Book," *Theosophist* 10.119 (August 1889) 701.

17. Most valuable on this point is William R. Hutchison's "Introduction" to his anthology, *American Protestant Thought in the Liberal Era* (Lanham, MD: University Press of America, 1968) 1–16.

18. *ODL*, 3.363.

19. Robert E. Speer, *Missionary Principles and Practice* (New York: Fleming H. Revell, 1910), quoted in William R. Hutchison, *Errand to the World,* 107–108.

20. Norbert Elias, *The Civilizing Process: The History of Manners,* Edmund Jephcott trans. (New York: Urizen Books, 1978). This important book was originally published as *Uber den Prozess der Zivilisation* (Basel: Haus zum Falken, 1939).

21. Pidgin and creole studies emerged as a field within the academic discipline of linguistics after World War II. "Creolistics," as scholars sometimes refer to creole and pidgin linguistics, has spawned over the past few decades a vast literature. For

recent work in the area, see *Journal of Pidgin and Creole Languages* (est. 1986). I have relied heavily here on John A. Holm, *Pidgins and Creoles* (Cambridge: Cambridge University Press, 1988). I vastly prefer the category "creolization" to "syncretism." While syncretism tells us simply that religious traditions have met and merged, creolization assists us in analyzing *how* that meeting and merger occurred. By attention to two levels of interaction (grammar and lexicon), creolization theory allows for richer and more sophisticated analyses. Creolization is also a more value-neutral category than syncretism, which continues to carry pejorative connotations. Finally, creolization, unlike syncretism, takes both the power to impose and the power to resist seriously.

22. On the creolization of culture, see Edward Brathwaite, *The Development of Creole Society in Jamaica, 1770–1820* (New York: Clarendon, 1971); and Charles Joyner: *Down by the Riverside: A South Carolina Slave Community* (Urbana: University of Illinois Press, 1984). I have been influenced here most markedly by Charles Joyner, who persuasively extends the concept of creolization not only to culture but also to religion. The quotation is from Joyner, *Down by the Riverside*, 239.

23. I am thinking here of Robert Orsi, who has been one of the most vocal critics of histories of American religion that put Protestants at their center. (See his contributions to "Forum: The Decade Ahead in Scholarship," in *Religion and American Culture: A Journal of Interpretation* 3.1 [Winter 1993] 1–8; and his *The Madonna of 115th Street: Faith and Community in Italian Harlem, 1880–1950* [New Haven: Yale University Press, 1985].) I share Orsi's interest in religions other than Protestantism and agree that Protestants should be displaced from the center of at least some of the stories constructed by historians of American religion. I also tend to agree with Orsi that "the study of religions in the United States is necessarily the study of improvisations" (1). I also think, however, that Orsi fails to understand how non-mainstream religious imports to the United States are themselves frequently improvised toward a mainstream. Consider, for example, Orsi's contention that the "real action" in the history of religion in America in the twentieth century occurred in the fringes, not the mainstream. One key assumption informing this contention is that the fringes and the mainstream are somehow radically distinct— in short, that they do not improvise upon one another. Orsi seems to believe (to improvise on Kipling) that fringe is fringe and mainstream is mainstream and never the twain shall meet. A whole host of studies of ostensibly non-mainstream religious traditions—e.g., Mechal Sobel, *The World They Made Together: Black and White Values in Eighteenth Century Virginia* (Princeton: Princeton University Press, 1987)—have shown, however, that this is not typically the case. In the "contestations of meaning" that comprise American religious history, mainstream and fringe groups have borrowed voraciously from one another. In the process, white, Anglo-Saxon Protestants have become undoubtedly more African and perhaps even more Asian. But so too have both Africans and Asians become Anglo-Saxonized and Protestantized. All too frequently, however, these exchanges have tilted in a mainstream direction because of unequal distributions of power in American society. Slaves improvised their religious beliefs and behaviors not in the abstract but in the real world, under slaveholder domination and typically Protestant hegemony. And recent Buddhist immigrants from Thailand have had to contend

with less coercive but no less real facts of Protestant hegemony, such as Sunday schools and voluntaryism. My book challenges Orsi's thesis by finding one instance where Protestant influence exerts itself in an unlikely place.

24. C. D. S. Siriwardane, "Olcott and the Buddhist Education Movement of Ceylon," *Buddhist* 25.10/11 (March–April 1965) 115–17.

25. This term was coined by anthropologist Gananath Obeyesekere in 1970 in "Religious Symbolism and Political Change in Ceylon," *Modern Ceylon Studies* 1.1 (January 1970) 43–63. Obeyesekere intended the term to convey two meanings: first, that this new form of Buddhism began as an anti-Christian protest; and second, that it mimicked Protestant Christianity in both structure and content. In the two decades since its coinage, this typology has enjoyed wide currency. It continues to dominate scholarly debate about the modernization of Theravada Buddhism in South Asia, and is beginning to inform scholarly analyses regarding transformations of the Buddhist tradition in the modern West. See, e.g., Kitsiri Malalgoda, *Buddhism in Sinhalese Society: 1750–1900* (Berkeley: University of California Press, 1976); George D. Bond, *The Buddhist Revival in Sri Lanka: Religious Tradition, Reinterpretation and Response* (Columbia: University of South Carolina Press, 1988); Richard Gombrich and Gananath Obeyesekere, *Buddhism Transformed: Religious Change in Sri Lanka* (Princeton: Princeton University Press, 1989); Philip A. Mellon, "Protestant Buddhism? The Cultural Translation of Buddhism in England," *Religion* 21 (January 1991) 73–92. I criticize this typology as overly reliant on sociologist Max Weber's understanding of Protestantism in "Henry Steel Olcott and 'Protestant Buddhism,' " forthcoming in the *Journal of the American Academy of Religion*.

26. "American Sponsor of Buddhism Honored at Memorials in Ceylon," *New York Times* (February 18, 1962) 29.

27. Readers interested in these matters might begin with Michael Gomes, *Theosophy in the Nineteenth Century: An Annotated Bibliography* (New York: Garland, 1994).

1. Universal Reformer

1. Ralph Henry Gabriel, *The Course of American Democratic Thought*, 2d edition (New York: Ronald, 1956), esp. 12–25. William McLoughlin, in *Revivals, Awakenings, and Reform* (Chicago: University of Chicago Press, 1978), summarized the core conceptions of this creed: "the chosen nation; the covenant with God; the millennial manifest destiny; the higher (biblical or natural) law, against which private and social behavior is to be judged; the moral law (the Ten Commandments, the Sermon on the Mount); the laws of science, presumed to be from the Creator, and evolutionary or progressive in their purpose; the free and moral responsible individual, whose political liberty and liberty of conscience are inalienable; the work ethic (or 'Protestant ethic'), which holds that equal opportunity and hard work will bring economic success and public respect to all who assert and discipline themselves; and the benevolence of nature under the exploitative or controlling hand of man" (103).

2. The most ambitious treatment of antebellum reform is Alice Felt Tyler's *Freedom's Ferment: Phases of American Social History from the Colonial Period to the Outbreak of the Civil War* (Minneapolis: University of Minnesota Press, 1944), but Whitney Cross's interpretation, *The Burned-Over District: The Social and Intellectual*

History of Enthusiastic Religion in Western New York, 1800–1850 (Ithaca: Cornell University Press, 1950) has most influenced me here. *Ante-bellum Reform*, a collection of essays edited by David Brion Davis (New York: Harper and Row, 1967) contains a number of helpful treatments, especially John L. Thomas's "Romantic Reform in America, 1815–1865," which originally appeared in *American Quarterly* 17 (Winter 1965) 656–81. A more specialized work that has also influenced my interpretation is Timothy L. Smith's *Revivalism and Social Reform: American Protestantism on the Eve of the Civil War* (Nashville: Abingdon, 1957).

3. Since the sixties, a number of scholarly works have appeared on utopianism and communitarianism in the United States. See, e.g., Wendy E. Chmielewski, Louis J. Kern, and Marlyn Klee-Hartzell, *Women in Spiritual and Communitarian Societies in the United States* (Syracuse: Syracuse University Press, 1993); Robert S. Fogarty, *All Things New: American Communes and Utopian Movements, 1860–1914* (Chicago: University of Chicago Press, 1990); Lawrence Foster, *Religion and Sexuality: Three American Communal Experiments* (New York: Oxford University Press, 1981); Louis J. Kern, *An Ordered Love: Sex Roles and Sexuality in Victorian America: The Shakers, the Mormons and the Oneida Community* (Chapel Hill: University of North Carolina Press, 1981).

4. O. A. Brownson, *Social Reform: An Address Before the Society of the Mystical Seven in the Wesleyan University, Middletown, Conn. August 7, 1844* (Boston: Waite, Peirce, 1844), quoted in Walter Hugins, ed., *The Reform Impulse, 1825–1850* (Columbia: University of South Carolina Press) 249.

5. In the 1960s, historians generally agreed that antebellum reformers came disproportionately from social groups whose social status was diminishing. Ministers and others in these groups, according to this interpretation, enlisted in moral crusades in an effort to alleviate "status anxieties." This view was decisively challenged, however, in William R. Hutchison, "Cultural Strain and Protestant Liberalism," *American Historical Review* 76.2 (April 1971) 386–411. There remains some agreement that antebellum reformers tended to come from evangelical Protestant homes in New England.

6. Francis Parkman, "The Failure of Universal Suffrage," *North American Review* 127 (July–August 1878) 19.

7. These terms appear throughout the historical literature. I borrow "universal reform" from Henry Steele Commager, *The Era of Reform, 1830–1860* (Princeton: Van Nostrand, 1960). John L. Thomas uses "romantic reform" somewhat synonymously in "Romantic Reform in America, 1815–1865."

8. The Davis quotation is from *The Progressive Annual for 1862. Comprising an Almanac, a Spiritual Register, and a General Calendar of Reform* (New York: A. J. Davis, 1862) 31; Higginson is quoted in Ronald G. Walters, *American Reformers, 1815–1860* (New York: Hill and Wang, 1978); Commager, *The Era of Reform*, 10.

9. One oft-cited example of the shift from reforming individuals to changing laws is the change in emphasis within the temperance movement from individual self-restraint to Prohibition.

10. Horace Greeley, *Recollections of a Busy Life* (New York: J. B. Ford, 1868) 527.

11. Philip Schaff, *The Principle of Protestantism as Related to the Present State of the Church*, John W. Nevin, trans. (Chambersburg, PA: Publication Office of the German Reformed Church, 1845) 114.

12. Olcott, "Old Diary Leaves," *Theosophist* 16.4 (January 1895) 205. There are hundreds of similar tips in Olcott's corpus.

13. Olcott, "Sorcery in Science," *Theosophist* 11.128 (May 1890) 443. This story comes from Olcott's pen and must be read with some skepticism. It sounds suspiciously like Luke 2:41–52, where Jesus, also twelve years old, goes to the temple in Jerusalem to sit among the scribes and ask them questions.

14. During his first and only year in attendance, Olcott earned a cumulative grade of 77.1, and an unspectacular ranking of 19 in a class of 31, according to *Catalogue of the Officers and Students of the University of the City of New York: 1847–48* (New York: Joseph H. Jennings, 1848); *Class Merit Book, July 1835–June 1888*, vol. 4. I am grateful to Angela Chin, an N.Y.U. archival assistant, for providing this information.

15. In *The Burned-Over District*, Whitney R. Cross defines "ultraism" as "a combination of activities, personalities, and attitudes creating a condition of society which could foster experimental doctrines" (173). Bracketed by anti-Masonry in the 1820s and spiritualism in the 1850s, ultraism gave rise, according to Cross, to a number of reform movements in the mid-nineteenth century.

16. This category includes not only liberal Protestants (certainly the most widely-studied "religious liberals" in America) but also modernist Catholics, reform Jews, and members of other faith communities who have rejected many beliefs and practices of their religious tradition because of their desire to accommodate themselves to the modern/postmodern world. Insofar as the category cuts across religious traditions, it bears some structural similarities to "fundamentalism" as understood by participants involved in the University of Chicago's comparative "Fundamentalism Project." Those scholars have found "fundamentalism" operating not only among fundamentalist Protestants in the United States but also, most conspicuously, in the Muslim World. See, e.g., Martin E. Marty and R. Scott Appleby, eds., *Fundamentalisms Observed* (Chicago: University of Chicago Press, 1991). (Other scholars are now finding Jewish and Catholic "fundamentalisms" also.) Robert Wuthnow has argued in *The Restructuring of American Religion: Society and Faith since World War II* (Princeton: Princeton University Press, 1988) that American religion since the 1960s has been characterized by a "two-party system" pitting religious liberals against religious conservatives. Previously Americans identified themselves as Protestants, Catholics, and Jews, or as members of particular Protestant denominations, but now, Wuthnow argues, they view themselves largely as liberals and conservatives (see esp. chapters 5 and 7). In referring to the existence of "religious liberalism" in the nineteenth century, I do not mean to argue that the fault line separating religious liberals and religious conservatives was more fundamental at the time than the divides between Protestants and Catholics or between Baptists and Episcopalians. Certainly that was not the case. All I intend is to highlight certain similarities in both religious belief and practice that did cut across those divides. Gilded Age liberal Protestants, Catholics, and Jews shared much more with one another *and* with adherents of supposedly nonmainstream faiths such as spiritualism, theosophy, and Buddhism than historians of American religion have previously recognized.

17. In interpreting American spiritualism, I have relied heavily on two sources: R. Laurence Moore, *In Search of White Crows: Spiritualism, Parapsychology, and Ameri-*

can Culture (New York: Oxford University Press, 1977) and Ann Braude, *Radical Spirits: Spiritualism and Women's Rights in Nineteenth-Century America* (Boston: Beacon, 1989). Howard H. Kerr's *Mediums, Spirit Rappers, and Roaring Radicals: Spiritualism in American Literature, 1850–1900* (Urbana: University of Illinois Press, 1972) is helpful on representations of spiritualism in American literature. Like many movements in American religion, spiritualism was a transatlantic phenomenon. Happily, spiritualism's later manifestation in England has also received the scrutiny of able scholars. Like Moore's *In Search of White Crows,* Janet Oppenheim's *The Other World: Spiritualism and Psychical Research in England, 1850–1914* (Cambridge: Cambridge University Press, 1985) interprets spiritualism in light of attempts by ostensibly "scientific" psychical researchers either to debunk or to legitimize the spiritualist movement. Alex Owen follows Braude in analyzing the role of women in the spiritualist movement in *The Darkened Room: Women, Power and Spiritualism in Late Victorian England* (Philadelphia: University of Pennsylvania Press, 1990). There is a voluminous literature on spiritualism, largely unhelpful to historians, that is preoccupied with either "proving" or "disproving" the genuineness of spiritual phenomena. One recent example of this genre is Ruth Brandon, *The Spiritualists: The Passion for the Occult in the Nineteenth and Twentieth Centuries* (New York: Knopf, 1983).

18. Jon Butler, *Awash in a Sea of Faith: Christianizing the American People* (Cambridge: Harvard University Press, 1990) 255; Ann Braude, *Radical Spirits,* 28–31; Lewis O. Saum, *The Popular Mood of Pre-Civil War America* (Westport: Greenwood, 1980) 50; R. Laurence Moore, *In Search of White Crows.* The final quotation is from Saum, *The Popular Mood of Pre-Civil War America,* 50. The argument for a more inclusive reading of the demography of American spiritualism is corroborated by the English case. In *The Darkened Room,* Alex Owen finds support for spiritualism not only among men and women but among working, middle, and aristocratic classes. She does note, however, that the majority of England's spiritualists were upper, working, and middle class (8, 246).

19. HSOD, October 10, 1891.

20. There is some disagreement about how to spell Olcott's middle name. The Steeles included a third "e" in their surname, and a statue of Olcott at Theosophical Society headquarters in Adyar spells his middle name as "Steele." Olcott rarely signed his full name. However, in the places he did that I have been able to find (e.g., Olcott, "To the Buddhists of Burma" [January 25, 1891], TSA) he signed it "Steel," so this is the spelling I have used. In a letter to the editor of the spiritualist periodical, *Banner of Light* (March 6, 1880), J. M. Peebles described the Steele brothers like this: "Frederic Steele was a classmate of Gen-Grant, and a General in the army; George Steele was a member of the Constitutional Convention, and is a Judge in the California Courts; E. W. Steele owns an extensive ranch; R. E. Steele is a thinker, and one of the best-read men in the ranks of Spiritualism; J. C. Steele, an excellent clear-headed man and a clairvoyant . . . has the gift of healing by the laying on of hands."

21. The literature on this cult is voluminous. See, e.g., Barbara Welter, "The Cult of True Womahoood, 1820–1860," *American Quarterly* 18 (1966) 151–74.

22. "The New York Conference of Spiritualists," *ST* 2.39 (January 28, 1854) 155; J. M. Peebles to editor, *BL* (March 6, 1880).

23. *National Cyclopaedia of American Biography,* vol. VIII (ed. James T. White; New

York: J. T. White, 1900) 464–65. The encyclopedia article was based on information provided by Olcott.

24. Amherst, "A Prophecy," *ST* 3.50 (April 14, 1855) 199.

25. See Robert C. Fuller, *Mesmerism and the American Cure of Souls* (Philadelphia: University of Pennsylvania Press, 1982) and *Alternative Medicine and American Religious Life* (New York: Oxford University Press, 1989). For mesmerism in Europe, consult Robert Darnton, *Mesmerism and the End of the Enlightenment in France* (Cambridge: Harvard University Press, 1968).

26. Olcott to Sarah D. Cape (September 27, 1894), HSOC; "Olcott the Theosophist," *New York Times* (September 24, 1891) 2:3; J. M. Peebles to editor, *BL* (March 6, 1880). Olcott's diary for August 30, 1882, also refers to a case of mesmeric healing in Ohio in 1852.

27. Many states boasted spiritualist societies in the 1850s, but spiritualists for the most part resisted national organizations. A Society for the Diffusion of Spiritualist Knowledge expired shortly after its birth in the 1850s. Founded in 1864, the National Organization of Spiritualists (later reorganized into the American Association of Spiritualists) folded in 1873. According to historian Ann Braude, American spiritualism was anti-institutional by design, since many participants in the movement saw spiritualist organizations as unwarranted attempts to enslave the individual spirit (*Radical Spirits*, esp. 162–91).

28. "New York Conference of Spiritualists," *ST* 2.27 (November 5, 1853) 106.

29. In a footnote in *ODL*, 1.322, Olcott wrote that he contributed articles to the *Spiritual Telegraph* under this pseudonym. Amherst is the northern Ohio town where Olcott had lived.

30. See, e.g., "Funeral of a Spiritualist" (2.12 [July 23, 1853] 47); "Two Spiritual Facts" (3.38 [January 20, 1855] 151); and "Manifestations in a German Castle" (3.42 [February 17, 1855] 166). These articles, for the most part unrevealing, do provide the careful reader with occasional hints about Olcott's thought. "Mental Telegraphy" (2.49 [April 8, 1854] 189), an article on the invention of a mental telegraph (a box—with batteries, a crank, and wire coated with fluid to conduct "nerve aura"—which facilitates "communication between minds without resorting to words") reveals Olcott's ebullient faith in progress through technological advances. "In the brightness of this dawn of science," Olcott wrote, "I see the harbingers of that glorious day that awaits the struggling sons of earth."

31. "Buchanan's Neurology" (3.43 [February 24, 1855] 169); "Our 'Spheres' " (3.46 [March 17, 1855] 182); "Magnetism" (3.40 [April 7, 1855] 193); "A Prophecy" (3.50 [April 14, 1855] 199); and "Psychometry—Its Origins and Claims" (4.6 [August 18, 1855] 61).

32. Amherst, "Amherst to Mr. Slayton," *ST* 4.38 (January 19, 1856) 149. The problem of "distinguishing" or "discerning" spirits goes back at least to the writing of 1 Corinthians 12:10, which describes this talent as a spiritual gift or charism. In the American context, Jonathan Edwards grappled most famously with this task in 1741 in "The Distinguishing Marks of a Work of the Spirit of God: A Discourse," in C. C. Goen, ed., *The Great Awakening* (New Haven: Yale University Press, 1972) 226–63. It is interesting that Olcott's pragmatic rule mirrors Edwards's insistence on testing the gifts of the spirit by their fruits.

33. Amherst, "Comparative Grades of Mediumship," *ST* 4.30 (November 24, 1855) 117.

34. Ibid.

35. See, e.g., Edward B. Tylor, *Primitive Culture* (London: J. Murray, 1871) and Herbert Spencer, *The Principles of Sociology* (New York: D. Appleton, 1881–).

36. Olcott, "The Spiritualist's Faith," *ST* 4.51 (April 19, 1856) 201.

37. As Braude notes in *Radical Spirits*, Davis's idea was itself an adaptation of Emmanuel Swedenborg's cosmology, which posited three heavens and three hells after death (40, 44).

38. Amherst, "Comparative Grades of Mediumship," *ST* 4.30 (November 24, 1855) 117. Perhaps the most direct correlation is Brisbane's "Associationism," which was embodied, as much as utopian ideals can be, in the Brook Farm experiment. See Albert Brisbane, *Social Destiny of Man: Or, Association and Reorganization of Industry* (Philadelphia: C. F. Stollmeyer, 1840).

39. See advertisements entitled "Olcott and Vail" and "Henry C. Vail—Consulting Agriculturalist" in *ST* 5.1 (May 3, 1856). Henry Vail shared Olcott's interest in spiritualism. He, too, was a frequent contributor to the *Spiritualist Telegraph*. Olcott and Vail's experiment was praised as "the only private school exclusively devoted to agricultural education" in George Ripley and Charles A. Dana, eds., *The New American Cyclopaedia* (New York: D. Appleton, 1859) 1.226. The school's course of instruction, it noted, "is designed to tend as much as possible to good practical results, and the theories of plant and animal growth and farm management are illustrated in the daily labor on the farm." The school's experiential pedagogy was modeled, according to Olcott, on a similar school in Hoffieyl, Switzerland. That school also supplemented book learning with practical experimentation.

40. Olcott, "What to do with them," *Ceylon Times* (November 26, 1881).

41. *Sorgho and Imphee, The Chinese and African Sugar Canes: A Treatise upon their Origin, Varieties and Culture* (New York: A. O. Moore, 1857). Although he had not yet traveled beyond his country's borders (his first excursion outside the country would come a year later, when he would visit Europe to report on its agriculture), Olcott displayed in this book a nascent cosmopolitanism. The solution to America's sugar shortage, he argued, lay in the importation and cultivation of Chinese and African sugar canes. A number of sources credit Olcott with writing an earlier volume. *Pulpit Sketches, or the Dreams of a Pew Holder* (Albany: Munsell and Tanner, 1845) was published anonymously but handwritten notations on the title pages of copies at Yale's Beinecke Library and the Boston Public Library credit "Henry S. Olcott" as the author. The National Union Catalog also lists Olcott as the work's author, as does William Cushing, *Initials and Pseudonyms: A Dictionary of Literary Disguises*, 2d series (New York: Thomas Y. Crowell, 1888) 119. *Pulpit Sketches* provides character outlines of six Albany area clergymen (among them the prominent Presbyterian cleric, William B. Sprague), and might possibly have been written by Olcott. He was, however, only thirteen years old at the time the book was apparently published.

42. "United States Agricultural Society," *ST* 5.51 (April 18, 1857). The medals are on display at the TSA.

43. Theophilus Roessle, *How to Cultivate and Preserve Celery*, Roessle's Gardener's Handbooks 1 (New York: C. M. Saxton, Banker, 1860).

44. Abbott's publishing career roughly parallels Olcott's childhood and adolescence. His first book, *The Young Christian* (1832), came out in the year of Olcott's birth. And Rollo, whose development Abbott charted in his first series of Rollo Books, from 1834 and 1843, was almost Olcott's exact contemporary. Early volumes

such as *Rollo Learning to Talk* (1839) and *Rollo Learning to Read* (1835) would have appeared roughly as Olcott himself was learning to talk and read. Olcott may well have grown up with Abbott's *The Rollo Code of Morals: or The Rules of Duty for Children* (1842). If not, he certainly praised most, if not all, of its values, which historian John B. Boles has catalogued as "conscience, justice, honesty, faithfulness, truth, obedience, industry, patience, forgiveness, purity, duty, conscientiousness, repentance, and duty to God" in "Jacob Abbott and the Rollo Books: New England Culture for Children," *Journal of Popular Culture* 6.3 (Spring 1973) 518. On the broader American tradition of success through self-help and moral uplift there is a vast literature. See, e.g., Irvin G. Wyllie, *The Self-Made Man in America: The Myth of Rags to Riches* (New Brunswick: Rutgers University Press, 1954); Richard Weiss, *The American Myth of Success: From Horatio Alger to Norman Vincent Peale* (New York: Basic, 1969); Daniel T. Rodgers, *The Work Ethic in Industrial America, 1850–1920* (Chicago: University of Chicago Press, 1978); John G. Cawelti, *Apostles of the Self-made Man: Changing Concepts of Success in America* (Chicago: University of Chicago Press, 1965); Richard M. Huber, *The American Idea of Success* (New York: McGraw-Hill, 1971); and Richard D. Mosier, *Making the American Mind: Social and Moral Ideas in the McGuffey Readers* (New York: King's Crown, 1947). Karen Halttunen provocatively integrates this literature into a broader argument regarding middle-class culture in antebellum America in *Confidence Men and Painted Women: A Study of Middle Class Culture in America, 1830–1870* (New Haven: Yale University Press, 1982).

45. Olcott, "Preface," in Roessle, *How to Cultivate and Preserve Celery*, iii, iii–iv, xi, xiii, xvii, xxv.

46. The scholarship on Greeley and the *Tribune* is immense. Suzanne Schulze, *Horace Greeley: A Bio-Bibliography* (Westport: Greenwood, 1992) is a good place to start.

47. One of his assignments was to transcribe and edit a series of lectures on farming techniques delivered at the Yale Scientific School. These lectures were later republished in Olcott, ed., *Outlines of the First Courses of Yale Agricultural Lectures* (New York: C. M. Saxton, Barber, 1860).

48. "The Execution on Friday Last," *Tribune* (December 5, 1859) 5.

49. Olcott was a member of Hugenot Lodge No. 448, chartered by the M. W. Grand Lodge of the State of New York. He was also a Royal Arch Freemason, a member of Corinthian chapter No. 159 of New York ("H. S. Olcott as a Freemason," in *Olcott Centenary Number* [Adyar, India: Theosophical Society, 1932] 478).

50. Olcott, "The War's Carnival of Fraud," in *Annals of the War* (Philadelphia: Times Publishing, 1879) 705.

51. This is probably the source of Olcott's title. Despite Olcott's repeated references to his rank of colonel, there is no record in the National Archives showing that he was an officer or, for that matter, an enlisted man in the Union Army (Trudy Huskamp Peterson, assistant archivist, letter to the author, November 3, 1988). One plausible explanation for this fact is that Olcott joined the war effort as a civilian aide—not an unusual practice at the time—and that Stanton conferred the title informally in an effort to facilitate Olcott's investigations. This theory is supported by a letter in which Olcott noted that he had been given a title in wartime "without there having been any such office created by law" (Olcott to Secretary of State William Evarts, [April 30, 1880], TSA).

52. A copy of the transcript of the civil trial of Solomon Kohnstamm is maintained at the National Archives in Case File 00–3655, Record Group 153, Records of the Judge Advocate General's Office. Records of Olcott's subsequent Army Department investigations are located at the National Archives in Case Files of Investigations by Levi C. Turner and Lafayette C. Baker, 1861–1866, Record Group 94, Records of the Adjutant General's Office, 1780s–1917.

53. Olcott, "The War's Carnival of Fraud," 706–707.

54. Ibid., 712. Two volumes of files of Olcott's Navy Department investigation are maintained at the National Archives in "Letters from Special Investigators of Frauds in Naval Procurement," entry 161, Record Group 45, Records of the Office of Naval Records and Library.

55. Olcott, "The War's Carnival of Fraud," 723.

56. Cited in Howard Murphet, *Hammer on the Mountain*, 18.

57. Records of Olcott's work investigating the Lincoln assassination conspiracy are housed in the National Archives in Washington, D.C. See *Investigation and Trial Papers Relating to the Assassination of President Lincoln* (National Archives Microfilm Publications: Pamphlet Accompanying Microcopy No. 599; Washington: National Archives, 1965). A verbatim account of Olcott's interrogation of Mrs. Surratt appears in Otto Eisenschiml, *Why Was Lincoln Murdered?* (Boston: Little, Brown, 1937) 287–89, and Theodore Roscoe, *The Web of Conspiracy* (Englewood Cliffs: Prentice-Hall, 1959) 245–49. Many now believe Mrs. Surratt was unjustly convicted.

58. Olcott, "A Memorial of Police Bravery," *New York Times* (July 20, 1871) 6:4. Most of the money was for the flag was donated by insurance companies, who had a pecuniary interest in maintaining law and order. See Olcott, "A Flag of Honor for the Police," *New York Times* (July 15, 1872) 8:4.

59. Olcott and Austin Abbott, *Official Revised Edition of the Outline of Draft of the General Insurance Law* (New York: J. H. and C. M. Goodsell, 1871).

60. Olcott, "The Insurance Superintendent," *New York Times* (September 5, 1871) S.3.

61. This was apparently a typical strategy of Protestant moralists in the Victorian period. See R. Laurence Moore's discussion of the theatre in *Selling God: American Religion in the Marketplace of Culture* (New York: Oxford University Press, 1994).

62. *Sun* (July 30, 1872) 95.

63. Olcott, "A Burlesque with Brains in It at Last," *Sun* (August 27, 1872) 105–107.

64. Olcott, "The Stars of the Stage" *Sun* (September 18, 1872).

65. *Tribune* (September 7, 1880) 4:4.

66. Robert Wiebe, *The Search for Order, 1877–1920* (New York: Hill and Wang, 1967); John Higham, *From Boundlessness to Consolidation: The Transformation of American Culture, 1848–1860* (Ann Arbor: William L. Clements Library, 1969). The quotation is from Higham, 15. Citing the impact of the European revolutions of 1848, Higham locates this shift in a single decade: the 1850s. Wiebe construes the transition more broadly, but places it later, in the last two decades of the nineteenth century and the first two decades of the twentieth. In *The Inner Civil War: Northern Intellectuals and the Crisis of the Union* (New York: Harper and Row, 1965), George Frederickson provides a more standard account, placing the shift in the immediate postbellum period. Historians of American religion have rightly criticized Wiebe for overarguing his "secularization" thesis. It is possible, however, to appropriate

Wiebe's broader "search for order" theme without adopting "secularity." The "search for order" was, in my view, influenced not only by the Enlightenment but also by liberal Protestantism.

67. Wiebe, *The Search for Order*, viii.

68. Butler, *Awash in a Sea of Faith*, 203.

2. From Spiritualism to Theosophy

1. Founded in 1870 as a literary alternative to the business-oriented (and more prestigious) Century Club, the Lotos Club, according to John Elderkin's *A Brief History of the Lotos Club* (New York: n.p., 1895), aimed "to promote social intercourse among journalists, literary men, artists and members of the musical and dramatic professions, and such merchants and professional gentlemen . . . as would naturally be attracted by such a club" (9). A number of Olcott's co-workers at the *Tribune*, including Whitelaw Reid, editor of the *Tribune* and a future vice-presidential nominee, were members. Olcott was active in the club, and for a time maintained an office at its headquarters. The name of the club derives from Tennyson's "Lotos Eaters" and was intended, according to Elderkin, to convey "an idea of rest and harmony" (9).

2. Thomas Bender, *New York Intellect: A History of Intellectual Life in New York City, from 1750 to the Beginnings of Our Own Time* (New York: Knopf, 1987), esp. 117–262.

3. Ibid., xvi. This tension is roughly analogous to Matthew Arnold's oft-cited distinction between "culture and anarchy."

4. Richard L. Bushman, *The Refinement of America: Persons, Houses, Cities* (New York: Knopf, 1992).

5. John Tomisch, *A Genteel Endeavor: American Culture and Politics in the Gilded Age* (Palo Alto: Stanford University Press, 1971) 24. See also Stow Persons, *The Decline of American Gentility* (New York: Columbia University Press, 1973).

6. Quoted in Bender, *New York Intellect*, 172.

7. *ODL*, 1.1–2.

8. Olcott, "The World of Spirits, Astounding Wonders that Stagger Belief," *Sun* (September 5, 1874). The *Daily Graphic* published twenty of Olcott's letters between September 29 and December 11, 1874.

9. Olcott, *People from the Other World* (1875; Rutland, VT: Tuttle, 1972).

10. D. D. Home, *Lights and Shadows of Spiritualism* (London: Virtue, 1878) 260, 258, 308, 271.

11. "Wallace and Spiritualism," *SS* 2.12 (May 27, 1875) 142.

12. There are a number of biographies of Blavatsky, all of them flawed. Apparently her enigmatic personality is as daunting to scholars as it was to Olcott, who noted after her death that she was to him "an insoluble riddle" (*ODL*, 2.viii). Early attempts to solve this riddle include *Incidents in the Life of Madame Blavatsky* (London: Redway, 1886) by theosophist A. P. Sinnett and *Priestess of the Occult: Madame Blavatsky* (New York: Knopf, 1946) by critic Gertrude M. Williams. Also widely read is Marion Meade, *Madame Blavatsky: The Woman Behind the Myth* (New York: Putnam's, 1980). Blavatsky scholarship lay relatively dormant until the early 1990s, when interest in women and religion sparked a biographical boom. Among the books that comprised this boom are: S. L. Cranston, *HPB: The Extraordinary Life and Influence of Helene Blavatsky, Founder of the Modern Theosophical Movement* (New

York: Putnam's, 1993); Peter Washington, *Madame Blavatsky's Baboon: Theosophy and the Emergence of the Western Guru* (London: Secker and Warburg, 1993); and K. Paul Johnson, *The Masters Revealed: Madam Blavatsky and the Myth of the Great White Lodge* (Albany: State University of New York Press, 1994).

13. *ODL*, 1.1.

14. *ODL*, 1.8.

15. *ODL*, 1.6. Olcott continued: "Neither then, at the commencement, nor ever afterwards, had either of us the sense of the other being of the opposite sex. We were simply chums; so regarded each other, so called each other." In response to allegations of Blavatsky's promiscuity, Olcott defended his friend's Victorian virtue: "Her every look, word, and action proclaimed her sexlessness." Later in her life Blavatsky would produce, in response to allegations that she had mothered an illegitimate child, a doctor's letter testifying both to her inability to have children and to her virginity. The image (alive and well among many theosophists today) of Blavatsky as a celibate saint is rejected by non-theosophical biographers. The contention that she and Olcott were not sexually intimate is more widely accepted.

16. HSOD, June 18, 1880. This description of Blavatsky as androgyne now enjoys wide currency in both theosophical and non-theosophical circles. But Blavatsky's androgyneity ought to be understood, in my view, not as fact but as imaginative construction. Independent, crude, and anything but maternal, Blavatsky was a gender anomaly even in Late Victorian New York City. She and her friends dealt with that anomaly by imaginatively constructing a mediating category between hardened Victorian taxonomies of male and female. Blavatsky was apparently not alone in constructing this mediating category. French novelist George Sand also smoked, wore male attire, and asked to be addressed as "mon frère."

17. New York County Court House, Index #1874–719. The complaint alleged that Olcott "committed adultry [sic] on the second day of May one thousand eight hundred and seventy three at a house of prostitution in the City of New York." The judge in the case forbade Olcott to marry again until after his ex-wife's death, and ordered him to pay $1,500 per year in alimony and unspecified additional monies in child support.

18. *ODL*, 1.56.

19. This idea is a hoary one; Blavatsky may have borrowed it from Edward Bulwer-Lytton's popular novel, *Zanoni* (1842). In this romance, the protagonist Zanoni—a member of a secret Rosicrucian fraternity obscured behind "the veil that hides the Isis of their wisdom from the world"—falls in love with the heroine Viola who all her life has dreamed of meeting a member of the occult brotherhood (quoted in Marion Meade, *Madame Blavatsky*, 170).

20. "Important to Spiritualists," *SS* 2.8 (April 29, 1875) 85.

21. Olcott, "Human Spirits and Elementaries," in Olcott, *Human Spirits and Elementaries and Eastern Magic and Western Spiritualism* (Adyar, India: Theosophist, n.d.), reprinted in *Theosophist*, 28.10 (July 1907) 721–29; 28.11 (August 1907) 801–10; and 28.12 (September 1907) 885–94.

22. Olcott, *Human Spirits and Elementaries*, 14, 11, 16; Olcott, "The Immortal Life," *Tribune* (August 30, 1875) 6; Olcott, "Spiritualism Rampant," *Tribune* (September 17, 1875) 3.

23. Olcott, "The Immortal Life," 6.

24. Olcott first advanced this argument in ibid., 6.

25. Olcott, *Human Spirits and Elementaries*, 40, 34. Scholars still await a persuasive critical interpretation of the complex role of women in theosophy. Mary Farrell Bednarowski provides some hint of what such an interpretation might look like in "Women in Occult America," in Howard Kerr and Charles L. Crow, eds., *The Occult in America* (Urbana: University of Illinois Press, 1983) 177–95.

26. R. Laurence Moore describes cultivating outsiderhood as a major theme in American religion and a "characteristic way of inventing one's Americanness" in *Religious Outsiders and the Making of Americans* (New York: Oxford University Press, 1986) xi.

27. Mary F. Davis, *Danger Signals: The Uses and Abuses of Modern Spiritualism* (New York: A. J. Davis, 1875), quoted in Olcott, "Occultism and its Critics," *SS* 3.6 (October 14, 1875) 63; S. B. Brittan, "Colonel Olcott and Spiritualism," *BL* (October 16, 1875), quoted in Michael Gomes, *The Dawning of the Theosophical Movement*, 80–81.

28. Reprinted in Olcott, "Col. Olcott Explains," *SS* 3.8 (October 28, 1875) 8.

29. Karen Halttunen, *Confidence Men and Painted Women*.

30. Olcott to Hiram Corson (January 8, 1876) in Eugene R. Corson, *Some Unpublished Letters of Helena Petrovna Blavatsky* (London: Rider, 1929) 173–74.

31. Rev. J. H. Wiggin, "Rosicrucianism in New York," *The Liberal Christian* 30.84 (September 4, 1875) 4.

32. Evidence of the fact that the theosophists appealed to and attracted this sort of audience appears throughout the theosophical literature. For example, in a note that appeared in the *Theosophist* 9.108 (September 1888), Olcott wrote, "We do not cater to the uneducated masses, but to that restricted class who think, analyze, synthesize, and lead contemporary opinion. Through them, we hope to elevate the people" (S.cvi).

33. Olcott, letter to the editor, *New York Daily Graphic* (May 4, 1875). Blavatsky, in a note in her scrapbook, wrote that she organized the club only after one of her Masters ordered her to start to tell "the truth" about spiritualism. "And now my martyrdom will begin!" she noted. "I shall have all the Spiritualists against me, in addition to the Christians and the Sceptics" (*ODL*, 1.25). See also Olcott, "Wallace and Spiritualism," *SS*, 2.12 (May 27, 1875) 142.

34. Olcott, *Human Spirits and Elementaries*, 40, 44.

35. Olcott, *Inaugural Address of the President of the Theosophical Society* (New York: Theosophical Society, 1875) 13.

36. Quoted in Olcott, "The First Leaf of T. S. Society," *Theosophist* 12.2 (November 1890) 67.

37. Olcott, *Human Spirits and Elementaries*, 16.

38. Olcott, *Inaugural Address*, 10–11, 7, 9.

39. See Eric Hobsbawm and Terence Ranger, eds., *The Invention of Tradition* (Cambridge: Cambridge University Press, 1983).

40. Olcott, *Inaugural Address*, 20–21.

41. Historical work on "separate spheres" is vast. A good place to start is Nancy F. Cott, *The Bonds of Womanhood: "Woman's Sphere" in New England, 1780–1835* (New Haven: Yale University Press, 1977). Linda K. Kerber reviews the literature in "Separate Spheres, Female Worlds, Women's Place: The Rhetoric of Women's History," *Journal of American History* 75.1 (June 1988) 9–39.

42. Olcott, "Eastern Magic and Western Spiritualism" (1875) in Olcott, *Applied Theosophy and Other Essays* (Adyar, India: Theosophical Publishing House, 1975) 249.

43. This thesis contradicts both the internal histories of theosophists and the external histories of other scholars of American religion. Theosophists are perennial philosophers who view their movement as a modern surfacing of an ancient hermetic tradition that runs through Swedenborgianism and mesmerism, Pythagoreanism and Neoplatonism, gnosticism and the Eleusian mysteries, the Jewish Cabbala and the Hindu Vedas, back to one primeval source of universal wisdom. More historically minded redactors have interpreted theosophy differently. Sydney E. Ahlstrom describes it as a type of "harmonial religion" in *A Religious History of the American People* (New Haven: Yale University Press, 1972) 1038, while Robert S. Ellwood, in *Alternative Altars: Unconventional and Eastern Spirituality in America* (Chicago: University of Chicago Press, 1979) 42–87, views it as part of an "alternative spirituality tradition" in America. Such interpretations tell us what theosophy is like, or to what category it belongs, but they finesse the more difficult historical question regarding from whence theosophy came.

44. R. Laurence Moore, *In Search of White Crows*, 61.

45. On Baron de Palm's obscure life and notorious death see *ODL*, 1.147–84; "A Theosophical Funeral," *New York Times* (May 29, 1876) 1; " 'Theosophical' Obsequies," *Tribune* (May 29, 1876) 4; "Baron de Palm's Funeral," *Tribune* (May 29, 1876) 5; and "De Palm's Incineration," *New York Times* (December 7, 1876) 6. The quotation is from *ODL*, 1.172.

46. *ODL*, 1.150.

47. *ODL*, 1.153.

48. "A Theosophical Funeral," *New York Times* (May 29, 1876) 1. All subsequent references to the funeral are from this source.

49. Scholarly works on Emerson and W. H. Channing are legion. I rely here on William R. Hutchison, *The Transcendentalist Ministers: Church Reform in the New England Renaissance* (New Haven: Yale University Press, 1959), and Stow Persons, *Free Religion, an American Faith* (New Haven: Yale University Press, 1947). Olcott shared with Emerson and W. H. Channing a number of additional ideas and impulses: a critique of materialism, a view of the moral and ethical basis of religion, a rejection of miracles and other forms of supernaturalism, optimism about human nature and confidence in the perfectibility of society, a belief in spiritual evolution, a practical emphasis on "works before doctrine," and a concern about preserving "culture" in the face of mass mediocrity. Olcott rejected, however, the transcendentalists' romantic intuitionism. Like O. B. Frothingham, he believed "that scientific demonstration, rather than intuition, must form the basis of religious faith" (Hutchison, 198). If, as Hutchison argues, the transcendentalists can be divided into individualists like Thoreau, utopian collectivists like Ripley and Channing, and radical reformers like Brownson, then Olcott clearly falls in the Fourier-influenced utopian collectivist (or associationist) camp. The Theosophical Society, in fact, would soon become something like a Fourier "phalanx"—an attempt to create "a divinely ordered harmony of human interests" (Hutchison, 170).

50. See "De Palm's Incineration," *New York Times* (December 7, 1876) 6; and "The Baron's Cremation," *New York Daily Graphic* (December 6, 1876) 2.

51. " 'Theosophical' Obsequies," *Tribune* (May 29, 1876) 4.

52. Karen Halttunen, *Confidence Men and Painted Women*, esp. 124–52.

53. In the summer of 1876, Olcott used the arrival in New York of nine shipwrecked and penniless "Mussulman Arabs" as an occasion to demonstrate publicly

the Theosophical Society's humanitarianism. Noting that these "Heathen" were unlikely to receive aid from Christian charities, Olcott appealed to New Yorkers to save these men from starvation. With the assistance of the mayor of New York, who personally contributed $25, Olcott raised $2000 from his "fellow Heathen." What he did with the money is surprising: he sent the Arabs home. *ODL*, 1.298–99; *New York Times* (July 10, 1876); *BL*, 39.20 (August 12, 1876); *Graphic* (August 3, 1876).

54. *ODL*, 1.330.

55. *American Bookseller* (October 1877), cited in *ODL*, 1.294.

56. Quoted in *ODL*, 1.296. Olcott himself described *Isis* as "a sort of literary rag-bag, with contents higgledy-piggledy" (Olcott to Blavatsky, January 19, 1886, Letters to Madame Blavatsky, 1885–1886, Add MSS 45,288, ff. 196–205, British Library, Manuscript Collections).

57. Helena P. Blavatsky, *Isis Unveiled: A Master-Key to the Mysteries of Ancient and Modern Science and Theology* (1877; Wheaton, IL: Theosophical Publishing House, 1972) 2.639. Blavatsky equivocated on whether Hinduism or Buddhism was the original religion. In one place she identified India as "the cradle of the race" and Hinduism as the root of all religion (1.576–89); elsewhere she called Buddhism religion's primeval source (2.142–43, 169, 205).

58. Although this criticism was not novel—it was popular among freethinkers from Thomas Paine to Robert Ingersoll—it is curious in light of arguments by Blavatsky's detractors that *Isis* itself was plagiarized. In a series of articles that began in volume 1, number 2 of *The Golden Way*, William Emmette Coleman, a member of the American Oriental Society and the Pali Text Society, argued that *Isis* contained no less than two thousand cases of plagiarism. Blavatsky herself admitted a sort of copying when she argued that she transcribed in her text messages she had received clairvoyantly from the "Astral Light." In a letter to a family member, Blavatsky wrote, "Somebody who knows all dictates to me. My Master, and occasionally others whom I knew on my travels years ago. . . . Whenever I write upon a subject I know little or nothing of, I address myself to them, and one of them inspires me, i.e., he allows me to simply copy what I write from manuscripts, and even printed matter that pass before my eyes, in the air, during which process I have never been unconscious one single instant" (*ODL*, 1.214).

59. Blavatsky, *Isis Unveiled*, 2.53, iv, 352.

60. C. Jinarajadasa, ed., *Letters from the Masters of the Wisdom* (Chicago: Theosophical Press, 1926) 2.19.

61. Ibid., 2.36–37.

62. *ODL*, 1.376. Subsequent descriptions of this event are from *ODL*, 1.376–81.

63. *ODL* 1.379.

64. Olcott, "Theosophy, the Scientific Basis of Religion," in Olcott, *A Collection of Lectures*, 164; *ODL*, 1.381.

65. Matthew Arnold, *Culture and Anarchy* (London: Smith, Elder, 1869), quoted in Bender, *New York Intellect*, 212.

3. An Errand to Asia

1. One recent book that gets this wrong is Mary Farrell Bednarowski's *New Religions and the Theological Imagination in America* (Bloomington: Indiana University Press, 1989) 13–14. The mistake is, however, understandable, since Blavatsky

herself claimed in *The Key to Theosophy,* Joy Mills, ed. (Wheaton, IL: Theosophical Publishing House, 1972) that the three objects were in place "from the beginning" (24).

2. Olcott notes in *ODL,* 1.280 that reincarnation was mentioned in the inaugural issue of the *Theosophist,* but was not taught until volume 3, 1881–82.

3. Olcott to Babu Peary Chand Mittra (June 5 and September 14, 1877), HSOC.

4. Olcott to Mittra (September 14, 1877), HSOC.

5. Henry F. May in *The Enlightenment in America* (New York: Oxford University Press, 1976) distinguishes among four European "Enlightenments" that influenced the American Enlightenment: the Moderate Enlightenment, the Skeptical Enlightenment, the Revolutionary Enlightenment, and the Didactic Enlightenment. Blavatsky was clearly most influenced by the Skeptical Enlightenment, characterized according to May by the virulent anticlericalism of Voltaire. Rooted in France, this Skeptical Enlightenment exerted little influence in America. Olcott, on the other hand, was influenced by a more measured type, which, according to May, flourished in America: the Didactic Enlightenment of Scotland, which survived, May notes, in the genteel tradition and, I would add, in New York City's metropolitan gentry.

6. *ODL,* 1.412.

7. James Turner, *Without God, Without Creed: The Origins of Unbelief in America* (Baltimore: Johns Hopkins University Press, 1985) 199.

8. "Notes from the Wide Field," *Missionary Herald* (October 1882) 394–95.

9. This discussion is analyzed in Thomas A. Tweed, *The American Encounter with Buddhism, 1844–1912: Victorian Culture and the Limits of Dissent* (Bloomington: Indiana University Press, 1992).

10. Olcott to Rev. Piyaratana Tissa Terunanse, in Ananda W. P. Guruge, ed., *From the Living Fountains of Buddhism: Sri Lankan Support to Pioneering Western Orientalists* (Colombo, Sri Lanka: Ministry of Cultural Affairs, 1984), 340, 338.

11. Ibid., 339.

12. Ibid., 340, 343.

13. Ibid., 339, 343.

14. HSOC. The letter is dated December 29, 1877.

15. Guruge, ed., *From the Living Fountains,* 341.

16. HSOC. The letter is dated August 16, 1878. Apparently Olcott took this translation plan seriously. In his diary of February 20, 1878, he recorded his hope to raise $10,000 to support "a series of publications of Oriental Works" and noted that Professor Alexander Wilder, a scholar who had assisted in editing *Isis,* had agreed to serve as the American editor of the series.

17. Saraswati to Olcott (April 21, 1878), in Olcott, "Swami Dayanand's Charges," *Theosophist* 3.10 (July 1882) S.4.

18. Ibid., S.4.

19. This letter appears in Bawa Chhajju Singh, *Life and Teachings of Swami Dayanand Saraswati* (New Delhi: Jan Gyan Prakashan, 1903) 58–64. The quote is from p. 62.

20. Olcott to Hurrychund Chintamon (February 22, 1878), in Olcott, "Swami Dayanand's Charges," S.4.

21. Olcott to Chintamon (May 29, 1878), in Olcott, "Swami Dayanand's Charges," S.4.

22. *Indian Spectator* (May 29, 1878), in Olcott, "Swami Dayanand's Charges," S.4–5.

23. *ODL*, 1.376.

24. The first hint regarding the litigation appears in HSOD, April 11, 1878: "More clouds from New Jersey. Telegram from District Attorney asking an interview. Wants my testimony. Got none to give." On June 10, Olcott received "a moral essay from Kali" and on August 8, a "threatening letter from Kali." Finally, and most ominously, Blavatsky herself noted in a December 13 entry that Kali, suspecting her ex-husband's departure, was considering "arresting H.S.O."

25. HSOD, May 15, October 22, October 23, November 27, December 1, 1878.

26. HSOD, December 6, 1878; *ODL*, 1.479.

27. *A Budget of American History* (Boston: Ellis, 1881) was published anonymously, but a copy located in the Adyar Library and Research Center in Adyar, Madras, India contains the handwritten notation, "by H. S. Olcott," and a February 10, 1878, entry in Olcott's diary reads, "H.S.O. finishing Report for Union Mutual Life Ins Co." That report may have been the manuscript for this pamphlet. Apart from this external evidence, there are numerous hints of Olcott's authorship in the text itself: an emphasis on Native American religion, praise for the doctrine of religious liberty, and an interest in inventions and industrial exhibitions. Two events in Olcott's life, the battle at Roanoke and the Lincoln assassination, are given considerable attention in the document. Moreover, the author (like Olcott himself) finds ample evidence of a conspiracy to assassinate Lincoln, and he judges Mary Surratt guilty. Finally, it should be remembered that Olcott's law firm specialized in insurance cases and that the Union Mutual Life Insurance Company was one of its clients. The weight of the evidence overwhelmingly supports Olcott's authorship.

28. See, e.g., Daniel Dorchester, *Christianity in the United States from the First Settlement Down to the Present Time* (New York: Phillips and Hunt, 1888); and Leonard Woolsey Bacon, *History of American Christianity* (New York: Christian Literature Company, 1897).

29. *ODL*, 1.376.

30. HSOD, November 14, 1878.

31. A dated but useful examination of the Disciples of Christ is Winfred E. Garrison and Alfred T. De Groot, *The Disciples of Christ, A History* (rev. ed.; St. Louis: Bethany, 1958).

32. "Damn the whole Catholic Church," Olcott wrote in his diary on June 8, 1878, "especially the Jesuits."

33. *ODL*, 1.376.

34. *ODL*, 2.13–14.

35. *Allahabad Pioneer* (April 28, 1880).

36. Guruge, ed., *From the Living Fountains*, 339, 343.

37. Olcott, "The Theosophical Society and its Aims," in Olcott, *A Collection of Lectures on Theosophy and Archaic Religions* (Madras, India: A. Thegaya Rajier, 1883) 1–17.

38. Ibid., 12, 15.

39. Olcott, *A Collection of Lectures*, 17.

40. Ibid., 7.

41. Olcott, *The Joint Labours of the Arya Samaj and Its American Sister, the Theosophical Society* (Roorkee, India: Thomason Civil Engineering College Press, 1879) 3, 2, 6, 7. Thomas Tweed notes in his *The American Encounter with Buddhism* that many Americans likened Buddhism's emergence out of Hinduism with Protestantism's

emergence out of Catholicism, and thus described Buddha as "a Luther-like re-former" (16). Olcott did this too, but he extended the compliment to Saraswati as well.

42. Ibid., 7, 4.

43. Ibid., 7.

44. The title comes from a note in the *Theosophist* 1.6. (March 1880) 133, which states that "Olcott . . . holds the appointment of United States Commissioner to the East Indies." Olcott had persuaded Secretary of State Evarts to receive his reports on U.S.–India trade, but received no official appointment. Olcott almost certainly invented the title himself.

45. Olcott to Secretary of State Evarts (April 30, 1880) in "Miscellaneous Letters," General Records of the Department of State (Record Group 59), National Archives, Washington, D.C.

46. Evarts to Olcott (December 11, 1878) in Domestic Letters, General Records of the Department of State (Record Group 59), National Archives, Washington, D.C.

47. Many of Blavatsky's letters were translated into English and published in her *From the Caves and Jungles of Hindustan* (London: Theosophical Publishing Society, 1892).

48. Olcott, "The Rising Storm in India," *Frank Leslie's Illustrated Newspaper* (June 22, 1878) 263. No author was credited with writing this article, but Olcott noted in his diary for May, 1878 that he was preparing the piece. In it, Olcott likened British colonialism to slavery and argued that the Indian people resembled not only African Americans but also "the unfortunate victims of Cortez, Pizarro, and those other Spanish ruffians who reared the Spanish American Empire upon the ruins of . . . the Aztecs and the Peruvians." Olcott prophesied disastrous consequences for Great Britain: "Her Indian Empire shakes under her hand like a giant rousing himself to burst its bonds. Hindoostan, from the Himalayas to Cape Comorin, is seething with suppressed excitement as it has not since the bloody days of 1857. . . . We are on the eve of a tragedy that will appall the world."

49. "Snake Charmers of India" *Sun* (August 31, 1879); "Serpent Worship in India" *Sun* (October 12, 1879); "The Hierophant in India," *Sun* (July 21, 1879); and "On India's Coral Strand," *Sun* (July 7, 1879).

50. Olcott, "On India's Coral Strand," *Sun* (July 7, 1879).

51. HSOD, April 29, 1879. According to Olcott's diary for May 7, 1879, the spy's name was John L. Laing.

52. My search of British colonial records in the India Office Library and the Public Records Office turned up no primary documents relating to British surveillance of Olcott and Blavatsky. In *"No Religion Higher than Truth,"* Maria Carlson speculates on the basis of documents recently located in Russia that British authorities, who "feared a Russian incursion into India" at the time, were convinced Blavatsky was a spy (40). See esp. note 6 on p. 214.

53. HSOD, January 25, 1879.

54. HSOD, May–June, 1879.

55. In his diary for September 29, 1879, Olcott noted the receipt of a letter from A. P. Sinnett stating that the viceroy "has become convinced that we are not spies and has issued an order through the Foreign Department that all police surveillance shall cease." This edict did not conclude the matter, however. While in Simla in 1880, Olcott found it necessary once again to lodge a series of official

protests regarding British surveillance of theosophists. Upon discovering that one of his private letters had been stolen and was about to be published by the *Times of India*, Olcott addressed a letter on October 24, 1880, to Mr. Primrose, the private secretary to the viceroy, Lord Ripon. "What I chiefly want you to realize is that our Society was founded for a good and legitimate purpose—that of promoting the study of ancient science and philosophy," Olcott explained. "It never had the least thing to do with politics in either of the countries where it has branches." The issue resurfaced one last time in 1883, when suspicions that the theosophists were harboring secret political designs arose in Madras. Olcott sought protection from the Government of Madras, and on September 13, 1883, Madras Government Order #1798 guaranteed members of the society full protection as long as they obeyed the law and abstained (as Olcott promised they would) from politics.

56. This saying appeared on the masthead of the *Theosophist* 1.1 (October 1879) 1.

57. "What Is Theosophy?" *Theosophist* 1.1 (October 1879) 3, 5; "Namastae!" *Theosophist* 1.1 (October 1879) 2.

58. "What Are the Theosophists?" *Theosophist* 1.1 (October 1879) 7, 5. The editors also took pains to distance themselves from politics in the second number of the *Theosophist*, where they noted that their policy of political nonpartisanship had compelled them to reject an article on the allegedly unfair treatment of natives by the Indian government. They then published an article arguing that the root cause of modern Indian decadence was neither foreign rule nor taxation but the destruction of forests! ("The Ruin of India," *Theosophist* 1.2 [November 1879] 42–43).

59. "What Are the Theosophists?" *Theosophist* 1.1 (October 1879) 5, 6.

60. *Theosophist* 1.5 (February 1880).

61. *Theosophist* 1.4 (January 1880) 83; *Theosophist* 1.11 (August 1880) 279.

62. Olcott "How Best to Become a Theosophist," *Theosophist* 1.6 (March 1880) 143–44.

63. *Bombay Guardian*, quoted in "Miscellany. India. Theosophy," *Missionary Herald* (September 1885), 360.

64. *ODL*, 2.129.

4. The Sinhalese Buddhist Revival

1. Kitsiri Malalgoda, *Buddhism in Sinhalese Society, 1750–1900* (Berkeley: University of California Press, 1976) 109.

2. *Classified Digest of the Records of the Society for the Propagation of the Gospel in Foreign Parts 1701–1892* (London: S.P.G., 1894) 664–65.

3. Ibid.

4. Ibid.

5. Olcott described Mohottivatte as "a middle-aged, shaven monk, of full medium stature, with a very intellectual head, a bright eye, very large mouth, and an air of perfect self-confidence and alertness . . . the most brilliant polemic orator of the Island, the terror of the Missionaries . . . more wrangler than ascetic, more Hilary than Hilarian . . . the boldest, most brilliant and powerful champion of Sinhalese Buddhism, the leader (originator) of the present revival" (*ODL*, 2.157).

6. At the two-day Panadura debate Mohottivatte reportedly bested DeSilva before a large partisan crowd, earning the nascent Buddhist revival movement its first

substantial victory. See J. M. Peebles, *Buddhism and Christianity Face to Face* (Boston: Colby and Rich, 1878) for an eyewitness account of the debate.

7. *ODL*, 2.158.

8. In a November 19, 1877, letter to Washington, D.C., newspaperman William Henry Burr, Blavatsky labeled herself a Buddhist: "Let us settle, once and for all if you please, as to the word 'Spiritualist.' I am not one—not least in the modern and American sense of the word. I am a Svabhavika, a Buddhist pantheist, if anything at all" (quoted in Michael Gomes, *The Dawning of the Theosophical Movement,* 178). Olcott later claimed that he had been "a declared Buddhist" since 1876 ("Interview with Colonel H. S. Olcott, P. T. S.," *Theosophist* 27.7 [April 1906] S.xxxix).

9. Tweed, *American Encounter with Buddhism,* 111, 90. On dissent, see especially chapter 4, and, on consent, especially chapters 5 and 6.

10. *ODL,* 2.167–69. Long after converting to Buddhism, in an interview in the *Kensington Churchman,* Olcott reaffirmed this stance: "If you ask me what my views are, they are those of the Esoteric Buddhist. I am not orthodox; I am too much of an eclectic for that" (quoted in *Theosophist* 11.122 [November 1889] S.xix).

11. "Theosophy and Buddhism" and "The Life of Buddha and Its Lessons," in Olcott *A Collection of Lectures,* 26–38, 39–46.

12. Olcott, *A Collection of Lectures,* 42, 36, 37, 45.

13. Ibid., 34.

14. *ODL,* 2.165.

15. *Ceylon Examiner,* June 1, 1880; "Gleanings from the Society's Annual Report," *Church Missionary Gleaner* 8.90 (June 1881) 54–65.

16. Olcott to E. R. Guneratue (August 19, 1881), HSOC.

17. *ODL,* 2.294.

18. *ODL,* 2.323.

19. HSOD, May 1, 1881; *ODL,* 2.298.

20. Edward Said, *Orientalism* (New York, Pantheon, 1978). Said confines his arguments to Orientalists' representations of Islam and the Near Orient, but Philip C. Almond applies Said's critique to Buddhism and the Far East in *The British Discovery of Buddhism* (Cambridge: Cambridge University Press, 1988). On Rhys Davids, see Ananda Wickremerante, *The Genesis of an Orientalist: Thomas William Rhys Davids in Sri Lanka* (Colombia, MO: South Asia Books, 1985).

21. "Namastae!" *Theosophist* 1.1 (October 1879); *ODL,* 2.298. This tract was first published in English as *A Buddhist Catechism, According to the Canon of the Southern Church* (Colombo, Ceylon: Theosophical Society, Buddhist Section, 1881). All subsequent references come from Olcott, *The Buddhist Catechism,* 47th ed. (Adyar, India: Theosophical Publishing House, 1947). Olcott's work has inspired a number of imitations. See, e.g., Bhikshu Subhadra, *A Buddhist Catechism* (London: Redway, 1890).

22. "Absurdities of 'A Buddhist Catechism,' by Henry S. Olcott," *Ceylon Catholic Messenger* (October 21, 1881) 408, 410–12.

23. Olcott, *Buddhist Catechism,* vii.

24. HSOD, May 16, 1881. Theravada Buddhist thinkers resolve the apparent but ultimately unreal self into five *skandhas* or "heaps": *rupa* or form; *vedana* or feelings; *samjna* or perceptions; *samskaras* or volitions; and *vijnana* or consciousness.

25. HSOD, June 16, 1881; Olcott, *Buddhist Catechism,* 38.

26. Ibid., 1.

27. HSOD, May 4, 1881.

28. Olcott, *Buddhist Catechism*, 3, 39, 72–73, 110.

29. Ibid., 43, 55, 183.

30. Ibid., 59.

31. On the miracles question, see ibid., 21, 51–53, 58, 70, 110, 119–20. The other quotations are from 109, 62, 63, 109, 95, 100. Thomas Tweed notes in *The American Encounter with Buddhism* (esp. 1–25) that other Buddhist adherents and sympathizers defined Buddhism largely in negative terms.

32. Olcott, *Buddhist Catechism*, 19, 54. Olcott's most extended description of the Buddha might have applied equally well to the liberals' man of Christian character: "he strives to subdue his passions, to gain wisdom by experience, and to develop his higher faculties. He thus grows by degrees wiser, nobler in character, and stronger in virtue . . . " (32).

33. Ibid., 111, 112, 20, 2. The women's rights theme was especially pronounced. According to Olcott, Buddhism put women "on a footing of perfect equality with men" (2). His *Catechism* contained paeans to the first Upasikas, or female lay Buddhists, to the first Bhikkhunis, or female monastic Buddhists, and to the famed daughter of Ashoka, Sanghamitta, who brought Buddhism to Ceylon. See 43, 66, 69, 20, 23, 100, 71.

34. Ibid., 45, 104.

35. Ibid., 25, 81.

36. Citing its alleged atheism, Daniel Gogerly, Max Müller, and Monier Monier-Williams all defined Buddhism as a philosophy rather than a religion. Orientalists were equally unanimous in terming this philosophy "moral" and in condemning monks for failing to follow its ethical precepts (Almond, *The British Discovery of Buddhism*, 93–96, 111–18, 119–23).

37. Almond, *The British Discovery of Buddhism*, 24–28. Said refers to a similar tendency among Islamicists as "synchronic essentialism" (*Orientalism*, 240).

38. Olcott, *Buddhist Catechism*, 62, 58, 106, 58.

39. Ibid., 58, 106, 58, 62, 58, 58, 104.

40. While the two had initially agreed to merge and form "The Theosophical Society of the Arya Samaj" they soon downplayed the importance of their joint venture by reinterpreting that organization as what Olcott called a "link-society" between the two. Olcott first publicly affirmed this subtlety on September 6, 1880 in Meerut, India, in his lecture on "The Theosophical Society and the Arya Samaj," but the idea also appeared in a July 26, 1880 letter from Saraswati to Olcott and in an 1880 circular by the Swami. The last two texts are reprinted in Olcott, "Swami Dayanand's Charges," *Theosophist* 3.10 (July 1882) S.7–8.

41. Olcott relates this dissolution in a chapter on "Swami Dayanand," *ODL*, 1.394–407. The quotation is from p. 398.

42. HSOD, July 18, 1882; *ODL*, 2.373.

43. *ODL*, 2.374–75.

44. *ODL*, 2.375.

45. *ODL*, 2.405–406.

46. *ODL*, 2.406–407. After this discovery, Olcott used an "auroemeter" to gauge the psychopathic sympathy between his clients and himself (*ODL*, 2.408).

47. This division of labor is well-attested in both the theosophical and the scholarly literatures. Drawing on Max Weber's typologies, Bruce F. Campbell argued in *Ancient Wisdom Revived: A History of the Theosophical Movement* (Berkeley: University of California Press, 1980) that Blavatsky exemplified "charismatic authority" and Olcott, "bureaucratic authority" (187–88). Annie Besant, Olcott's successor as Theosophical Society president, expressed a similar idea in a more pious idiom: "H.P.B. gave to the world Theosophy, H. S. Olcott gave to the world the Theosophical Society. Each was chosen by the Masters: which brought the greater gift?" (*Olcott Centenary Number, Theosophist* 53.1 [August 1932] n.p.). Olcott himself expressed this "separate spheres" theory many times in *Old Diary Leaves.* "Under the Hindu classification, she would be the teaching Brahmin, I the fighting Kshattriya," he wrote. "Under the Buddhist one, she would be the Bhikshu, I the working Dyakya or laic" (*ODL*, 3.22–23). Elsewhere he added humorously that he was "the practical brain to plan, the right hand to work out the practical details" (*ODL*, 4.23). "Her sphere was the literary and spiritual one. . . . She was as unfit for platform and pioneer organising work as she was for cooking; and when we remember that she thought to get boiled eggs by laying them, raw, on the hot coals, her culinary aptitude is easily gauged. Moreover, she had too much sense to try it, but kept strictly to her own department, as I did to mine" (*ODL*, 3.11–12).

48. *ODL*, 2.326; HSOD, December 18, 1881; *ODL*, 2.326.

49. "Statistics of Col. Olcott's Bengal Tour," *Theosophist* 4.9 (June 1883) S.11–12. These healings were, according to Olcott, "the chief sensational feature of the Society's year's history" (*ODL*, 2.425).

50. "Col. Olcott's Healing Stopped," *Theosophist* 5.2 (November 1883) S.n.p.; "Col. Olcott's Healings," *Theosophist* 6.1 (October 1884) 11–12.

51. Longden, "The Buddhist Idea of the Approaching Termination of English Domination in Ceylon," CO/54/542/960, PRO.

52. Longden to Governor Duff, Madras (February 26, 1883), CO/54/547/9598, PRO.

53. See K. H. M. Sumathipala, "The Kotahena Riots and their Repercussions," *Ceylon Historical Journal* 19.1 (July 1969) 65–81.

54. Cited in Olcott, "Theosophy and Religious Riots," *Theosophist* 4.8 (May 1883) 197–200. Olcott himself argued that the true cause of the riot was "the ungenerous and unlawful attitude of the Christian padris [*sic*] and bigots of Ceylon toward Buddhist religion" (198).

55. Olcott, *The Government and the Buddhists of Ceylon* (London: n.p., 1884) 6; CO/54/547/13518, PRO. The strongest government statement regarding Catholic culpability appeared in a report sent by Longden to Secretary of State Derby on April 2, 1883. "It is manifest from the reports I have received that the Roman Catholics were the aggressors in this riot," Longden wrote. "The Buddhists were conducting their Perahera peaceably enough when they were furiously attacked by the Roman Catholics collected near *their* Cathedral, and though when attacked they retaliated, the blame of the first commencement of the riot must be laid on the Catholics" (CO/54/546/6807, PRO). Body counts tend to confirm this analysis. The only man killed in the riot was a Buddhist, and of the thirty people hospitalized only seven were Catholics.

56. "Report of the Riots Commission," *Indian Mirror* (n.d.), and Major Transchell, inspector general of police to Bombay *Gazette* (April 7, 1883), both extracted

in "The Final Result of the Savage Attack of the Roman Catholics on the Buddhists at Colombo," *Theosophist* 4.12 (September 1883) 325.

57. Longden to Colonial Secretary Derby (June 26, 1883), CO/54/547/13518, PRO.

58. Olcott, *The Government and the Buddhists of Ceylon*, 17.

59. Gordon to Colonial Secretary Derby (February 18, 1884), CO/54/552/4170, PRO.

60. Cited in Malalgoda, *Buddhism in Sinhalese Society*, 245.

61. Longden to Colonial Secretary Derby (June 26, 1883), CO/54/547/13518, PRO.

62. Longden to Colonial Secretary Derby (June 24, 1883), CO/54/547/13518, PRO.

63. Longden to Colonial Secretary Derby (June 28, 1883), CO/54/547/13519, PRO.

64. R. H. Meade note, CO/54/547/13519, PRO. The legislation they were discussing was the Buddhist Temporalities Ordinance, a law mandating government regulations for the administration of monastic temples and temple lands, which authorities referred to as "Buddhist Temporalities." The problem of the Buddhist Temporalities is discussed often and at great length in Public Record Office documents; in fact, no religious topic arose more frequently in the Colonial Office records of the 1880s than this dispute. At issue was the administration of these temple estates. Colonial administrators in favor of the legislation were convinced that Buddhist monks could not administer their holdings efficiently, and that their inefficiency would lead to social unrest. Many Christian missionaries, on the other hand, opposed the legislation on the grounds that it amounted to government support for Buddhism. After much procrastination, colonial administrators passed a compromise version of the Buddhist Temporalities Ordinance in 1889.

65. Olcott, *The Government and the Buddhists of Ceylon*, 19–20.

66. J. R. DeSilva to Olcott (March 23, 1884), CO/54/556/8274, PRO.

67. Edward F. Perera to Governor Gordon (February 5, 1884), CO/54/556/8274, PRO.

68. R. H. Meade to Olcott (June 17, 1884), in Olcott, *The Government and the Buddhists of Ceylon*, 23.

69. R. H. Meade to Olcott (June 27, 1884) in Olcott, *The Government and the Buddhists of Ceylon*, 28.

70. R. H. Meade to Olcott (June 17, 1884) in Olcott, *The Government and the Buddhists of Ceylon*, 23. After long negotiations, Pandid Batuvantudawe became the first Buddhist registrar in 1888 ("Controversy Regarding Buddhist Registrarship," *Buddhist* 8.3 [March 6, 1896]).

71. Gordon to Colonial Secretary Derby (August 29, 1884), CO/54/554/16173, PRO.

72. Olcott to A. P. Dharma Goonewardhane Muhandiram (July 7, 1884) in Olcott, *The Government and the Buddhists of Ceylon*, 2.

73. Gordon claimed the idea to make Wesak a public holiday had not originated with Olcott. "It was I myself," Gordon wrote, "who first mentioned [the idea] to Col Olcott" (Gordon to Colonial Secretary Derby [August 1884], CO/54/554/III/16173, PRO). An unsigned note (probably by R. H. Meade) in the Colonial Office records for September 20, 1886, corroborates Gordon's claims: "The Buddhists are very grateful to Col. Olcott whose mission really did absolutely nothing, for the only result . . . viz. the making of the Full Moon Day of Wesak a Public Holiday, was originally suggested to Col. Olcott by the Governor himself" (CO/54/566/IV/16903, PRO).

74. "The Buddhist Defence Committee" (September 20, 1886), CO/54/566/IV/16903, PRO. The credit Olcott earned was not spent for a number of years. On Wesak in 1888, villagers in Panadura offered thanks to Olcott, and Buddhists throughout the island sang a song in which the Buddha and the Colonel received near-equal

billing: "Let us worship the holy feet of the chief sage who has taught and declared the great thirty-two blessings. And may long life, health and happiness be unto Col. Olcott for helping to make the Full Moon Day of the month of Wesak a government holiday, wherein to exalt and spread the glories and virtues of the Omniscient Buddha" ("Buddha's Birthday in Ceylon," *Theosophist* 9.106 [July, 1888] 626).

75. " 'I Am Not a Dog,' " *Church Missionary Gleaner* 10.118 (October 1883) 110; "Ceylon: Extracts from Annual Letters," *Church Missionary Intelligencer and Record* 6 (1881) 174.

76. Olcott, "An United Buddhist World," *Theosophist* 13.4 (January, 1892) 239-43.

5. A United Buddhist World

1. K. H. M. Sumathipala, "The Kotahena Riots and their Repercussions" *Ceylon Historical Journal* 19.1 (July 1969) 78. Olcott is often credited with designing the flag, but he did little more than suggest that the pennant-like shape of the original flag be abandoned in favor of "the usual shape and size of national flags" (*ODL*, 3.364, 4.469). Olcott advanced his suggestion too late for the 1885 celebrations. But when the flags were hoisted the following year their dimensions mirrored those of the flags of most nation-states.

2. *ODL*, 3.363.

3. HSOD, April 28, 1881.

4. Olcott, "Old Diary Leaves," *Theosophist* 16.12 (September 1895) 745.

5. HSOD, January 28, 1885.

6. HSOD, January 29, 1885.

7. HSOD, February 2, 1885.

8. HSOD, February 5, 1885.

9. *ODL*, 3.227.

10. George Patterson, "The Collapse of Koot Hoomi," *Christian College Magazine* (September 10, 1884).

11. Society for Psychical Research Committee, *First Report of the Committee of the Society for Psychical Research, Appointed to Investigate the Evidence for Marvelous Phenomena Offered by Certain Members of the Theosophical Society* (London, n.p., 1885) 6.

12. *ODL*, 3.232; HSOD, August 7, 1885; *ODL*, 3.231.

13. Olcott to Miss Francesca Arundale (August 7, 1885), HSOC. In an attempt to allay his anxiety, Olcott wrote to Blavatsky, now in Würzburg, asking her to come clean: "*Are* there any more soiled petticoats to be washed in front of the Chateau Grundy? If so, let us have them all out at once and empty the brick-basket" (Olcott to Blavatsky [January 19, 1886], Add. MSS 45,288, ff.196-205, MCBL).

14. Quoted in "Editorial Paragraphs," *Missionary Herald* (May 1886) 171; Society for Psychical Research, "Report of the Committee Appointed to Investigate Phenomena Connected with the Theosophical Society," *Proceedings of the Society for Psychical Research* 3 (December 1885) 207. This document is commonly referred to as the "Hodgson Report."

15. Olcott to Blavatsky (March 17, 1886), Add. MSS 45,288, ff.216-17, MCBL.

16. Olcott to Miss Francesca Arundale (April 1, 1885), HSOC.

17. Olcott, "Special Orders of 1885," *Theosophist* 6.8 (May 1885) S.196-97. At the next Theosophical Society convention, Olcott proposed and the delegates accepted language stating that the occult objective was pursued only "by a portion

of the members of the Society" ("Official Report of the Decennial Convention and Anniversary of the Theosophical Society," *Theosophist* 7.75 [December 1885] S.lxxxix).

18. Olcott, "Infallibility," *Theosophist* 6.9 (June 1885) 200.

19. Olcott to Blavatsky (March 17, 1886), Add. MSS 45,288, ff.216–27, MCBL.

20. HSOD, September 20 and August 2, 1890; Olcott to Bertram Keightley (September 5, 1890), TSA.

21. Olcott, "Address of the President of the Theosophical Society," *Theosophist* 8.88 (January 1887) xliv.

22. Blavatsky to Olcott (n.d., 1888), HSOC.

23. Olcott, "The President-Founder's Address," *Theosophist* 7.76 (January 1886) S.xliii.

24. *ODL*, 3.419. Later Mohottivatte would start his own newspaper as an alternative to the B.T.S.-run and Olcott-influenced *Saravasi Sandaresa*.

25. *ODL*, 4.86; Blavatsky to Olcott (n.d., 1888), HSOC; "The President in Ceylon," *Theosophist* 10.113 (February 1889) S.xxxvii.

26. Dharmapala's fiery rhetoric survives in "Reminiscences of My Early Life," *JMBS* 41 (1933) 151–62; "Diary Leaves of the Late Ven. Dharmapala," *JMBS* 51–72 (1943–1964); and Ananda Guruge, ed., *Return to Righteousness: A Collection of Speeches, Essays, and Letters of the Anagarika Dharmapala* (Colombo, Ceylon: Government Press, 1965). Gananath Obeyesekere provides a controversial psychoanalytic perspective on the Dharmapala's life in "Personal Identity and Cultural Crisis: The Case of Anagarika Dharmapala of Sri Lanka," in Frank Reynolds and Donald Capps, eds., *The Biographical Process* (The Hague: Mouton, 1976) 221–52. Dharmapala's many contributions to the Sinhalese Buddhist Revival and to "Protestant Buddhism" are discussed in George Bond, *The Buddhist Revival in Sri Lanka*; Richard Gombrich and Gananath Obeyesekere, *Buddhism Transformed*; Kitsiri Malalgoda, *Buddhism in Sinhalese Society*; and L. A. Wickremeratne, "Religion, Nationalism and Social Change in Ceylon, 1865–1885," *Journal of the Royal Asiatic Society (GB and I)* 2 (1969) 123–50.

27. *ODL*, 4.100–101.

28. "Translation of the Sanskrit Letter of H. Sumangala Maha Thero to the Buddhists of Japan," TSA.

29. "The President's Japanese Tour," *Theosophist* 10.115 (April 1889) S.lxiii.

30. Ibid., S.lxiv.

31. Ibid.

32. A Buddhist, "Colonel Olcott in Japan," *Japan Weekly Mail* 11.11 (March 16, 1889) 262.

33. Olcott, "To the Chief Priests of the Japanese Buddhist Sects" (May 27, 1889), TSA.

34. *ODL*, 4.159, 134. The Y.M.B.A. would later find its way to the United States through the efforts of the Jodo Shinshu-based Buddhist Mission of North America (later, the Buddhist Churches of America). See Tetsuden Kashima, *Buddhism in America: The Social Organization of an Ethnic Religious Institution* (Westport: Greenwood, 1977) 13–15, 152–53.

35. "Editorial Paragraphs," *Missionary Herald* (May 1889); "Japan Mission," *Missionary Herald* (May 1889); J. T. Cole, "Colonel Olcott and Ghost Stories," *Japan Weekly Mail* 11.14 (April 6, 1889) 333. These judgments are reiterated in Otis Cary, *A History of Christianity in Japan* (New York: Revell, 1909) 2.224–25.

36. Quoted in *ODL*, 4.134, 165.

37. "The President's Return," *Theosophist* 10.118 (July 1889) S.cxiv.

38. *ODL*, 4.150.

39. Olcott, "The President's Address," *Theosophist* 12.2 (November 1890) S.12.

40. Quoted in Olcott, "The Buddhist Revival in Japan," in *Theosophical Pamphlets Collection, 1875–1929* (Madras: Theosophical Publishing House, 1921) 8–12.

41. HSOD, January 26, 1891.

42. Olcott, "Suggestions for the Burmese Buddhist League," TSA.

43. Olcott, "Burma Revisited," *Theosophist* 12.6 (March 1891) 329.

44. Olcott, "To the Buddhists of Burma," TSA.

45. Olcott, "Burma Revisited," *Theosophist* 12.6 (March 1891) 329.

46. The lack of Sinhalese interest in international Buddhist affairs was a chronic problem for Olcott. "I have never been able to get the Sinhalese interested in [foreign propaganda]," Olcott later lamented, "their whole sympathies and endeavors being concentrated on the regulation of Buddhist affairs in their own country" (*ODL*, 4.287).

47. *ODL*, 4.412.

48. Unlike the Buddhist representatives of Ceylon, Burma, and Chittagong who endorsed Olcott's fourteen propositions unreservedly, the Japanese accepted them merely as "included within the body of Northern Buddhism" (*ODL*, 4.420).

49. *ODL*, 6.155.

50. "The President-Founder's Birthday in Ceylon," *Theosophist* 23.10 (July 1902) xliii; "The President in Japan," *Theosophist* 10.119 (August 1889) S.cxliii.

51. Although Theosophists have written (and continue to write) reams about the "Judge Case" and the schism it engendered, there is no critical biography of the man himself. There is, however, a theosophical rendition of his life: Sven Eek and Boris de Zirkoff, eds., *William Quan Judge* (Wheaton, IL: Theosophical Publishing House, 1969).

52. *ODL*, 4.313, 315.

53. Olcott, "H.P.B.'s Death," *Theosophist* 12.10 (July 1891) 575, 577, 578.

54. Consider also *ODL*, 1.viii: "If there ever existed a person in history who was a greater conglomeration of good and bad, light and shadow, wisdom and indiscretion, spiritual insight and lack of common sense, I cannot recall the name, the circumstances or the epoch."

55. "First International Convention in Europe," *Theosophist* 12.12 (September 1891) 708.

56. *ODL*, 4.404.

57. Olcott, "The President's Address," *Theosophist* 12.12 (September 1891) 707; Olcott, "The President's Address," *Theosophist* 13.3 (December 1891) S.11.

58. Olcott, "Letter of Resignation," *Theosophist* 13.6 (March 1892) S.xliii–sliv; Olcott, "The Olcott Pension Fund: A Personal Explanation," *Theosophist* 13.12 (September 1892) S.xcvi–xcvii. Olcott dubbed his three-room Ootacamund retreat "Gulistan." In grand Victorian style, Olcott stuffed the cottage with Burmese lacquered bowls, diplomas from learned societies, statues of the Buddha, and other souvenirs of his work and travel. But the most striking collection on display was a group of portraits documenting the course of his public life. Sumangala, Thomas Edison, Max Müller, William Judge, Annie Besant, Professors Leon de Rosny and M. E. M. Burnouf, and psychologists Babinski, Liebault, Bernheim, and Charcot

were all included in Olcott's gallery of the saints. Somehow Olcott also found wall space for two Buddhist flags, as well as a picture of a seventeenth-century Salem witch trial—a reminder, no doubt, of his Protestant past.

59. Olcott did receive a few Mahatma revelations in 1885 and 1886. On January 7, 1886, Olcott wrote to Mrs. Mary Arundale, "I have a lion's heart now for my Master came to me on the night of [December] 17th and said he and the Maha Sahib were satisfied with me. I felt the dreadful strain so suddenly removed that I fell to sobbing for joy like a fisherman's bride on his return after a storm! It's all right now" (HSOC). Consider also Olcott's diary for June 7, 1886: "A joyful day! This morning, upon opening a letter from Torkanam Tatya . . . I find an entire page of [Koot Hoomi's] writing. . . . It is, in truth a glorious proof for . . . all doubters that the Blessed Ones still watch over us."

60. HSOD, February 10, 1892. Olcott provides a lengthier description of the message in *ODL*, 4.442.

61. HSOD, March 14, and April 8, 1892.

62. Olcott himself flirted with both interpretations. In *Old Diary Leaves* he described the February 10 voice as a Mahatmic message, but his diary for that date contains the admission that "all this may mean nothing."

63. Olcott, "The President's Address," *Theosophist* 12.12 (September 1891) 708.

64. Olcott, "The President's Address," *Theosophist* 13.3 (December 1891) 3.

6. The Indian Renaissance

1. William Theodore de Bary devotes one-third of the readings in the section on "Modern Hindu India" in his influential *Sources of the Indian Tradition* (New York: Columbia University Press, 1958) to the Indian Renaissance. David Kopf has authored two influential monographs on the movement: *British Orientalism and the Bengal Renaissance* (Berkeley: University of California Press, 1969); and *The Brahmo Samaj and the Shaping of the Modern Indian Mind* (Princeton: Princeton University Press, 1979). The Indian Renaissance is also sometimes referred to (less precisely, in my view) as the Hindu Renaissance.

2. The Brahmo Samaj, for example, was the first Hindu group to follow the Protestant example and conduct worship services congregationally. In those services, members sang hymns, read from the scriptures, and listened to sermons. In fact, one leader of the Brahmo Samaj, Keshub Chunder Sen, published a book of *Psalms* (London: C. Green, 1870). Rammohun Roy, who founded the Brahmo Samaj in 1828, was educated in the ways not only of Hinduism but also of Buddhism, Zoroastrianism, Christianity, and Islam. He and his followers came to believe in one universal religion.

3. Olcott, "The Theosophical Society and Its Aims," in Olcott, *A Collection of Lectures on Theosophy and Archaic Religions* (Madras, India: A. Theyaga Rajier, 1883) 11.

4. According to the *Indian Mirror* (January 7, 1902), "a small group of Theosophists thought out and launched the Congress into being. Mr. Allan Hume [the first I.N.C. president] was himself a member of the Theosophical Society when he took the Congress in Hand. The idea of holding a Congress was suggested by Theosophical Conventions. . . . Thus all national movements for India's spiritual and material welfare are both indirectly and directly due to the Theosophical Society and to its founders." One contemporary scholar of the I.N.C., John R. McLane, lists four

theosophists—Kashinath Telang, Mahadev Ballal Namjoshi, Narendranath Sen, and P. Ananda Charlu—among important early congressmen in his *Indian Nationalism and the Early Congress* (Princeton: Princeton University Press, 1977) 46.

5. Kewal Motwani, *Colonel H. S. Olcott: A Forgotten Page of American History* (Madras, India: Ganesh, 1955) 13.

6. HSOD, January 25, 1879.

7. Olcott to E. F. Webster, quoted in "The Government and Theosophy," *Theosophist* 5.1 (October 1883) 2.

8. *ODL*, 2.112.

9. Olcott, "The President's Address," *Theosophist* 23.12 (September 1902) S.12.

10. Olcott to Chicago *Record-Herald* (July 17, 1901), reprinted in *Theosophist* 22.3 (December 1901) S.vii–viii.

11. Ambedkar is only beginning to receive the attention of scholars of religion. See Sudarshan Agarwal, ed., *Dr. B. R. Ambedkar, the Man and his Message: A Commemorative Volume* (New Delhi: Prentice-Hall of India, 1991); Gail Omvedt, *Dalits and the Democratic Revolution: Dr. Ambedkar and the Dalit Movement in Colonial India* (New Delhi: Sage, 1994); Bhikshu Sangharakshita, *Ambedkar and Buddhism* (Glasgow: Windhorse Publications, 1986); Sanghasen Singh, ed., *Ambedkar on Buddhist Conversion and Its Impact* (Delhi: Eastern Book Linkers, 1990).

12. "General Report of the Twenty-Ninth Anniversary and Convention of the Theosophical Society," 26.12 (September 1905) S.55. See also the reports for the two previous conventions in *Theosophist* 24.12 (September 1903) S.41; and *Theosophist* 25.12 (September 1904) S.17, 42.

13. Olcott, "The President's Address" *Theosophist* 16.12 (September 1895) S.3.

14. "General Report of the Twenty-Fifth Anniversary and Convention of the Theosophical Society," *Theosophist* 22.12 (September 1891) S.35.

15. "Olcott Free School," *Theosophist* 18.7 (April 1897) S.xxv.

16. "Notes and Comments," *ABB* 2.6 (June 1896) 141.

17. James E. Tennent, *Christianity in Ceylon* (London: John Murray, 1850) 205; Olcott, "Religion in the Ceylon Census," *Theosophist* 14.1 (October 1892) 54–58.

18. Olcott, "Burma Revisited," *Theosophist* 12.6 (March 1891) 326; *ODL*, 5.15–16. Olcott's *Theosophist* published a number of articles on esoteric racial theories. See, e.g., "Racial Development," 7.73 (October 1885) 76–77: "The year 2000 will probably see the Aryan race sole possessors of this world, the older races having died out from want of stamina."

19. Olcott, "President's Closing Address," *Theosophist* 13.3 (December, 1891) S.55.

20. "Instruction in the 'Olcott Panchama Free Schools,'" *Theosophist* 26.6 (March 1905) 383.

21. See Bushnell, *Christian Nurture* (Hartford: Edwin Hunt, 1847).

22. *ODL*, 5.413–14; "Colonel Olcott at the Theological School," *ABB* 2.12 (December 1896) 324.

23. Pundit C. Iyotheethoss, "A Unique Petition," *JMBS* 7.3 (July 1898) 23–24. Olcott claimed in his written reminiscences that the organization was a spontaneous indigenous initiative. However, this petition was outlined not by Madras' untouchables but by Olcott himself, who wrote a letter on May 22, 1898, to the groups' leaders "instructing them as to drafting their Petition to me" (HSOD, May 21, 22, 1898).

24. Olcott, "Buddhistic Revival in Madras, *ABB* 4.8 (August 1898) 217–19. See

also Olcott, "The Revival of Buddhism in Southern India," *Theosophist* 19.9 (June 1898) 629–30.

25. Iyotheethoss, "A Unique Petition," 24.

26. Quoted in "The Revival of Buddhism in Southern India," *JMBS* 7.4 (August 1898) 36.

27. Ibid.

28. "Petition from Southern India Sakya Buddhist Society Representatives to Sri H. Sumangala Maha Nayaka Colombo," in TSA.

29. *ODL*, 6.346.

30. The final version, "To the Committee of the Panchama Community of Madras" (TSA), was signed by Sumangala, Subhuti, Weligama, and many other high-ranking Sinhalese monks. See also "The Reply of the Chief Priests," *Buddhist* 10.1 (September 1896) 13–14.

31. Quoted in "The Revival of Buddhism in Southern India," 37.

32. Olcott, "The President's Address," *Theosophist* 21.12 (September 1890) S.4. See also *ODL*, 6.345.

33. Olcott, "Address of the President-Founder," *Theosophist* 8.88 (January 1887) S.19.

34. Richard T. Hughes, "Introduction: On Recovering the Theme of Recovery," in Richard T. Hughes, ed., *The American Quest for the Primitive Church* (Urbana: University of Illinois Press, 1988) 1.

35. Olcott, *A Collection of Lectures*, 13, 15, 82.

36. Olcott, "Nett Results of Our Indian Work," *Theosophist* 12.1 (October 1890) 2.

37. Ibid.

38. Olcott, "Transfer of the *Bodhini*," *ABB* 6.11 (November 1900) 281. Olcott had attempted earlier to instill "manliness and self-reliance" in Indian boys through local Boys' Aryan Leagues, but those institutions failed (*ODL*, 5.62). David I. Macleod discusses analogous attempts to "civilize" modern American boys in *Building Character in the American Boy: The Boy Scouts, the YMCA, and Their Forerunners, 1870–1920* (Madison: University of Wisconsin Press, 1983). Jeffrey Hantover looks at the Boy Scouts from the perspective of the emerging field of the history of masculinity in America in "The Boy Scouts and the Validation of Masculinity," in Elizabeth H. Pleck and Joseph H. Pleck, eds., *The American Man* (Englewood Cliffs: Prentice-Hall, 1980) 293–99.

39. "Constitution and Rules of the Hindu Boys Association," *ABB* 1.1 (January 1895) 12.

40. Pandurang Hari, "The Building of Character," *ABB* 1.10 (October 1895) 253–55; and Vasanji Premji, "The Formation of Character," *ABB* 2.7 (July 1896) 171–83.

41. Olcott, *An Epitome of Aryan Morals*, 1, 12.

42. Olcott, "The President-Founder's Address," *Theosophist* 7.76 (January 1886) S.xxxvi–xxxix. Regarding Buddhism, Olcott wrote, "The rapid increase of Indian work has compelled me to neglect that so successfully begun in Ceylon . . . and the effects have been bad" (S.xliii).

43. Olcott "Address of the President of the Theosophical Society," *Theosophist* 8.88 (January 1887) xliv, xlvii.

44. Olcott, ed., *Dwaita Catechism* (Madras, India: n.p., 1886). The *Theosophist* eventually published a "Shin-shu Catechism" and a "Vishishtadvaita Catechism" (*ODL*, 5.117).

45. *ODL*, 3.402.

46. Stow Persons described this piece as the "most widely distributed document of free religion" (*Free Religion: An American Faith* [New Haven: Yale University Press, 1947] 23). Higginson first published it in *The Radical* in 1871. He later delivered it on numerous occasions, most notably at the World's Parliament of Religions in Chicago in 1893. My quotations are from Jackson, *Oriental Religions and American Thought*, 114; and John H. Barrows, ed., *The World's Parliament of Religions* (Chicago: Parliament Publishing, 1893) 2.780–84.

47. Olcott, *A Collection of Lectures*, 119.

48. *ODL*, 2.30–31.

49. Olcott, "The Spirit of Zoroastrianism," in Olcott, *Applied Theosophy and Other Essays* (Adyar, India: Theosophical Publishing House, 1975) 99, 99, 110, 122.

50. Ibid., 108.

51. Ibid., 110, 135.

52. The classic monograph here is Sacvan Bercovitch, *The American Jeremiad* (Madison: University of Wisconsin Press, 1978).

53. Olcott, "The Spirit of Zoroastrianism," 133, 100.

54. Olcott, "Zoroastrian Revival," *Theosophist* 17.6 (March 1896) 369–71. Olcott followed up this correspondence with a July 15, 1896 letter that is reprinted in *ODL*, 6.56–57. He discusses Zoroastrianism at length in *ODL*, 5.416–30.

55. *ODL*, 5.420.

56. Olcott, "The Spirit of Zoroastrianism," 139.

57. N. F. Bilimoria, "Colonel Olcott's Services to Zoroastrianism," *Theosophist* 28.6 (March 1907) 468.

58. *ODL*, 3.296–97.

59. Olcott, "Nett Result of Our Indian Work," 4; Olcott, "The President's Address," in "General Report of the Twenty-Fifth Anniversary and Convention," *Theosophist* 22.12 (September 1901) 7.

60. Church Missionary Society, *Proceedings of the Church Missionary Society for Africa and the East, Eighty-Fifth Year, 1883–1884* (London: Church Missionary House, 1884) 141, 142.

61. Olcott, "The Hindu Revival," *Theosophist* 15.7 (April 1894) 424.

62. "Notes from the Wide Field, India. The Revival of Hinduism," *Missionary Herald* (April 1889) 163.

63. "Colonel Olcott at the Theological School," *ABB* 2.12 (December 1896) 326.

7. Things Fall Apart

1. Lafcadio Hearn, *Occidental Gleanings; Sketches and Essays Now First Collected by Albert Mordell* (New York: Dodd, Mead, 1925) 2.84–88.

2. Church Missionary Society, *Proceedings of the Church Missionary Society for Africa and the East, Eighty-Fifth Year, 1883–1884* (London: Church Missionary House, 1884) 141.

3. Eugene Stock, *The History of the Church Missionary Society* (London: Church Missionary Society) 3.543.

4. One of Olcott's Christian friends was the Roman Catholic bishop, Father Paul Ambrose Bigandet. Olcott befriended Bigandet, the author of *The Life or Legend of Gaudama, the Budha of the Burmese, with Annotations* (Rangoon: Ranney, 1858),

during his 1885 tour of Burma. He called the priest "a staunch Christian" but added that "he deserves and has all my respect and affectionate regard" because of "his unselfishness and loyalty to conscience" (Olcott, "Burma Revisited," *Theosophist* 12.6 [March 1891] 332). See also Olcott, "Good Bishop Bigandet," *Theosophist* 15.8 (May 1894) 490–92.

5. HSOD, March 9, 1893. Olcott even contributed money to the Salvationists—for "rescue work," he noted, not missions (*ODL*, 4.462–63).

6. "General Report of the Sixteenth Convention and Anniversary of the Theosophical Society," *Theosophist* 13.3 (December 1891) 2–3.

7. Olcott, "The President-Founder's Address," in "Official Report of the Decennial Convention and Anniversary of the Theosophical Society," *Theosophist* 7.76 (January 1886) S.xxix.

8. Julius Richter, *A History of Missions in India* (New York: Fleming H. Revell, 1908) 381.

9. D. Hevavitarana, "The Buddha-Gaya Maha Bodhi Society," *Buddhist* 4.5 (January 25, 1892) 40.

10. "Vandalism on Buddhist Shrines," *Theosophist* 12.11 (August 1891) 677–86; and "General Report of the Sixteenth Convention and Anniversary of the Theosophical Society," *Theosophist* 13.3 (December 1891) S.41–42.

11. Dharmapala, "Memories of an Interpreter of Buddhism to the Present-Day World," in Guruge, ed., *Return to Righteousness*, 688. Alan Trevithick offers an anthropologically informed analysis of the struggle to regain and restore Bodhgaya in "A Jerusalem of the Buddhists in British India: 1874–1949" (Ph.D. diss., Harvard University, 1989).

12. This campaign is discussed in Reginald L. Rajapakse, "Christian Missions, Theosophy and Trade: A History of American Relations with Ceylon, 1815–1915" (Ph.D. diss., University of Pennsylvania, 1973). Kitsiri Malalgoda overlooks this important early element of the nineteenth-century revival in his otherwise exhaustive *Buddhism and Sinhalese Society*.

13. Gordon to Colonial Secretary Stanhope (Aug. 11, 1886), CO/54/566/IV/15958, PRO.

14. HSOD, July 15, 1885.

15. Olcott, "The Kinship between Hinduism and Buddhism," in Guruge, ed., *Return to Righteousness*, 371, 375, 368, 384. Apparently swayed by Olcott's arguments, a group of Hindu theosophists founded a new periodical called *The Theosophic Thinker*, which aimed, according to its inaugural issue of February 25, 1893, to demonstrate that while "Theosophy is pure Hinduism in its essence," Hinduism and Buddhism should be friends rather than enemies (1).

16. Ibid., 386.

17. An attorney in Gaya informed Olcott and Dharmapala that the Bodhgaya temple and its lands could be purchased for about 80,000 rupees (HSOD, April 3, 1893). So they traveled together to Rangoon to raise the revenue. But their efforts stalled, since "the whole body of middle men in the rice trade are in the grip of the foreign merchants" (HSOD, April 11, 1893).

18. HSOD, 1896: January 21, 29, 30; February 14, 15, 19, 20; March 1; May 20.

19. HSOD, December 1, 1897.

20. *ODL*, 6.348.

21. Curiously, Dharmapala was surprised when Olcott construed this motion as a

personal attack. Perhaps he was recalling Olcott's previous criticism of Ceylon's B.T.S. branches—that "properly speaking, not one of them is a *Theosophical* society, as the word is commonly understood, for they are . . . strictly Buddhist societies"—and was merely attempting to conform the organization's nomenclature to that institutional reality (Olcott, "The President's Address," *Theosophist* 17.12 [September 1896] S.4).

22. *ODL*, 6.349.

23. Theosophists are loath to discuss their community's many controversies, but they harbor no similar compunction about scrutinizing their scandals in print. Only the Coulomb affair exceeds the Judge case in ink spilled, so I will not attempt an exhaustive bibliography here. The original arguments appear in William Q. Judge, *Charges against William Q. Judge* (privately published, 1894); and Annie Besant, *The Case against W. Q. Judge* (London: Theosophical Publishing Society, 1895). Emmett A. Greenwalt recounts the history of Judge's schismatic Theosophical Society in America in *California Utopia: Point Loma: 1897–1942* (San Diego: Point Loma, 1978).

24. *ODL*, 5.314–15.

25. *ODL*, 5.317.

26. On Vivekananda and other Asians at the Parliament, see Richard Hughes Seager, *The World's Parliament of Religions: The East/West Encounter, Chicago, 1893* (Bloomington: Indiana University Press, 1995). On Vivekenanda's influence in America, see Carl T. Jackson, *Vedanta for the West: The Ramakrishna Movement in the United States* (Bloomington: Indiana University Press, 1994).

27. *Hindu* (February 8–11, 1897); Swami Vivekananda, *The Complete Works of Swami Vivekananda* (Calcutta: Advaita Ashrama, 1955) 3.208–209, 4.318. For Olcott's gentlemanly response to the Swami's criticisms, see his March 7, 1897 letter to the *Hindu*. Also, *ODL*, 6.128–29, 136–37; and Olcott, "Death of Swami Vivekananda," *Theosophist* 23.11 (August 1902) 696–97.

28. Quoted in *ODL*, 5.42.

29. Olcott, "The 'Wail' of Dharmapala," *Theosophist* 19.7 (April 1899) S.xxviii–xxx. The authors of at least one recent book apparently agree with this assessment. In *A History of the World's Religions* (New York: Macmillan, 1994), David S. Noss and John B. Noss contend that "Theosophy is, in spite of its professed hospitality to all religions, Hindu at heart" (152).

30. Olcott, "The 'Wail' of Dharmapala," *Theosophist* 19.7 (April 1899) S.xxviii–xxx. Olcott was even more ruthless in his private correspondence. In a letter to Charles Leadbeater, another American convert to theosophy and Buddhism, Olcott described "that spoilt suckling Dhammapala Dhamapada" as "vain to a degree and more kinds of an ass . . . than are enumerated by Linnaeus in his classification of the varieties in the family *Equus Asinus*" (November 9, 1902, HSOC).

31. Dharmapala to Olcott (August 5, 1905), HSOC.

32. Olcott to Dharmapala (August 18, 1905), HSOC.

33. Ibid.

34. Olcott to Leadbeater (November 9, 1902), TSA.

35. Olcott, "Letter of Resignation," *Theosophist* 13.6 (March 1892) S.xliii–xliv.

36. Olcott, "Old Diary Leaves," *Theosophist* 26.12 (September 1905), revised in *ODL*, 6.164–66. This diatribe was at least partially motivated by good intentions. More chauvinistic Sinhalese Buddhists had in the past used the fact that this relic of the Buddha resided in their country as evidence for the specialness of Ceylon and the chosen-ness of the Sinhalese people. As a creole Buddhist, Olcott was op-

posed to the notion—a notion that Dharmapala was gradually coming to share—that Sinhalese Buddhism was somehow more pure and more authentic than the Buddhism of, for example, Burma or Japan.

37. Dharmapala to Olcott (September 21, 1905), HSOC.

38. Sumangala to Olcott (September 22, 1905), HSOC, reprinted in *JMBS* 14.4 (April 1906) 57–58.

39. Olcott to Mirando (September 25, 1905), HSOC. Olcott expressed the same sentiment in an October 2, 1905 letter to Leadbeater. The resignation of "that pertinacious popinjay, Dharmapala," Olcott wrote, was a "small matter" but Sumangala's complaint had turned it into a "serious one" (HSOC).

40. Olcott to D. B. Jayatilaka (August 16, 1906), HSOC.

41. "Theosophical Degenerates," *JMBS* 14.7 (July 1906) 105–106.

42. "Ceylon, Past and Present," *JMBS* 14.3 (March 1906) 38; "The Parting of the Ways," *JMBS* 14.8 (August 1906). See also Dharmapala, "Can a Buddhist Be a Member of the Theosophical Society?" *JMBS* 14.3 (March 1906) 42–43.

43. Olcott, "Theosophy: An Outline of Its Teachings," *Theosophy* 23.1 (October 1901) 30.

44. In addition to the "rationalistic" and the "esoteric" sympathizer, Tweed includes in his scheme a "romantic" type. See his *The American Encounter with Buddhism*, esp. 48–77, 164–65. Tweed includes Olcott among the "esoteric" Buddhists.

45. HSOD, December 17, 1895, December 9, 1901.

46. HSOD, September 17 and October 7, 1895; May 28 and October 26, 1901. Olcott took these speculations seriously enough to consult histories and legends regarding Ashoka's life (HSOD, September 22 and October 7, 1895; November 16, 1896).

47. Olcott, "The Coming Calamities," *Theosophist* 18.7 (April 1897) 414–17.

48. Leadbeater was charged, among other things, with advising masturbation to a boy he was tutoring. The Executive Committee of the British Section of the Theosophical Society accepted Leadbeater's resignation on May 16, 1906. See Gregory Tillett, *The Elder Brother: A Biography of Charles Webster Leadbeater* (London: Routledge, 1982).

49. HSOD, November 24, 1906; "The President-Founder's Dangerous Illness: His Hearty Welcome in Ceylon," *Theosophist* 28.3 (December 1906) S.xvi; Annie Besant, "The Last Days of the President-Founder," *Theosophist* 28.6 (March 1907) 425.

50. HSOD, January 12, 1907. Olcott's diary refers to visitations from the Mahatmas on December 21, 1906; January 5, 11, 12, 13, 29, 30, 1907; and February 3, 1907. Beginning on January 11, Olcott's diary entries were made by his friend Mrs. Marie Russak.

51. Olcott, "A Recent Conversation with the Mahatmas," *Theosophist* 18.5 (February 1907) 388. This communication was dated January 13, 1907.

52. Olcott, "To the Theosophical Society," *Theosophist* 28.5 (February 1907) S.xix–xx.

53. "Copy of Letter Sent to Friends by Colonel Olcott a Few Days Before His Death," *Theosophist* 28.6 (March 1907) S.xxviii.

54. Besant, "The Last Days of the President-Founder," *Theosophist* 28.6 (March 1907) 426.

55. "There Is No Religion Higher Than Truth: Cremation of the Late Col. Olcott," *Hindu Organ* (February 27, 1907).

56. Besant, "The Last Days of the President-Founder," *Theosophist* 28.6 (March 1907) 431.

57. "In Memoriam," *JMBS* 15.1–3 (January–March 1907) 19; "Colonel Olcott and the Buddhist Revival Movement," *JMBS* 15.1–3 (January–March 1907) 26–28.

Conclusion

1. "General Report of the Thirty-Second Anniversary and Convention of the Theosophical Society," *Theosophist* 29.4 (January 1908) S.7. Some of these branches were dormant. This report found 567 active and 88 inactive branches, though the number of dormant branches was probably much higher.

2. Jules Richter, *History of Indian Missions* (London: Oliphant Anderson and Ferrier, 1908) 379, 385. This judgment was echoed elsewhere. C. F. Andrews, for example, admitted in *The Renaissance in India: Its Missionary Aspect* (Madras: Christian Literature Society for India, 1913) that the Theosophical Society "has exercised considerable influence in the south" (101). John P. Jones was even more generous. In *India: Its Life and Thought* (New York: Laymen's Missionary Movement, 1909), he admitted that "Theosophy has exercised considerable influence upon the educated classes in this country. . . . [It] is not represented by a very large number of organizations and members. But the movement has the sympathy of many who have not taken upon them its name" (406, 409).

3. The D.O.P.I. report is cited in "General Report of the Thirty-Second Anniversary and Convention of the Theosophical Society," *Theosophist* 29.4 (January 1908) S.64; those numbers are confirmed in *Ceylon Blue Book, 1907* (Colombo, Ceylon: Cottle, 1908). Because the government did not provide grants to all schools, the total number of Buddhist schools and Buddhist students was certainly higher. C.D.S. Siriwardane accounts for 215 total schools and 23,975 total students in "Olcott and the Buddhist Education Movement of Ceylon," *Buddhist* 35.10/11 (March–April 1965) 115–17.

4. Gananath Obeyesekere, "Buddhism and Conscience: An Exploratory Essay," *Daedalus* 120.3 (Summer 1991) 223.

5. Church Missionary Society, *Proceedings of the Church Missionary Society for Africa and the East, Ninety-Seventh Year, 1895–1896* (Church Missionary Society: Church Missionary House, 1896) 292.

6. This quote is from Japanese Buddhist Zenshiro Nogouchi and appears in *ODL*, 4.85.

7. Olcott, "The Genesis of Theosophy," 213.

8. Historians have settled the celebrated debate between Melville J. Herskovits's thesis of African "survivals" in the New World (*The Myth of the Negro Past* [Boston: Beacon, 1958]) and E. Franklin Frazier's thesis of African cultural obliteration (*The Negro Church in America* [New York: Schocken, 1964]) by agreeing that African American religion is a cultural and religious amalgamation. See, e.g., Albert H. Raboteau, *Slave Religion: The 'Invisible Institution' in the Antebellum South* (New York: Oxford University Press, 1978).

9. "Official Report of the Decennial Convention and Anniversary of the Theosophical Society," *Theosophist* 7.75 (December 1885) S.lxxxvii.

10. HSOD, April 21, 1887.

11. Olcott was not the only man of his time to make such claims. Paul Carus

(1852–1919), the German-American editor of *Open Court* and also a Buddhist sympathizer, claimed in an 1896 letter to Anagarika Dharmapala that "I am a Buddhist, but you must not forget that I am at the same time a Christian in so far as I accept certain teachings of Christ. I am even a Taoist. . . . I am an Israelite [sic]. . . . In one word, I am, as it were, a religious parliament incarnate" (quoted in Tweed, *The American Encounter with Buddhism*, 101).

12. CO/54/552/1/4170, CO/54/615/3/12101 and CO/54/619/7/14218, PRO.

13. John Murdoch, *Theosophy Unveiled* (Madras, India: Tract Depot, 1885) 84. The Twain remark is quoted in Tweed, *American Encounter with Buddhism*, 112.

14. Ashis Nandy, *The Intimate Enemy: Loss and Recovery of Self under Colonialism* (Delhi: Oxford University Press, 1983), esp. his essay on "The Psychology of Colonialism," 1–63. One main theme of Nandy's book is summarized in a quotation he reprints from Northcote Parkinson's *East and West* (New York: Mentor, 1965): "It was the knowledgeable, efficient, and polite Europeans who did the serious damage" (6).

15. Olcott, "Old Diary Leaves," *Theosophist* 17.3 (December 1895) 131.

16. See William R. Hutchison's discussion of "anticivilizing" and "Christ only" missionary theories in *Errand to the World: American Protestant Thought and Foreign Missions* (Chicago: University of Chicago Press, 1987) 77–90, 146–75. While Hutchison criticizes the American missionary movement for contributing to imperialism, he notes that many missions theorists were "remarkably enlightened about the dangers of cultural imposition" (205).

17. Tzvetan Todorov, *The Conquest of America: The Question of the Other,* Richard Howard, trans. (New York: Harper and Row, 1984).

18. W. O. Carver, "Baptists and the Problem of World Missions," *Review and Expositor* 17 (July 1920) 327, quoted in William R. Hutchison, *Errand to the World,* 92.

19. Genuine interreligious dialogue must in my view assume not only human equality (which Olcott affirmed) but also religious difference (which he denied). It must presume, moreover, that the discussants are willing to listen as well as to speak, to learn as well as to teach.

20. Clifford Geertz, in "Religion as a Cultural System," in *The Interpretation of Cultures* (New York: Basic, 1973), defines a religion as: "(1) a system of symbols which acts to (2) establish powerful, pervasive, and long-lasting moods and motivations in men by (3) formulating conceptions of a general order of existence and (4) clothing these conceptions with such an aura of factuality that (5) the moods and motivations seem uniquely realistic" (90).

Selected Bibliography

Bibliographic Notes

The most important unpublished sources on Olcott's life are his diary, letters, and miscellaneous papers housed at the Archives of the International Headquarters of the Theosophical Society in Adyar, Madras, India. Olcott's diary, which covers the period from 1878 to 1907, consists of thirty bound volumes, typically written in English but occasionally in French. Many entries in the first few years are in Blavatsky's handwriting and in the last two years of Olcott's life entries were made by his friend, Mrs. Marie Russak Hotchener. The diary is also something of a scrapbook, with business cards, invitations to governor's balls, and letters pasted in. Around the time of the centennial of Olcott's birth there were efforts to publish these volumes (see, e.g., "Diary of Colonel Olcott, 1878," *Theosophist* 55.3 [December 1933] 304–309), so some of the early books are transcribed into typewriting. These transcriptions are the versions that I read at the archives, though I did check the typewritten books against the originals on occasion and, in those instances, found them to be exactly the same.

Also tremendously useful are a set of twenty large scrapbooks containing thousands of newspaper and magazine clippings assembled and annotated by Helena Blavatsky. These scrapbooks cover roughly a decade, from the time of Blavatsky's initial encounter with Olcott in 1874 through 1884, and are an extremely important source for reconstructing Olcott's activities before he commenced his diary in 1878.

For Olcott's work in Asia, the extensive records of the Colonial Office, housed at the Public Records Office in London, are invaluable. Material related to Olcott in India and Ceylon, including letters written in his own hand and frank administrative comments on his activities, can be found in the following files: Colonial Office Original Correspondence; Government of Ceylon, Administrative Reports; Government of Ceylon, Sessional Papers; Government of Ceylon, Blue Books; and Government of Ceylon, Censuses. Some key theosophical papers, including reputed Mahatma letters to A. P. Sinnett, are located at the Department of Manuscripts at the British Library in London. The India Office Library may also contain important information on Olcott's work in India and Ceylon, though I was not able to locate anything of significance during my research there.

In the United States, researchers should consult two official theosophical repositories: the Olcott Library, which is housed in Wheaton, Illinois at the headquarters of the American Section of the Theosophical Society; and the Archives and Library of the Theosophical Society in Pasadena, California. Some important letters of Helena Blavatsky are housed in the Department of Manuscripts at the Andover-Harvard Theological Library of the Harvard Divinity School in Cambridge, Massachusetts.

Records of Olcott's college years can be viewed in New York City at the Univer-

Selected Bibliography

sity Archives, New York University. Various documents related to Olcott's work for the Army and Navy are housed at the National Archives in Washington, D.C. Especially relevant are the Records of the Office of Naval Records and Library, Record Group 45, Entry 161, "Letters from Special Investigators of Fraud in Naval Procurement"; Records of the Adjutant General's Office, 1780s–1917, Record Group 94, "Case Files of Investigations by Levi C. Turner and Lafayette C. Baker, 1861–1866,"; Records of the Office of the Judge Advocate General (Army), Record Group 153, "Investigation and Trail Papers Relating to the Assassination of President Lincoln," Case File 00-3655. Letters sent by Colonel Olcott to Lt. Col. Mallery of the Smithsonian Institution are on file at the Smithsonian Institution, National Anthropological Archives, National Museum of Natural History, BAE Correspondence File (Letters Received, 1879–88).

Among the published sources, Olcott's *Old Diary Leaves,* which chronicles the history of the theosophical movement from 1874 through 1898, is most important. Originally published serially in the *Theosophist* between March 1892 and December 1906, portions of these historical recollections later appeared in six volumes beginning in 1895 and culminating in 1935. The *Theosophist* entries were revised, however, when the books were published. Here I have typically used the 1974–1975 edition of *Old Diary Leaves,* but have quoted at times from the earlier articles. Readers interested in the transmigration of the *Theosophist* articles into book form should consult the 1941 edition of *Old Diary Leaves.* It contains a guide to additions and deletions.

Three overlapping collections of shorter works by Olcott—*A Collection of Lectures on Theosophy and Archaic Religions* (1883), *Theosophy, Religion and Occult Science* (1885), and *Applied Theosophy and Other Essays* (1975)—are the place to start for his speeches, pamphlets, and articles.

Although there is no comprehensive bibliography of Olcott's published work, historian of theosophy Michael Gomes has recently produced an extremely helpful bibliography of theosophy: *Theosophy in the Nineteenth Century: An Annotated Bibliography* (New York: Garland, 1994). Researchers looking for the best repository of published material on Olcott must travel to India to the Adyar Library, which Olcott himself founded in 1886. Housed at Theosophical Society headquarters in Adyar (outside Madras), this library is described in Gomes's bibliography as "a sort of Theosophical Library of Congress" (7). In the United States, the best collections on theosophical matters outside of theosophical libraries are in New York City at the New York Public Library and in Cambridge, Massachusetts, at the Andover-Harvard Theological Library of the Harvard Divinity School.

Primary Sources

Newspapers and Periodicals

Annual Report of the Baptist Missionary Society
Arya Bala Bodhini
Banner of Light

Selected Bibliography

Ceylon Catholic Messenger
Church Missionary Gleaner
Church Missionary Intelligencer and Record
Frank Leslie's Illustrated Newspaper
Hindu
Indian Mirror
Japan Weekly Mail
Journal of the Maha Bodhi Society
Lucifer
Missionary Herald
Missionary Review of the World
National Review
New York Times
New York Tribune
The Path
Religio-Philosophical Journal
Saturday Review
Spirit Messenger
Spiritual Scientist
Spiritual Telegraph
Spiritualist
The Theosophic Thinker
The Theosophist
Times of India
Working Farmer

Publications by Henry Steel Olcott

An Address by Col. Henry S. Olcott, President of the Theosophical Society, To the Arya Samaj of Meerut. Roorkee, India: Thomason Civil Engineering College Press, 1879.

Applied Theosophy and Other Essays. Adyar, India: Theosophical Publishing House, 1975.

Asceticism: A Word of Friendly Counsel. Madras, India: Theosophical Society, 1892.

[Anon.] *A Budget of American History.* Boston: Ellis, 1881.

A Buddhist Catechism, According to the Canon of the Southern Church. Colombo, Ceylon: Theosophical Society, Buddhist Section, 1881. Revised 47th edition. Adyar, India: Theosophical Publishing House, 1947.

A Collection of Lectures on Theosophy and Archaic Religions, Delivered in India and Ceylon by Colonel H. S. Olcott, President of the Theosophical Society. Madras, India: A. Theyaga Rajier, 1883.

The Descendants of Thomas Olcott. Albany: J. Munsell, 1874.

Eastern Magic and Western Spiritualism. Adyar, India: Theosophical Publishing House, 1933.

"Explanatory Preface." In Babu Madhowdasji, *The Sayings of the Grecian Sages.* Allahabad, India: Namwur Press, 1885.

"The Genesis of Theosophy." *National Review* 14.80 (October 1887) 213.

Selected Bibliography

The Golden Rules of Buddhism, Compiled from the Bana Books. Madras, India: Theosophical Society, 1887.

The Government and the Buddhists of Ceylon. [London]: n.p., [1884].

A Historical Retrospect—1875–1896—of the Theosophical Society. Madras, India: Theosophical Society, 1896.

Human Spirits and Elementaries and Eastern Magic and Western Spiritualism. Adyar, India: Theosophist, n.d.

Inaugural Address of the President of the Theosophical Society. New York: Theosophical Society, 1875.

"Introduction." In N. C., *Psychometry and Thought Transference, with Practical Hints for Experiments.* Madras, India: Theosophist, 1886.

"Introduction." In Tookaram Tatya, ed., *The Yoga Philosophy.* Bombay: Subodha-Prakash Press, 1885.

The Joint Labours of the Arya Samaj and Its American Sister, The Theosophical Society. Roorkee, India: Thomason Civil Engineering College Press, 1879.

The Kinship between Hinduism and Buddhism. Calcutta: The Maha-Bodhi Society, 1893.

A Letter on the Taxation of Loans as Capital, to the Commissioner of Internal Revenue, in Behalf of the Bankers and Brokers of New York. New York: n.p., 1869.

The Life of Buddha and Its Lessons. Colombo, Ceylon: n.p., 1880.

Official Revised Edition of the Outline of Draft of the General Insurance Law. New York: J. H. and C. M. Goodsell, 1871.

Old Diary Leaves: The History of the Theosophical Society. 6 vols. 1895–1935. Reprinted Adyar, India: Theosophical Publishing House, 1974–1975.

Outlines of the First Courses of Yale Agricultural Lectures. New York: Saxton, Barber, 1860.

People from the Other World. Hartford: American Publishing, 1875. Reprinted, Rutland, VT: Tuttle, 1972.

The Peril of Indian Youth. Madras, India: Premier Press, 1892.

The Poor Pariah. [Madras, India: Addison, 1902.]

[Anon.] *Preamble and By-Laws of the Theosophical Society.* [New York: Theosophical Society, 1875.]

"Preface." In Theophilus Roessle, *How to Cultivate and Preserve Celery.* New York: Saxton, Barker, 1860.

"Preface." In C. W. Leadbeater, *The Aura.* Madras, India: Theosophist, 1895.

The Safety Fund Law of the State of New York, in Relation to Fire Insurance. Its Advantages Explained. New York: Continental Insurance Company of the State of New York, 1875.

Sorgho and Imphee: The Chinese and African Sugar Canes. A Treatise upon Their Origin, Varieties and Culture. New York: A. O. Moore, 1857.

A Supplement to Sorgho and Imphee, the Chinese and African Sugar Canes, . . . Containing the American Experiments of 1857. New York: n.p., 1858.

"Theosophy and Theosophists." *Overland Monthly* 37.5 (May 1901) 992–98.

Theosophy, Religion and Occult Science. London: Redway, 1885.

A United Buddhist World. Being Fourteen Fundamental Buddhistic Beliefs. Madras, India: Scottish Press, 1892.

Selected Bibliography

The Vampire. Adyar, India: Theosophical Publishing House, 1920.

"The War's Carnival of Fraud." In *Annals of the War.* Philadelphia: Times Publishing, 1879.

Works Edited, Translated and Co-Authored by Henry Steel Olcott

[With P. Sreenevasa Row.] *Dwaita Catechism. The Dwaita Philosophy of Stiman Madwacharyar.* Madras, India: n.p., 1886.

[Ed.] *Official Report of the Proceedings of the National Insurance Convention (Second Session).* New York: n.p., 1872.

[Trans.] *Posthumous Humanity: A Study of Phantoms.* London: Redway, 1887.

Other Primary Sources

Arnold, Edwin. *India Revisited.* London: Kegan Paul, 1899.

———. *The Light of Asia; or, The Great Renunciation.* New York: A. L. Burt, 1879.

Barker, A. Trevor, ed. *The Mahatma Letters to A. P. Sinnett.* Pasadena: Theosophical University Press, 1975.

Barrows, John Henry. *A World Pilgrimage.* Chicago: A. C. McClurg, 1897.

———. *The World's Parliament of Religions.* Chicago: Parliament Publishing, 1893.

Blavatsky, Helena Petrovna. *From the Caves and Jungles of Hindustan.* Translated by Vera Johnston. New York: The Path, 1892.

———. *Isis Unveiled: A Master-Key to the Mysteries of Ancient and Modern Science and Theology.* 1877. 2 vols. Wheaton, IL: Theosophical Publishing House, 1972.

———. *The Secret Doctrine: The Synthesis of Science, Religion, and Philosophy.* 1888, 1897. 3 vols. Pasadena: Theosophical University Press, 1974.

Britten, Emma Hardinge. *Nineteenth Century Miracles; or Spirits and Their Work in Every Country of the Earth.* New York: Lovell, 1884.

Conway, Moncure. *My Pilgrimage to the Wise Men of the East.* Boston: Houghton Mifflin, 1906.

Copleston, R. S. *Buddhism: Primitive and Present in Magadha and in Ceylon.* London: Longmans, Green, 1892.

Corson, Eugene R., ed. *Some Unpublished Letters of Helena Petrovna Blavatsky.* London: Rider [1929].

Davis, Mary F. *Danger Signals: The Uses and Abuses of Modern Spiritualism.* New York: A. J. Davis, 1875.

de Zirkoff, Boris., ed. *H. P. Blavatsky: Collected Writings.* 14 vols. Wheaton, IL: Theosophical Press, 1950–87.

Dharmapala, Anagarika. "Diary Leaves of the Late Ven. Dharmapala." *The Maha Bodhi* 51–72 (1943–54).

———. "Reminiscences of My Early Life." *The Maha Bodhi* 41 (1933) 151–62.

Guruge, Ananda, ed. *From the Living Fountains of Buddhism: Sri Lankan Support to Pioneering Western Orientalists.* Colombo, Sri Lanka: Ministry of Cultural Affairs, 1984.

———, ed. *Return to Righteousness: A Collection of Speeches, Essays and Letters of the Anagarika Dharmapala.* Colombo, Ceylon: Government Press, 1965.

Hearn, Lafcadio. *Occidental Gleanings; Sketches and Essays Now First Collected by Albert Mordell.* 2 vols. New York: Dodd, Mead, 1925.

Selected Bibliography

Home, D. D. *Lights and Shadows of Spiritualism*. London: Virtue, 1878.

Jinarajadasa, C., ed. *Letters from the Masters of the Wisdom*. Two Series. Adyar, India: Theosophical Publishing House, 1919, 1925.

Müller, F. Max. "Esoteric Buddhism." *The Nineteenth Century* 33 (May 1893) 767–88.

———. "Esoteric Buddhism: A Rejoinder." *The Nineteenth Century* 33 (August 1893) 296–305.

Murdoch, John. *Theosophy Unveiled*. Madras, India: Tract Depot, 1885.

Peebles, J. M. *Buddhism and Christianity Face to Face*. Boston: Colby and Rich, 1878.

Sinnett, A. P. *Incidents in the Life of Madame Blavatsky*. London: Redway, 1886.

Society for Psychical Research Committee. *First Report of the Committee of the Society for Psychical Research, Appointed to Investigate the Evidence for Marvelous Phenomena Offered by Certain Members of the Theosophical Society*. London: n.p., 1885.

———. "Report of the Committee Appointed to Investigate Phenomena Connected with the Theosophical Society." *Proceedings of the Society for Psychical Research* 3 (December 1885) 201–207.

Tennent, James E. *Christianity in Ceylon; Its Introduction and Progress under the Portuguese, the Dutch, the British, and American Missions*. London: John Murray, 1850.

Vivekananda, Swami. *The Complete Works of Swami Vivekananda*. Calcutta: Advaita Ashrama, 1955.

Wiggin, Rev. J. H. "Rosicrucianism in New York." *Liberal Christian* 30.84 (September 4, 1875) 4.

Secondary Sources

Spiritualism, Theosophy and Buddhism in the West

Agarwal, Hridaya Narain, ed. *Reminiscences of Colonel H. S. Olcott by Various Writers*. Adyar, India: Theosophical Publishing House, 1932.

Almond, Philip C. *The British Discovery of Buddhism*. Cambridge: Cambridge University Press, 1988.

Bednarowski, Mary Farrell. *New Religions and the Theological Imagination in America*. Bloomington: Indiana University Press, 1989.

———. "Outside the Mainstream: Women's Religion and Women Religious Leaders in Nineteenth-Century America." *Journal of the American Academy of Religion* 48 (1980) 207–31.

Braude, Ann. *Radical Spirits: Spiritualism and Women's Rights in Nineteenth-Century America*. Boston: Beacon, 1989.

Buddhist Churches of America. *Buddhist Churches of America: Seventy-Five-Year History, 1899–1974*. 2 vols. Chicago: Nobart, 1974.

Campbell, Bruce F. *Ancient Wisdom Revived: A History of the Theosophical Movement*. Berkeley: University of California Press, 1980.

Carlson, Maria. *"No Religion Higher Than Truth": A History of the Theosophical Movement in Russia, 1875–1922*. Princeton: Princeton University Press, 1993.

Cranston, S. L. *HPB: The Extraordinary Life and Influence of Helena Blavatsky, Founder of the Modern Theosophical Movement*. New York: Putnam, 1993.

Selected Bibliography

Darnton, Robert. *Mesmerism and the End of the Enlightenment in France*. Cambridge: Harvard University Press, 1968.

Delp, Robert W. "Andrew Jackson Davis: Prophet of American Spiritualism." *Journal of American History* 54 (1967) 43–56.

Ellwood, Robert S. *Alternative Altars: Unconventional and Eastern Spirituality in America*. Chicago: University of Chicago Press, 1979.

———. *Theosophy: A Modern Expression of the Wisdom of the Ages*. Wheaton, IL: Theosophical Publishing House, 1986.

Fields, Rick. *How the Swans Came to the Lake: A Narrative History of Buddhism in America*. Boulder: Shambala, 1981.

Fuller, Robert C. *Mesmerism and the American Cure of Souls*. Philadelphia: University of Pennsylvania Press, 1982.

Gomes, Michael. *The Dawning of the Theosophical Movement*. Wheaton, IL: Quest, 1987.

———. *Theosophy in the Nineteenth Century: An Annotated Bibliography*. New York: Garland, 1994.

Greenwalt, Emmett A. *The Point Loma Community in California: 1897–1942*. Berkeley: University of California Press, 1955. Reprinted as *California Utopia: Point Loma: 1897–1942*. San Diego: Point Loma Publications, 1978.

Humphreys, T. Christmas. *The Development of Buddhism in England*. London: The Buddhist Lodge, 1937.

———. *Sixty Years of Buddhism in England*. London: The Buddhist Society, 1968.

Hunter, Louise H. *Buddhism in Hawaii: Its Impact on a Yankee Community*. Honolulu: University of Hawaii Press, 1971.

Jackson, Carl T. "The Influence of Asia upon American Thought: A Bibliographic Essay." *American Studies International* 22.1 (April 1984) 3–31.

———. *The Oriental Religions and American Thought: Nineteenth-Century Explorations*. Westport: Greenwood, 1981.

———. *Vedanta for the West: The Ramakrishna Movement in the United States*. Bloomington: Indiana University Press, 1994.

Jinarajadasa, C., ed. *The Golden Book of the Theosophical Society*. Adyar, India: Theosophical Publishing House, 1925.

Johnson, K. Paul. *The Masters Revealed: Madame Blavatsky and the Myth of the Great White Lodge*. Albany: State University of New York Press, 1994.

Judah, J. Stillson. *The History and Philosophy of Metaphysical Movements in America*. Philadelphia: Westminster, 1967.

Karunaratne, Saddhamangala, ed. *Olcott Commemoration Volume*. Ceylon: Olcott Commemoration Society, 1967.

Kashima, Tetsuden. *Buddhism in America: The Social Organization of an Ethnic Religious Organization*. Westport: Greenwood, 1977.

Kerr, Howard. *Mediums, Spirit Rappers, and Roaring Radicals: Spiritualism in American Literature, 1850–1900*. Urbana: University of Illinois Press, 1972.

Kerr, Howard, and Charles L. Crow, eds. *The Occult in America: New Historical Perspectives*. Urbana: University of Illinois Press, 1983.

Kirthisinghe, Buddhadasa P. *Colonel Olcott: His Service to Buddhism*. Kandy, Sri Lanka: Buddhist Publication Society, 1981.

Selected Bibliography

————. "Henry Steel Olcott Is a Bodhisattva." *Modern Review* 140.4 (Oct 1976) 201–207.

Kuhn, Alvin Boyd. *Theosophy: A Revival of Ancient Wisdom.* New York: Henry Holt, 1930.

Lavan, Spencer. *Unitarians and India: A Study in Encounter and Response.* Boston: Beacon, 1977.

Layman, Emma McCloy. *Buddhism in America.* Chicago: Nelson-Hall, 1976.

Meade, Marion. *Madame Blavatsky: The Woman Behind the Myth.* New York: Putnam, 1980.

Mills, Joy. *One Hundred Years of Theosophy: A History of the Theosophical Society in America.* Wheaton, IL: Theosophical Publishing House, 1987.

Moore, R. Laurence. *In Search of White Crows: Spiritualism, Parapsychology, and American Culture.* New York: Oxford University Press, 1977.

Motwani, Ketal. *Colonel Henry Steel Olcott: A Forgotten Page in American History.* Madras, India: Ganesh, 1955.

Murphet, Howard. *Hammer on the Mountain: Life of Henry Steel Olcott (1832–1907).* Wheaton, IL: Theosophical Publishing House, 1972. Reprinted as *Yankee Beacon of Buddhist Light.* Wheaton, IL: Quest, 1988.

Nethercot, Arthur H. *The First Five Lives of Annie Besant.* Chicago: University of Chicago Press, 1960.

————. *The Last Four Lives of Annie Besant.* Chicago: University of Chicago Press, 1963.

Oppenheim, Janet. *The Other World: Spiritualism and Psychical Research in England, 1850–1914.* Cambridge: Cambridge University Press, 1985.

Owen, Alex. *The Darkened Room: Women, Power and Spiritualism in Late Victorian England.* Philadelphia: University of Pennsylvania Press, 1990.

Prebisch, Charles. *American Buddhism.* North Scituate, MA: Duxbury Press, 1979.

Prothero, Stephen Richard. "Henry Steel Olcott (1832–1907) and the Construction of 'Protestant Buddhism.'" Ph.D. diss., Harvard University, 1990.

Rajapakse, Reginald L. "Christian Missions, Theosophy and Trade: A History of American Relations with Ceylon, 1815–1915." Ph.D. diss., University of Pennsylvania, 1973.

Schwab, Raymond. *The Oriental Renaissance: Europe's Rediscovery of India and the Far East, 1680–1880.* Translated by Gene Patterson-Black and Victor Reinking. New York: Columbia University Press, 1984.

Seager, Richard H. *The World's Parliament of Religions: The East-West Encounter, Chicago, 1893.* Bloomington: Indiana University Press, 1995.

Sellon, Emily B., and Renée Weber. "Theosophy and the Theosophical Society." In Antoine Faivre and Jacob Needleman, eds., *Modern Esoteric Spirituality*, pp. 311–29. New York: Crossroads, 1992.

Solovyov, Vsevolod S. *A Modern Priestess of Isis.* London: Longmans, Green, 1895.

Starr, Frank Farnsworth. *The Olcott Family of Hartford, Connecticut.* Hartford, CT: n.p. 1899.

Taylor, Anne. *Annie Besant: A Biography.* New York: Oxford University Press, 1992.

Tillett, Gregory. *The Elder Brother: A Biography of Charles Webster Leadbeater.* London: Routledge and Kegan Paul, 1982.

Selected Bibliography

Tweed, Thomas A. *The American Encounter with Buddhism, 1844–1912: Victorian Culture and the Limits of Dissent.* Bloomington: Indiana University Press, 1992.

Wickremeratne, L. A. "An American Bodhisattva and an Irish Karmayogin: Reflections on Two European Encounters with Non-Christian Religious Cultures in the Nineteenth Century." *Journal of the American Academy of Religion* 50.2 (June 1982) 237–54.

———. "Olcott, Sri Lankan Buddhism, and the Buddhist Raj." *The American Theosophist* 68.4 (April 1980) 68–77.

Williams, Gertrude M. *Priestess of the Occult: Madame Blavatsky.* New York: Knopf, 1946.

Yates, Frances A. *The Rosicrucian Enlightenment.* London: Routledge and Kegan Paul, 1972.

American Religion and Culture

Ahlstrom, Sydney E. *A Religious History of the American People.* New Haven: Yale University Press, 1972.

Bender, Thomas. *New York Intellect: A History of Intellectual Life in New York City from 1750 to the Beginnings of Our Own Time.* New York: Knopf, 1987.

Boles, John B. "Jacob Abbott and the Rollo Books: New England Culture for Children." *Journal of Popular Culture* 6.3 (Spring 1973) 518.

Boylan, Anne M. *Sunday School: The Formation of an American Institution, 1790–1880.* New Haven: Yale University Press, 1988.

Brathwaite, Edward. *The Development of Creole Society in Jamaica, 1770–1820.* New York: Clarendon, 1971.

Bushman, Richard L. *The Refinement of America: Persons, Houses, Cities.* New York: Knopf, 1992.

Butler, Jon. *Awash in a Sea of Faith: Christianizing the American People.* Cambridge: Harvard University Press, 1990.

Carter, Paul A. *The Spiritual Crisis of the Gilded Age.* Dekalb: Northern Illinois University Press, 1971.

Cauthen, Kenneth. *The Impact of American Religious Liberalism.* New York: Harper and Row, 1962.

Christensen, Torben, and William R. Hutchison, eds. *Missionary Ideologies in the Imperialist Era: 1880–1920.* Cambridge: Harvard Theological Review, 1984.

Commager, Henry Steele, ed. *The Era of Reform, 1830–1860.* Princeton: Van Nostrand, 1960.

Cott, Nancy F. *The Bonds of Womanhood: "Woman's Sphere" in New England, 1780–1835.* New Haven: Yale University Press, 1977.

Cross, Whitney. *The Burned-Over District: The Social and Intellectual History of Enthusiastic Religion in Western New York, 1800–1850.* Ithaca: Cornell University Press, 1950.

Davis, David Brion, ed. *Ante-bellum Reform.* New York: Harper and Row, 1967.

Douglas, Ann. *The Feminization of American Culture.* New York: Knopf, 1977.

Dumenil, Lynn. *Freemasonry and American Culture, 1880–1930.* Princeton: Princeton University Press, 1984.

Selected Bibliography

Elderkin, John. *A Brief History of the Lotos Club.* New York: n.p., 1895.

Gabriel, Ralph Henry. *The Course of American Democratic Thought.* 2d edition. New York: Ronald, 1956.

Gaustad, Edwin Scott. *Dissent in American Religion.* Chicago: University of Chicago Press, 1973.

Gottschalk, Stephen. *The Emergence of Christian Science in American Religious Life.* Berkeley: University of California Press, 1973.

Halttunen, Karen. *Confidence Men and Painted Women: A Study of Middle-Class Culture in America, 1830–1870.* New Haven: Yale University Press, 1982.

Hatch, Nathan O. *The Democratization of American Christianity.* New Haven: Yale University Press, 1989.

Higham, John. *From Boundlessness to Consolidation: The Transformation of American Culture, 1848–1860.* Ann Arbor: William L. Clements Library, 1969.

Hofstadter, Richard. *The Age of Reform.* New York: Vintage, 1955.

———. *Social Darwinism in the United States: 1860–1915.* Philadelphia: University of Pennsylvania Press, 1959.

Houghton, Walter E. *The Victorian Frame of Mind, 1830–1870.* New Haven: Yale University Press, 1957.

Howe, Daniel Walker, ed. *Victorian America.* Philadelphia: University of Pennsylvania Press, 1976.

Hughes, Richard T., ed. *The American Quest for the Primitive Church.* Champaign: University of Illinois Press, 1988.

Hughes, Richard T., and C. Leonard Allen. *Illusions of Innocence: Protestant Primitivism in America, 1630–1875.* Chicago: University of Chicago Press, 1988.

Hutchison, William R. *Errand to the World: American Protestant Thought and Foreign Missions.* Chicago: University of Chicago Press, 1987.

———. *The Modernist Impulse in American Protestantism.* Cambridge: Harvard University Press, 1976.

———. *The Transcendentalist Ministers: Church Reform in the New England Renaissance.* New Haven: Yale University Press, 1959.

Joyner, Charles. *Down by the Riverside: A South Carolina Slave Community.* Urbana: University of Illinois Press, 1984.

Kasson, John F. *Rudeness and Civility: Manners in Nineteenth-Century Urban America.* New York: Hill and Wang, 1990.

Kerber, Linda K. "Separate Spheres, Female Worlds, Women's Place: The Rhetoric of Women's History." *Journal of American History* 75.1 (June 1988) 9–39.

Kuklick, Bruce. *Churchmen and Philosophers: From Jonathan Edwards to John Dewey.* New Haven: Yale University Press, 1985.

Lears, T. J. Jackson. *No Place of Grace: Antimodernism and the Transformation of American Culture, 1880–1920.* New York: Pantheon, 1981.

Levine, Lawrence W. *Highbrow/Lowbrow: The Emergence of Cultural Hierarchy in America.* Cambridge: Harvard University Press, 1988.

Macleod, David I. *Building Character in the American Boy: The Boy Scouts, the YMCA, and Their Forerunners, 1870–1920.* Madison: University of Wisconsin Press, 1983.

May, Henry F. *The Enlightenment in America.* New York: Oxford University Press, 1976.

Selected Bibliography

McLoughlin, William G. *The Meaning of Henry Ward Beecher: An Essay on the Shifting Values of Mid-Victorian America, 1840–1870.* New York: Knopf, 1970.

———. *Revivals, Awakenings and Reform.* Chicago: University of Chicago Press, 1978.

Mead, Sydney E. *The Lively Experiment: The Shaping of Christianity in America.* New York: Harper and Row, 1963.

Miller, Perry. *Errand into the Wilderness.* Cambridge: Harvard University Press, 1956.

Moore, R. Laurence. *Religious Outsiders and the Making of Americans.* New York: Oxford University Press, 1986.

Mosier, Richard D. *Making the American Mind: Social and Moral Ideas in the McGuffey Readers.* New York: King's Crown, 1947.

Persons, Stow. *The Decline of American Gentility.* New York: Columbia University Press, 1973.

———. *Free Religion: An American Faith.* New Haven: Yale University Press, 1947.

Raboteau, Albert H. *Slave Religion: The 'Invisible Institution' in the Antebellum South.* New York: Oxford University Press, 1978.

Saum, Lewis O. *The Popular Mood of Pre-Civil War America.* Westport: Greenwood, 1980.

Schlesinger, Arthur M. "A Critical Period in American Religion, 1875–1900." *Massachusetts Historical Society Proceedings* 64 (June 1932) 523–47.

Sobel, Mechal. *The World They Made Together: Black and White Values in Eighteenth Century Virginia.* Princeton: Princeton University Press, 1987.

Szasz, Ferenc Morton. *The Divided Mind of Protestant America, 1880–1930.* University: University of Alabama Press, 1982.

Thomas, John L. "Romantic Reform in America, 1815–1865." *American Quarterly* 17.4 (Winter 1965) 656–81.

Todorov, Tzvetan. *The Conquest of America: The Question of the Other.* Translated by Richard Howard. New York: Harper and Row, 1984.

Tomsich, John. *A Genteel Endeavor: American Culture and Politics in the Gilded Age.* Stanford: Stanford University Press, 1971.

Trachtenberg, Alan. *The Incorporation of America: Culture and Society in the Gilded Age.* New York: Hill and Wang, 1982.

Turner, James. *Without God, Without Creed: The Origins of Unbelief in America.* Baltimore: Johns Hopkins University Press, 1985.

Tyler, Alice Felt. *Freedom's Ferment: Phases of American Social History from the Colonial Period to the Outbreak of the Civil War.* Minneapolis: University of Minnesota Press, 1944.

Walters, Ronald G. *American Reformers, 1815–1860.* New York: Hill and Wang, 1978.

Weiss, Richard. *The American Myth of Success: From Horatio Alger to Norman Vincent Peale.* New York: Basic, 1969.

Welter, Barbara. "The Cult of True Womanhood, 1820–1860." *American Quarterly* 18 (1966) 151–74.

Wiebe, Robert H. *The Search for Order: 1877–1920.* New York: Hill and Wang, 1967.

Williams, Raymond. *Culture and Society, 1780–1950*. New York: Harper and Row, 1966.

Buddhism and Hinduism in Asia

Ames, Michael M. "Ideological and Social Change in Ceylon." *Human Organization* 22 (963) 45–53.

———. "The Impact of Western Education on Religion and Society in Ceylon." *Pacific Affairs* 40 (1967) 19–42.

———. "Westernization or Modernization: The Case of Sinhalese Buddhism." *Social Compass* 20.2 (1973) 139–70.

Bastiampillai, Bertram. "American Activity and Influence in Nineteenth-Century Ceylon." In Robin W. Winks, ed., *Other Voices, Other Views*, pp. 113–24. Westport: Greenwood, 1978.

Bechert, Heinz, ed. *Buddhismus, Staat und Gesellschaft in den Landern des Theravada-Buddhismus*. 3 vols. Wiesbaden: Otto Harrassowitz, 1973.

———. "Sangha, State, Society, 'Nation': Persistence of Traditions in 'Post-Traditional' Buddhist Societies." *Daedalus* 102.1 (1973) 85–95.

Bond, George D. *The Buddhist Revival in Sri Lanka: Religious Tradition, Reinterpretation and Response*. Columbia: University of South Carolina Press, 1988.

Cary, Otis. *A History of Christianity in Japan*. 3 vols. New York: Fleming H. Revell, 1909.

Farquhar, John N. *Modern Religious Movements in India*. Delhi: Munshiram Manoharlal, 1967.

French, Hal W., and Arvind Sharma. *Religious Ferment in Modern India*. New York: St. Martin's, 1981.

Gombrich, Richard. *Precept and Practice: Traditional Buddhism in the Rural Highlands of Ceylon*. Oxford: Clarendon, 1971.

———. *Theravada Buddhism: A Social History from Ancient Benares to Modern Colombo*. New York: Routledge and Kegan Paul, 1988.

Gombrich, Richard, and Gananath Obeyesekere. *Buddhism Transformed: Religious Change in Sri Lanka*. Princeton: Princeton University Press, 1988.

Goonetileke, H. A. I. *Lanka, Their Lanka: Cameos of Ceylon through Other Eyes*. New Delhi: Naurans, 1984.

Jones, Kenneth W. *Arya Dharm: Hindu Consciousness in 19th-Century Punjab*. Berkeley: University of California Press, 1976.

Kopf, David. *The Brahmo Samaj and the Shaping of the Modern Indian Mind*. Princeton: Princeton University Press, 1979.

———. *British Orientalism and the Bengal Renaissance*. Berkeley: University of California Press, 1969.

Malalgoda, Kitsiri. *Buddhism in Sinhalese Society: 1750–1900*. Berkeley: University of California Press, 1976.

McLane, John R. *Indian Nationalism and the Early Congress*. Princeton: Princeton University Press, 1977.

Obeyesekere, Gananath. "Personal Identity and Cultural Crisis: The Case of Anagarika Dharmapala in Sri Lanka." In Frank E. Reynolds and Donald Capps, *The Biographical Process: Studies in the History and Psychology of Religion*, 221–52. The Hague: Mouton, 1976.

——. "Religious Symbolism and Political Change in Ceylon." *Modern Ceylon Studies* 1.1 (January 1970) 43–63.

Rahula, Walpola. *History of Buddhism in Ceylon.* Colombo, Ceylon: M. D. Gunasena, 1956.

Said, Edward. *Orientalism.* New York: Pantheon, 1978.

Sumathipala, K. H. M. "The Kotahena Riots and Their Repercussions." *Ceylon Historical Journal* 19.1 (July 1969) 65–81.

Tambiah, S. J. "Buddhism and This-worldly Activity." *Modern Asian Studies* 7.1 (1973) 1–20.

——. "The Persistence and Transformation of Tradition in Southeast Asia, with Special Reference to Thailand." *Daedalus* 102.1 (Winter 1973) 55–84.

——. *Sri Lanka: Ethnic Fratricide and the Dismantling of Democracy.* Chicago: University of Chicago Press, 1986.

——. *World Conqueror and World Renouncer: A Study of Buddhism and Polity in Thailand against a Historical Background.* Cambridge: Cambridge University Press, 1976.

Thelle, Notto R. *Buddhism and Christianity in Japan: From Conflict to Dialogue, 1854–1899.* Honolulu: University of Hawaii Press, 1987.

Trevithick, Alan. "A Jerusalem of the Buddhists in British India: 1874–1949." Ph.D. diss., Harvard University, 1989.

Weber, Max. *The Religion of India: The Sociology of Hinduism and Buddhism.* Glencoe: Free Press, 1958.

Wickremeratne, L. A. "Annie Besant, Theosophism and Buddhist Nationalism in Sri Lanka." *Ceylon Journal of Historical and Social Studies* 6.1 (January–June 1976) 62–79.

——. "Religion, Nationalism and Social Change in Ceylon, 1865–1885." *Journal of the Royal Asiatic Society (GB and I)* 2 (1969) 123–50.

Index

Abbott, Jacob, 193–94n.44
Abolitionism, 32
Adepts, spiritualist, 45–46
Adyar Library, 146–48, 221, 222
African-Americans, and Protestantism in American South, 175, 219n.8
Agarwal, Sudarshan, 213n.11
Agriculture: and Olcott as journalist, 24; Olcott and reform movement, 29–32, 193n.39
Ahlstrom, Sydney E., 199n.43
Allahabad Pioneer (newspaper), 75
Almond, Philip C., 105, 205n.20, 206nn.36, 37
Ambedkar, Dr. Bhimrao Ramji, 137, 139, 141, 213n.11
Ames, Michael M., 185n.6
Andover-Harvard Theological Library (Cambridge, Massachusetts), 221, 222
Andrews, C. F., 219n.2
Anthony, Susan B., 21
Applied Theosophy and Other Essays (Olcott, 1975), 222
Arnold, Sir Edwin, 143, 159
Arnold, Matthew, 7, 39, 61, 145, 196n.3, 200n.65
Arya Bala Bodhini (magazine), 145
Aryan Temperance Society, 83
Arya Samaj: merger of with Theosophical Society, 68–69, 77–78, 135, 206n.40; and resistance to Olcott's Buddhist heterodoxy, 67; Saraswati and, 106–107
Avesta (sacred text of Zoroastrianism), 149

Bacon, Leonard Woolsey, 202n.28
Barnum, P. T., 21
Barrows, John H., 215n.46
Bary, William Theodore de, 212n.1
Bednarowski, Mary Farrell, 186n.7, 198n.25, 200n.1
Bender, Thomas, 38–39, 196n.2
Bercovitch, Sacvan, 215n.52
Besant, Annie Wood, *94*: eulogy for Olcott, 171; and leadership of Theosophical Society, 130, 133, 135, 170, 207n.47; and revival of Hinduism, 162
Betanelly, Michael, 43
Bigandet, Father Paul Ambrose, 215–16n.4
Bigelow, William Sturgis, 125, 177, 185n.2
Biography: of Blavatsky, 196–97n.12; of Olcott, 2, 186n.7
Blavatsky, Helena Petrovna, *89, 90*: biographies of, 196–97n.12; as Buddhist, 205n.8; criticism of Christianity, 64; criticism of Olcott's focus on Buddhism, 106, 157–58; death of, 130–33, 157; and eastern orientation of Theosophical Society, 59–61; establishment of Theosophical Society, 5, 25, 48–50, 62, 198n.33; letters of, 63, 203n.47, 221; Olcott's relationship with, 11, 98, 108–109, 119–23, 197n.15, 202n.24; and Olcott's role in Theosophical Society, 207n.47; Olcott and spiritualism, 41–44, 47–48; and Olcott's tour of Burma, 117–18; and Olcott's visits to Asia, 70–71, 72, 75; question of authenticity of spiritual phenomena, 173, 209n.13; role of in theosophy movement, 51–54; scrapbooks of, 221; and Skeptical Enlightenment, 201n.5; Theosophical Society and *Isis Unveiled*, 57–59, 197n.19, 200n.58; tour of Ceylon, 85, 95, 97, 99
Blithedale Romance (Hawthorne, 1852), 16
Bodhgaya, restoration of Bo tree temple at, 158–60, 161–62, 216n.17
Boles, John B., 194n.44
Bond, George D., 188n.25, 210n.26
Brahmo Samaj, 51, 122, 212n.2
Brandon, Ruth, 191n.17
Brathwaite, Edward, 187n.22
Braude, Ann, 21, 191nn.17, 18, 192n.27, 193n.37
Brisbane, Albert, 29, 193n.38
British Library (London), 221
Brown, E. Gerry, 44
Brown, John, 32
Brownson, Orestes A., 16, 189n.4
Bryant, William Cullen, 21

Index

Stephen Prothero is Assistant Professor in the Religion Department at Boston University. He has published articles in *Religion and American Culture,* the *Harvard Theological Review,* and the *Journal of the American Academy of Religion.* This is his first book.